GREAT LIVES OBSERVED

Gerald Emanuel Stearn, *General Editor*

EACH VOLUME IN THE SERIES VIEWS THE CHARACTER AND ACHIEVEMENT OF A GREAT WORLD FIGURE IN THREE PERSPECTIVES—THROUGH HIS OWN WORDS, THROUGH THE OPINIONS OF HIS CONTEMPORARIES, AND THROUGH RETROSPECTIVE JUDGMENTS—THUS COMBINING THE INTIMACY OF AUTOBIOGRAPHY, THE IMMEDIACY OF EYEWITNESS OBSERVATION, AND THE OBJECTIVITY OF MODERN SCHOLARSHIP.

FREDERIC B. M. HOLLYDAY, *the editor of this volume in the Great Lives Observed series, is Associate Professor of History at Duke University. He has written on Bismarck and also on the politics of communism.*

GREAT LIVES OBSERVED

BISMARCK

Edited by
FREDERIC B. M. HOLLYDAY

Politics does not have the task of Nemesis.
—BISMARCK

A SPECTRUM BOOK

PRENTICE-HALL, INC., ENGLEWOOD CLIFFS, N. J.

Copyright © 1970 by PRENTICE-HALL, INC.,
Englewood Cliffs, New Jersey.

A SPECTRUM BOOK

Current printing (last number): 10 9 8 7 6 5 4 3 2

C–13–077362–x

P–13–077354–9

Library of Congress Catalog Card Number: 77–126816

Printed in the United States of America

PRENTICE-HALL INTERNATIONAL, INC. (*London*)
PRENTICE-HALL OF AUSTRALIA, PTY. LTD. (*Sydney*)
PRENTICE-HALL OF CANADA, LTD. (*Toronto*)
PRENTICE-HALL OF INDIA PRIVATE LIMITED (*New Delhi*)
PRENTICE-HALL OF JAPAN, INC. (*Tokyo*)

Contents

v

5

Imperial Foreign Policy 67

Defeated France, 67   Between Austria and Russia, 72   The Colonial Question, 75   The Bases of Foreign Policy, 76

6

The Jews 81

GREAT LIVES OBSERVED

BISMARCK

Introduction

The old fable of the elephant and the blind men relates that one blind man felt only the trunk, another only an ear, and the third only the tail, and each believed he could describe the animal. Can a historian hope to do better with Otto von Bismarck, whose political career spanned half a century and who, for nearly thirty years, dominated the German, European, and world scene? A study of his life involves complex questions of the nature of his genius and of his philosophy, aims, and methods—whether in fighting the liberals over parliamentary control, unifying Germany by successive wars with Denmark, Austria, and France, asserting civil control over the military in the determination of policy, establishing a new governmental structure, battling the clericals and socialists, meeting new economic problems, or reconciling Europe to the existence of the new German Empire. It is hardly surprising that the answers proposed have clashed radically with one another.

The difficulty of solving these problems is compounded by Bismarck's pragmatic approach to men and events. It is true that he became associated with a Christian fundamentalist sect—the Pietists—which included some of the most influential, as well as ultraconservative, men in Prussia. But it is hard to trace the concrete effects of his beliefs on his policy. Doubtless, his belief in God tended to bolster his considerable self-confidence and his paternalistic attitude toward the poor, so frequently expressed during debates over social welfare. But he believed that God operated through power politics and that the statesman, whatever his private convictions, should not act according to abstract beliefs, but in line with realities. His contempt for Christian humanitarianism, conservative doctrine, and liberal ideology as guides for the statesman, and his reliance upon state interest alone as the determinant of policy, are usually termed *realpolitik*. However, *realpolitik* describes his aims and methods in only the most general way. He adhered to no single articulated philosophy; at best his own views must be inferred from his deeds and words.

Bismarck became Prussian minister president and minister of foreign affairs in 1862, at the age of 47. Like most men, his views had been formed during earlier years. Dominating the late nineteenth century, he was a product of an earlier epoch. He had reacted violently to the bourgeois inheritance of his unsympathetic and intel-

1

ligent mother and had learned to look with favor upon the noble, Junker traditions of his affable and mediocre father. His affinities lay with the existing social system, with rural Prussia, ruled by the king and administered by the nobles and the upper middle class. He was summoned to office to maintain the power of the Prussian monarchy by repulsing liberal attempts to control the army, and his position depended on the successful achievement of this goal.

Bismarck never deviated from the course of championing the monarchy, the army, and the existing system. It was his fate to appear on the political stage at a time when, as an urban society developed, these fulcrums of power were coming under heavy attack from most of the middle class and the masses. During his early years, diplomacy had barely passed beyond the stage in which the king made decisions in private, in his "cabinet." And although the monarch now tended also to estimate and respond to the reactions of the educated classes, Bismarck still tended to think in terms of cabinet diplomacy. Experience with manipulation of public opinion only increased his disdain for it and caused him to undervalue it. He did not believe that Anglo-German commercial rivalry or the forbidding of the Berlin bourse to float Russian loans could exercise a significantly unfavorable influence on foreign public opinion and thus on the sphere of "high policy." And he still thought almost exclusively in terms of the continent, although he inaugurated German colonial expansion and regarded the United States in an amicable fashion as a great power of the future. Conservative preconceptions of the inherent instability of liberal and democratic government caused him to view the French republic and the British parliamentary monarchy as essentially weak governments.

Thus, in 1862, the future arbiter of Europe seemed to be the representative of repression, and for four years he administered affairs in opposition to the majority of the Prussian Chamber of Deputies. Intertwined with the question of the king's control of the army was the legality not of collecting taxes without a budget (which had constitutional justification), but of spending the proceeds. Bismarck pursued his liberal opponents in the Progressive party with great dialectical skill and with harsh invective, but he always tried to leave the door open for a settlement. This accorded well with his pragmatic philosophy of always keeping at least two irons in the fire. He refused to be bound by the neo-absolutist and Metternichian philosophy of his Conservative allies, did not reject the idea of a pact with either the middle class liberals or the masses, and did not feel that solidarity on the basis of conservative antinational principles with Russia and Austria necessarily reflected Prussia's true interests.

The circle was squared by Bismarck's resourcefulness in adapting the nationalist-liberal aspiration of a united Germany to his ends. His diplomatic masterpiece is often considered to be his maintaining ties with the tsar and conciliating the rest of the powers while, always keeping his immediate purposes in view, he maneuvered Austria into one untenable position after another. He made clear to all of Europe the impossibility of a multinational Austrian monarchy's pursuing a national policy in Germany. In alliance with Italy, but with few German allies, the Prussian armies crushed Austria in the Seven Weeks' War of 1866. At Nikolsburg, Bismarck successfully fought against territorial demands on Austria that would have disturbed the European powers, though he had to accept Prussian annexation of some German states, which alarmed particularist domestic opinion.

How devoted was he to German nationalism? Was it merely a cloak for Prussian hegemony in Germany? These questions have often been asked. The National Liberals, who appeared in 1866 after the split in the Progressive party, believed his nationalism sincere and were willing to work for the achievement of a united country. This alliance was to last a decade, with the particularist Conservatives turning to opposition, though a small splinter group, the Free Conservatives, became the Bismarck faction. If, as has often been conjectured, the personal effect on the new North German chancellor of the Conservatives' estrangement was to deprive him of the friends of his youth and to embitter him, this willingness to cooperate with whatever party which would support him was the result of the belief that he, as a statesman and servant of the king, stood above partisan politics.

The North German Constitution of 1867, which in its essentials continued as the German Constitution of 1871, represented Bismarck's attempt to institutionalize the existing system, incorporating novel features to conciliate liberal and democratic forces. One innovation, which the new chancellor was to regret, was the introduction of universal suffrage. Contemporaries were inclined to see this as an imitation of Napoleon III's Caesarist regime, in which liberal and democratic forms masked dictatorial power. A national assembly, the Reichstag, was established. But counterweights appeared also. A federal council or Bundesrat was set up as, in Bismarck's view, the repository of German sovereignty. In this body, representatives of the twenty-five separate states, presided over by the chancellor, voted on legislation and exercised some judicial and executive powers as well. Prussia, though in a minority, could block constitutional amendments. Above all, the king of Prussia, who bore the additional title of German emperor after 1870, kept control of policy-making and the army and initiated the appointment of the chancellor. Perhaps the gravest defect of this constitutional system was that it required for its effective and responsible functioning a man of Bismarck's energy and manifold genius and a monarch of the stamp of William I.

William I was the most sympathetic of the three king-emperors under whom Bismarck worked. In politics, William was basically a conservative of the old Prussian particularist school, but he was at the same time susceptible to some modern trends. While it is possible that he found Bismarck's personality, methods, and some of his aims personally antipathetic, William recognized and was grateful for the chancellor's great achievements and was content to let him occupy the public limelight. The king's age—approaching sixty-four when he ascended the Prussian throne in 1861—made Bismarck's tenure in office precarious. Fear of William's death and, consequently, of his own dismissal account for the chancellor's obsession with potential rivals, the hatred with which he pursued them, and the pressure he brought by threats of resignation. The heir to the throne, William's son, the crown prince, the future Frederick III, found Bismarck's high-handed manner repellent and frequently swore he would not reign with him. In the conflict of the sixties, influenced by his liberal wife, Victoria, he publicly denounced Bismarck's domestic policy and privately worked against his foreign policy. Yet he agreed with Bismarck at Nikolsburg. Advancing age, the counsel of advisers, and Bismarck's great prestige and influence persuaded the reluctant crown prince by 1885 to retain the chancellor. Although informed of this decision, Bismarck still felt unsure of the future monarch's favor. The crown prince had seen the Kulturkampf as a disaster, opposed the chancellor's brief flirtation with the anti-Semites, was sympathetic to Great Britain, hostile to Russia, and disliked the bellicose tone of the government's statements and attitudes in foreign affairs. Dying when he ascended the throne in 1888, Frederick III's desire for a more unitary national state than the chancellor wished and his extreme consciousness of the emperor's prerogative might well have brought a decisive clash, had he reigned for more than ninety-nine days. Frederick's son and successor, William II, was an acknowledged adherent of the chancellor. But Bismarck's dictatorial ways clashed with his own and, fortified by the general feeling that the aging chancellor had exhausted his ideas and was an anachronism in a new age, William dismissed Bismarck over conflicts of policy and the proper stance to take toward the workingman. Without the first chancellor's clear grasp of objectives and masterful personality, the constitutional foundation of 1867 subsided toward chaos.

The state established in 1867 was not only framed to maintain the monarchy, the army, and the existing sytem and to win over liberal opinion, it aimed at calming European fears of a strong Germany, while encouraging the South German states to coalesce with it. Bismarck, then and in 1871, was careful to construct a nation made up of existing states and not to pander to the most extreme nationalist elements, who hungrily eyed German populations in Austria and in Russia's Baltic provinces. The existing European state system was altered dramatically, but not destroyed. If acquisition of Alsace-Lorraine pleased nationalist elements, Bismarck's justification was the military security of the new empire. If many European statesmen accepted Bismarck's moderation at Nikolsburg as a sign of good faith, France still seemed a bar to complete unity.

Unity was achieved by the common military effort of both North Germany and the South German states in the Franco-German War of 1870–1871. Territorial unification in Bismarck's sense was achieved, but, in his view, if the new national state was really to be established, it must set up common institutions. Bismarck's approach was, as usual, pragmatic. The institutions that developed grew up as the need arose. If one expedient did not work well, another was tried. His attempts were complicated by constitutional differences in the offices of minister president of Prussia, which dated from 1848, and imperial chancellor, which Bismarck himself instituted in 1867. The minister president was not a prime minister who proposed a cabinet to the king. He simply presided over the ministers, who were appointed by the king and organized in the Prussian Ministry of State. Bismarck worked over the years to displace ministers who disagreed with him, and it was not until about 1878 that he was close to his goal. An experiment of dividing responsibility in 1872 by appointing War Minister Roon to the post of minister president, while Bismarck remained in the Ministry of State as Prussian minister of foreign affairs, proved unworkable and was abandoned. As imperial chancellor, Bismarck bore the entire responsibility to the Emperor for the conduct of imperial affairs. At first, he kept firm control of foreign affairs, while delegating immediate supervision of domestic matters to the freetrader Rudolf Delbrück, as president of the Imperial Chancellery from 1867. Delbrück's dismissal in 1876 marked Bismarck's shift toward a new imperial organization. The office of vice chancellor was instituted to handle ever-increasing business, and secretaries of state appeared as the chancellor's chief subordinates. Restricted imperial tax revenues, a condition Bismarck was able to remedy but not to cure, made imperial officials few in number, and the German government acted primarily through the state governments, depending especially on Prussian aid in making policy. To dominate this intricate and cumbersome governmental system, Bismarck remained simultaneously Prussian minister president and imperial chancellor. Also, the secretaries of state were often made Prussian ministers without portfolio. The Prussian Ministry of State—there was none for the empire—considered and often determined matters of imperial policy. If there was much intergovernmental rivalry and confusion, with even Bismarck himself sometimes uncertain of which particular capacity he was acting in, greater unity was achieved through these institutional arrangements, themselves the result of trial and error.

One of the greatest opponents of this unity, in the chancellor's eyes, was the Catholic Center party, which had sounded the first discordant note in the new German Reichstag in 1871. The Center represented to a large degree the particularist elements in Germany, who had opposed unification under Prussian leadership and seemed to underscore this fact by tactical alliances with opposition parties and with the separatist factions of the Poles, Alsatians, and adherents of the deposed Guelf dynasty in Hanover. Bismarck's attention was also riveted by fear of what he believed to be the desire of the international Catholic church to control national Germany by means of the papal claim to infallibility, announced in 1870. If, as has been argued, there was no papal desire for international political hegemony and Bismarck's resistance to it may be described as shadowboxing, many statesmen of the time were of the chancellor's persuasion. The result was the Kulturkampf, which, with its largely Prussian measures, complemented by similar actions in several other German states, sought to curb the clerical danger by legislation restricting the Catholic church's political power. Backed by the Free Conservatives, National Liberals, and most of the Progressives, Bismarck waged an unrelenting battle that produced great bitterness on both sides. But, as the Center party increased in numbers and the economic situation worsened with the onset of the great depression of the latter nineteenth century, the chancellor's attitude changed. The German Catholics had been early advocates of modifying capitalism to improve working conditions. Now Bismarck looked to the Center party for support of his remedies for the depression: protective tariffs and, later, state intervention to aid the workers. Despite papal pressure, this potential alliance was never realized by him, though he was even in contact with the Centrist leader Windthorst at the time of his dismissal from office in 1890, but the Center did give tactical support on many measures.

Bismarck's reversal of policy away from laissez-faire and free trade, signaled by Delbrück's dismissal in 1876, caused a break with the majority of the National Liberals, who split, with the larger left wing amalgamating with the Progressives in 1884 as a new German Left Liberal or Radical party. As in the sixties, Bismarck faced an opposition majority, now composed in the Reichstag of the Center, the

Left Liberals, the Social Democrats, and splinter groups, which he compared to the heterogeneous elements in Great Britain who followed the detested Gladstone and had no common policy except opposition to Bismarck. He apparently believed mistakenly that they backed the formation of a "Gladstone Ministry," a coalition of all the many rivals he felt wanted to replace him. Ever conscious of the perilousness of his position and the allegedly frail physique of William I, Bismarck excoriated the opposition parties as traitors, as "enemies of the empire." Always quick to repay an injury, real or imagined, he never forgave opponents. Unrelenting vendettas are a distinguishing characteristic of his statecraft. With the shifts in party support and the dismissal of independent men, his position became more isolated. The opposition's power was broken in 1887 when the putative danger of war from France was used by him to drum up patriotic support for a third septennate, a third army budget voted for seven years. His backers joined in a formal alliance, the Cartel, made up of the Free Conservatives, Conservatives, and rump National Liberals, to support his national and military policy.

Only part of the charge of the Declaration of Independence against George III applies to Bismarck: "He has affected to render the military independent of, and superior to, the civil power." Possessing no technical military knowledge, he correctly and coolly relied on the capability of the army to overcome Prussia's enemies. He defended the monarch's powers of command over the army, pushed through the military's demands, and contributed to the continuance of military agencies removed from parliamentary scrutiny. Military policy continued to be made by Prussian military authorities; there was no imperial secretary of state for war. Bismarck identified himself with the army by appearing in uniform in public, disingenuously explaining that it made expensive changes of dress unnecessary. But, at the same time, he insisted on the dominance of the civil over the military power in determining general policy. This struggle became more heated during the Franco-German War over the issues of the bombardment of Paris, annihilation of the French, and the peace treaty. Despite William I's military predilections, Bismarck's victory was complete. He was equally successful in resisting efforts of the military to wage "prophylactic war" against France and Russia. Wars, he felt, were dangerous adventures whose outcome contained too many unpredictable elements and were best avoided or, if they were necessary, ended as soon as possible. Never should Germany fight a war of prestige.

Rational calculation was, indeed, the keystone of his thought. The statesman had to estimate the true interests of his country and act upon them, defending himself against other rational statesmen. With this belief, he often misunderstood his counterparts, seeing rational conniving where there was only confusion or stupidity. And he tended to underestimate or ignore the irrational. This emerges clearly in his social policy. His concern with the economic depression, which caused him to add the office of Prussian minister of commerce to his other posts as Prussian minister of foreign affairs, minister president, and German chancellor, not only swayed him to adopt protective tariffs, but brought the Social Democratic or Marxist party to his notice, as the party grew with the depression. In 1878, he was able to push an anti-Socialist law through the Reichstag in the teeth of National Liberal resistance and Centrist, Progressive, and of course, Social Democratic opposition. Repressive measures were periodically renewed and only lapsed after his dismissal in 1890. Approaching the problem reasonably, he believed repression must be tempered by reform; correction of capitalism's worst abuses, provided employers were not touched, would wean the workers from pernicious revolutionary leadership. Thus he inaugurated the social welfare state with insurance to protect the workingman from the financial burdens of illness, accidents, and old age. These rational measures failed to stem growing support for the Social Democrats. One might argue, however, that after repressive measures expired, social welfare measures, extended by his successors, aided the rise of revisionist Marxism and helped reconcile the workers to the German state.

It is as the acknowledged master of foreign policy that Bismarck is most remembered, although foreign and domestic motivations were frequently intermingled in his actions, as in the septennate struggle of 1887. After the Franco-German War, Bismarck was faced with the task of reconciling Europe to the existence not only of an expanded Prussia, but also of a German Empire which was the most powerful continental state. If his ideal solution to this problem came to be the establishment of a new concert excluding France and bound together by formal alliances to maintain the European peace Germany needed for consolidation, he never achieved it. Instead he was forced to content himself with a complicated mixture of alliances with informal understandings, which, at least, usually assured the effective isolation of France. Whether correctly or incorrectly, he considered France the irreconcilable enemy of the German Empire and the inveterate disturber of European peace. He might, as has often been claimed, temporarily trifle with France to discomfort Great Britain, or back French colonial expansion to divert France from the continent, but he never considered it a potential loyal friend, let alone a possible ally.

His initial preference was for a league of the three emperors of Russia, Austria, and Germany. This policy floundered on the perennial problem of the opposing ambitions in the Balkans of Germany's two allies. Neither would conscientiously adhere formally to a division of spheres of influence which he desired. When the Russo-Turkish War resulted in an impressive expansion of Russian power, Bismarck intervened to call a European conference to prevent general war and preserve peace by allowing Russia to retain as much as the other powers would allow. As the "honest broker" at the Congress of Berlin, he believed he had achieved this. When the Russians, however, came to feel that they had been cheated and adopted a hostile attitude, he quickly forced through the fateful Dual Alliance with Austria-Hungary. He was impelled not only by fear of possible Russian action and a feeling of community of interests with Austria, but also by a desire to appeal to national wishes by an alliance with the fellow German Austrians, and perhaps by overestimation of his ally's stability. Whether German interests would not have been better served by adhesion to Russia is still debated. In any case, he felt that he would be able to reconcile the Dual Alliance and Russia, and he enjoyed uneasy success for a time by resurrecting the League of Three Emperors. When this arrangement fell apart, he took the unusual course of continuing the Dual Alliance, now enlarged to the Triple Alliance by the addition of Italy, while making the secret Reinsurance Treaty with Russia.

With Great Britain he usually saw no basic conflicts, nor did he entertain any prospects of firm support from it. Believing that Britain's parliamentary monarchy was unstable, he made no alliance. Except when briefly plagued by Britain's blundering and obtuse response to German colonial aspirations in Africa, he attempted to work hand in hand, particularly viewing German backing of British policy in Egypt as a means to secure cooperation elsewhere. He worked to bring Britain into his alliance system implicitly by encouraging close ties with Austria and with Italy, which he never saw as a reliable ally or a significant factor in European affairs.

Criticism of Bismarck has often focused on his constructing the system of secret alliances which led to World War I. He did not, however, look at the system as a necessarily permanent one, but simply as an arrangement which imperfectly served Germany's, and Europe's, interests in his time. Moreover, he did not see an alliance as committing Germany beyond its terms. He was careful to keep Austria on the leash, avoided involvement in any Balkan adventures, and stressed, generally, the defensive nature of the alliances. Indeed, the secrecy of the alliance system—except for the Reinsurance Treaty whose existence Bismarck himself disclosed in 1896—was limited. European statesmen knew of the alliances and their approximate terms, and Bismarck valued opportunities to make them known, as in the publication of the Dual Alliance in 1888.

Bismarck's heritage is an ambiguous one. In foreign affairs, he created a system which he manipulated to preserve German interests and European peace. In the hands of others, it led to tension and conflict. In domestic affairs, he contributed greatly to the perpetuation of an antiquated social system and to the failure to develop effective parliamentary government. The liberal parties abandoned classical liberal principles, and they became more nationalistic, as did the formerly particularist Conservatives. Government by conciliating economic interests rather than by securing firm political party backing became the imperial system. Bismarck's insistence upon the correctness of his policy and his utter ruthlessness toward opponents removed men of character from German public life at a time when they were most needed and sharpened a tragic tradition of intolerance of dissent. He left no real successor. The constitutional institutions which he erected were too rigid to accommodate successfully to changing times and new stresses. Yet to have unified a great people and to have preserved the general peace of Europe are no mean achievements and, despite his belief that the statesman can only steer the ship of state upon the streams of time, Bismarck remains one of the conspicuous examples of men who have altered the course of history.

Chronology of
the Life of Bismarck

1815	(1 April, 1:00 P.M.) Born at Schönhausen, province of Brandenburg, Prussia, son of the landed proprietor Ferdinand v. Bismarck and Wilhelmine, née Mencken.
	(8 June) German Confederation established.
	(18 June) Battle of Waterloo.
1832	(10 May) Matriculated at the University of Göttingen.
1833	(11 September) Leaves Göttingen.
1833–35	Hears lectures at the University of Berlin.
1835	(20 May) Passes legal examination.
	(4 June) Enters Prussian civil service.
1838–39	Military service.
1839	Manages family estates.
1840	(7 June) Death of King Frederick William III of Prussia. Accession of Frederick William IV.
1845	Proprietor of Schönhausen and Kniephof.
1847	(11 April) Enters Prussian United Landtag.
	(28 July) Marries Johanna v. Puttkamer.
1848	(18 March) Revolt in Berlin.
1849	(5 February) Elected to Prussian Second Chamber.
1850	(31 January) Elected to Erfurt Parliament.
	(30 November) Punctation of Olmütz.
1851	(15 July) Minister plenipotentiary at Frankfort.
1854	(21 November) Life member of the Prussian Chamber of Peers.
1858	(7 October) William, Prince of Prussia becomes prince Regent.
1859	(29 January) Ambassador at St. Petersburg.
1861	(2 January) Death of Frederick William IV. Accession of William I.
1862	(22 May) Ambassador at Paris.
	(23 September) Acting minister president of Prussia.
	(30 September) "Iron and blood" speech.
	(8 October) Prussian minister president and minister of foreign affairs.
1863	(1 June) Press Ordinances.

1864	(18 January) War with Denmark.
	(30 October) Peace of Vienna.
1865	(14 August) Convention of Gastein.
	(16 September) Created count.
1866	(8 April) Alliance with Italy.
	(7 May) Blind's assassination attempt.
	(16 June) War with Austria.
	(3 July) Battle of Königgrätz.
	(26 July) Preliminary Peace of Nikolsburg.
	(23 August) Peace of Prague.
	(14 September) Indemnity Bill.
1867	Acquires estate of Varzin in Pomerania.
	(April–May) Luxemburg Crisis.
	(16 April) North German constitution proclaimed.
	(14 July) Appointed North German chancellor.
1870	(13 July) Ems Dispatch.
	(19 July) French declaration of war delivered in Berlin.
	(2 September) Capitulation of Napoleon III at Sedan.
	(4 September) Second Empire falls. Third Republic established in France.
	(13 September) Demands Alsace-Lorraine as a condition of peace.
1871	(18 January) William I proclaimed German emperor at Versailles.
	(26 February) Preliminary Peace of Versailles.
	(21 March) Created prince and appointed imperial chancellor.
	(16 April) Imperial constitution proclaimed.
	(10 May) Treaty of Frankfort.
1872	(2 July) Imperial law expelling the Jesuits.
	(21 December) Surrenders post as Prussian minister president.
1873	(11 May) First Prussian May laws.
	(22 October) League of Three Emperors.
	(9 November) Reappointed Prussian minister president.
1874	Acquires estate of Friedrichsruh near Hamburg.
	(14 April) First septennate.
	(13 July) Kullmann's assassination attempt.
	(4 October) Arrest of Count Harry von Arnim.
1875	(April) "War-in-Sight" Crisis.
1878	(2 June) Assassination attempt on William I.
	(4 June–5 December) Crown prince regent.
	(13 June–13 July) Congress of Berlin.
	(21 October) First anti-Socialist law.
1879	(25 July) Protective tariff in force.
	(15 October) Dual Alliance with Austria.

1880	(6 May) Second septennate.
	(23 August) Appointed Prussian minister of commerce.
1881	(18 June) Revival of the League of Three Emperors.
1882	(20 May) Triple Alliance concluded.
1883	(15 June) Workers' health insurance law.
1884	(27 May) Renewal of the Triple Alliance for three years.
	(23 June) Proclamation of colonial policy.
	(6 July) Workers' accident insurance law.
1887	(20 January) Renewal of the Triple Alliance.
	(11 March) Third septennate.
	(18 June) Reinsurance Treaty with Russia.
1888	(9 March) Death of William I. Accession of the crown prince as Frederick III.
	(15 June) Death of Frederick III. Accession of William II.
1889	(18 May) Last speech in the Reichstag.
	(22 May) Law insuring the aged.
1890	(25 January) Renewal of anti-Socialist law defeated in the Reichstag.
	(31 January) Surrenders post as Prussian minister of commerce.
	(20 February) Cartel defeated in Reichstag elections.
	(18 March) Requests dismissal from the offices of Prussian foreign minister and minister president and German imperial chancellor.
	(20 March) Dismissed. Created duke of Lauenburg.
1894	(26 January) Reconciliation with William II.
	(27 November) Death of Johanna v. Bismarck.
1895	(23 March) Reichstag defeats a motion to congratulate him on his eightieth birthday.
1898	(30 July, 11:00 P.M.) Dies at Friedrichsruh.

BISMARCK LOOKS AT THE WORLD

A national hero can expect that his words will be widely circulated, and Bismarck is no exception. There is no single, complete compilation of what he said and wrote, although Die gesammelten Werke *contains much of importance, but there are myriad publications of his letters, official reports, and dispatches, as well as his speeches. Bismarck was far removed from the popular notion of a successful nineteenth-century orator. His soft, high-pitched voice, which contrasted so markedly with his massive frame, did not carry far, and listeners had to strain to hear him. He sometimes took minutes to find a correct word and often dropped a sentence in the middle of a speech to start anew. It was the forcefulness of his language and the vigor of his thought that enraptured or antagonized his listeners. Other valuable sources are the numerous records of his conversations, reflecting a tradition of table talk that goes back to Luther at least. His memoirs, though incomplete and highly prejudiced, are also indispensable to understanding him. Often the chancellor used frankness as other statesmen did guile or obscurity to win over others or to mislead them. Few believed, particularly at first, that any statesman would reveal his plans, especially ones that appeared to contemporaries as so bold and so novel. Unlike many other national heroes, Bismarck was a master of his language, as well as being proficient in French, Russian, Polish, and English.*

1

Unification

Bismarck's unchallenged achievement was German unification. Unlike many of the liberals, he did not believe that unification could come about peacefully, and he accomplished it only by three wars. Part of his task was to win over the nationalist liberals, who were repelled by his actions in the Prussian constitutional conflict. He did this by adopting some liberal measures and, after Austria had been conquered by force of arms, by acknowledging in the Indemnity Bill of 1866 that the government had acted illegally in spending taxes without a budget. Unity was achieved by the common war of the North German Confederation and the South German states against the French. It was sealed by the incorporation of Alsace-Lorraine, not into Prussia as was the case with the acquisitions of 1866, but into the new German Empire.

THE NEW CONSERVATISM [1]

Before he took office, Bismarck had broken with traditional conservative principles. In this letter, he attacks the notion of the solidarity of conservative powers in foreign affairs. He also feels alienated from the announced program of the Prussian Conservative party, which he helped found in 1848, and even advocates a German national parliament. This document raises the question of how much Bismarck's later policy was the result of reasoned calculation aimed at specific goals and how much he responded simply to the needs of the moment. Did he follow a plan for unification, or did he merely swim with the tide?

. . . I approve completely of your criticisms with regard to the Conservative program. From the beginning, the prevading *negative* cast of the sentences drafted should have been avoided. A political party cannot endure merely on the feeble defensive, much less gain ground and adherents. —Every party maintains it detests the filth of the German republic, and the opponents . . . also honestly strive not to desire it, especially not the filth. A mode of speech which goes so far beyond the needs of the moment says either nothing at all or conceals what one does not want to say. . . . Among our best friends we have so many doctrinaires, who desire from Prussia entirely the same obligation to protect legally foreign princes and countries as in the case of its own subjects. This system of the solidarity of the conservative interests of all countries is a dangerous fiction, as long as the most complete and most honorable reciprocity does not exist in the countries of all rulers. Carried out by Prussia in isolation it would be quixotic and would only weaken the King and his government in the implementation of their own task, for the Prussian crown

[1] Letter from Bismarck to Alexander von Below-Hohendorf, Stolpmünde, 18 September 1861. In Bismarck, *Die gesammelten Werke* 15 vols. in 19 (Berlin: Deutsche Verlagsgesellschaft m.g. H, 1933), xiv-1, 578–79. Translated by the editor.

manages the God-given defense *of Prussia* against injustices, coming
from within and from without. We are coming to the point where
the entirely unhistoric, godless, and unjust sovereignty swindle of
the German princes uses our Confederation relationships as a pedestal from which they play at being a European power in order to
make the Prussian Conservative party their pet. Moreover, our *government* is liberal in Prussia and legitimist abroad. We protect
foreign crownrights with more persistence than our own, and about
particularist sovereignty, created by Napoleon and sanctioned by
Metternich, we are enthusiastic to the point of blindness to the
dangers with which Prussia's and Germany's independence is threatened, as long as the nonsense of the *present* Confederation constitution exists, which is nothing but a hothouse and preserve factory
for dangerous and revolutionary particularist efforts. Instead of giving
public expression in the program to the vague attack against the
German republic, I would have wished [a statement of] what we in
Germany desire to be altered and established, be it through aspirations of legally achieved changes in the Confederation constitution,
be it by way of well-known associations on the analogy of the Zollverein and the Coburg military convention. We have the double task
of bearing witness that the existent Confederation constitution is *not*
our ideal, that we openly seek necessary changes but in a legal manner
and will not go *beyond* the limit requisite for the security and success of all. We need a tight consolidation of German military power
which is as necessary as our daily bread; we need a new and flexible
organization in the customs' area and a number of common institutions to protect material interests against the disadvantages which
arise from the unnatural configuration of German domestic state
boundaries. —Moreover, I don't see why we *shrink back so prudishly
from the idea of representation of the people, be it in the Confederation, be it in a Zollverein parliament.* We really could not combat
as revolutionary an institution which has legitimate value in every
German state, and which in Prussia we Conservatives ourselves are
not able to dispense with. Up to now very moderate concessions in
the national area would still be recognized as valuable. One could
create a truly conservative national representation and yet even
harvest liberal thanks for that.

IRON AND BLOOD [2]

*One of Bismarck's most famous utterances is also one of the
most imperfectly recorded. Reproduced here is a selection from*

[2] Bismarck's speech to the Budget Committee of the Prussian Chamber of
Deputies, 30 September 1862. In H. Kohl, ed., *Die politischen Reden des Fürsten*

the report of the parliamentary correspondent of the newspaper,
Berliner Allgemeine Zeitung *of 1 October 1862. Only the thread
of Bismarck's argument is given, and the reporter varies between
direct and indirect discourse. Bismarck is attempting both to conciliate the Progressive majority and to show the government's
firmness. In speeches twenty years later he altered "iron and
blood" to the more familiar "blood and iron."*

He would like to go into the budget for 1862, without, however,
giving a binding explanation. Misuse of constitutional rights could
be maintained from all sides; that led to reaction from the other side.
For example, the crown could dissolve [the Chamber of Deputies]
twelve times successively; that, certainly was permissible according
to the letter of the constitution, but it would still be an abuse. Likewise it could reject deletion of the budget without limit. There the
boundary was difficult to draw; was it already set at 6 millions? At
16? Or at 60? —There were members of the National League, a league
which was respected for the justice of its demands, esteemed members,
who declared all standing armies to be superfluous. Indeed, now if a
representation of the people had this view! Would not a government have to reject that? —There had been discussion of the "calm-
ness" of the Prussian people. Indeed, the great independence of the
individual in Prussia made it difficult to govern with the constitution
. . . ; in France it was different, there this individual independence
was lacking. A constitutional crisis was no disgrace, but an honor.
—Further we are perhaps too "educated" to support a constitution.
We are too critical. The capability of forming an opinion of governmental measures and acts of representation of the people is too general. In the country there are a great number of "Cataline-like
beings," who have a great interest in revolutions. That may sound
paradoxical, but still proves to everyone how difficult constitutional
life in Prussia is. —Further, one is too sensitive to governmental
errors; as if it were enough to say such and such a minister had
made mistakes, as if one himself did not sympathize! —Public opinion
changes. The press is not public opinion; we know how the press
originated. The deputies had the lofty duty of leading opinion, of
standing above it. —Again concerning our people: our blood is too
hot, we prefer to carry too great an armament for our body; only
we should use it too. Germany does not look to Prussia's liberalism,
but to its power; Bavaria, Württemberg, and Baden may indulge in

Bismarck 14 vols. (Stuttgart: J. G. Cotta'schen Buchhandlung Nachfolger, 1892),
2:28–30. Translated by the editor.

liberalism; no one will assign them Prussia's role because of that. Prussia must concentrate and maintain its power for the favorable moment which has already slipped by several times. Prussia's boundaries according to the treaties of Vienna are not favorable to a healthy state life. The great questions of the time will not be resolved by speeches and majority decisions—that was the great mistake of 1848 and 1849—but by iron and blood.

PARTICULARISM AND UNIFICATION [3]

Looking back upon unification in his memoirs, Bismarck saw one of the greatest barriers to unity in particularism, or states' rights. Here he defends his policy of erecting a federal state with arguments about German dynastic loyalties and discusses the conflict between Prussian and national goals. He points out that the particularist forces in Prussia, represented by the Conservative party and often personified in William I, often worked against his national policy.

Never, not even at Frankfort, did I doubt that the key to German politics has to be found in princes and dynasties, not in publicists, whether in parliament and the press, or on the barricades. The opinion of the cultivated public as uttered in parliament and the press might promote and sustain the determination of the dynasties, but perhaps provoked their resistance more frequently than it urged them forward in the direction of national unity. The weaker dynasties leant for shelter upon the national cause, rulers and houses that felt themselves more capable of resistance mistrusted the movement, because with the promotion of German unity there was a prospect of the diminution of their independence in favor of the central authority or the popular representative body. The Prussian dynasty might anticipate that the hegemony in the future German Empire would eventually fall to it, with an increase of consideration and power. It could foresee its own advantage, so far as it were not absorbed by a national parliament, in the lowering of status so much dreaded by the other dynasties. From the time that the idea of the dual entity, Austria-Prussia, under the influence of which I had come to the Frankfort Federal Diet, had given place to a sense of the necessity of defending our position against attacks and stratagems on the part of the [Austrian] president, when once I had received the im-

[3] A. J. Butler, trans., *Bismarck: The Man and the Statesman* 2 vols., by Otto von Bismarck (New York and London: Harper and Brothers, 1899), 1: 318-27.

pression that the mutual support of Austria and Prussia was a youthful dream, resulting from the after-effects of the war of liberation and the notions of schools, and had convinced myself that the Austria with which I had until then reckoned did not exist for Prussia, I acquired the conviction that on the basis of the authority of the Federal Diet it would not be possible even to recover for Prussia that position which she had held in the *Bund* before the events of March, to say nothing of such a reform of the Federal Constitution as might have afforded the German people a prospect of the realization of their pretension to a position recognized by international law as one of the great European nations. . . .

. . . The Gordian knot of German circumstances was not to be untied by the gentle methods of dual policy [and], could only be cut by the sword; it came to this, that the King of Prussia, conscious or unconscious, and with him the Prussian army, must be gained for the national cause, whether from the "Borussian" point of view one regarded the hegemony of Prussia or from the national point of view the unification of Germany as the main object: both aims were coextensive. So much was clear to me, and I hinted at it when in the budget committee (September 30, 1862) I made the much misrepresented deliverance concerning iron and blood. . . .

Prussia was nominally a Great Power, at any rate the fifth. The transcendent genius of Frederick the Great had given her this position, and it had been re-established by the mighty achievements of the people in 1813. . . . Prussia's material weight did not then correspond to her moral significance and her achievement in the war of liberation.

In order that German patriotism should be active and effective, it needs as a rule to hang on the peg of dependence upon a dynasty; independent of dynasty it rarely comes to the rising point, though in theory it daily does so, in parliament, in the press, in public meeting; in practice the German needs either attachment to a dynasty or the goad of anger, hurrying him into action; the latter phenomenon, however, by its own nature is not permanent. It is as a Prussian, a Hanoverian, a Würtemberger, a Bavarian or a Hessian, rather than as a German, that he is disposed to give unequivocal proof of patriotism; and in the lower orders and the parliamentary groups it will be long before it is otherwise. We cannot say that the Hanoverian, Hessian, and other dynasties were at any special pains to win the affections of their subjects; but nevertheless the German patriotism of their subjects is essentially conditioned by their attachment to the dynasty after which they call themselves. It is not differences of stock, but dynastic relations upon which in their origin the centrifugal elements repose. It is not attachment to Swabian, Lower Saxon, Thu-

ringian, or other particular stock that counts for most, but the dynastic incorporation with the people of some severed portion of a
ruling princely family, as in the instances of Brunswick, Brabant,
and Wittelsbach dynasties. . . . The German's love of Fatherland has
need of a prince on whom it can concentrate its attachment. Suppose
that all the German dynasties were suddenly deposed; there would
then be no likelihood that German national sentiment would suffice to
hold all Germans together from the point of view of international
law amid the friction of European politics, even in the form of
federated Hanse towns and imperial village communes. The Germans
would fall a prey to more closely welded nations if they once lost the
tie which resides in the princes' sense of community of rank.

History shows that in Germany the Prussian stock is that of which
the individual character is most strongly stamped, and yet no one
could decisively answer the question whether, supposing the Hohenzollern dynasty and all its rightful successors to have passed away,
the political cohesion of Prussia would survive. . . . Some dynasties
have many memories which are not exactly of the kind to inspire attachment in the heterogeneous fragments out of which their states
have, as a matter of history, been formed. Schleswig-Holstein has
absolutely no dynastic memories, least of all any opposed to the House
of Gottorp, and yet the prospect of the possible formation there of a
small, independent, brand-new little court with ministers, court-mar-
shals, and orders, in which the life of a petty state should be sustained at the cost of what Austria and Prussia could manage in the
Bund, called forth very strong Particularist movements in the Elbe
duchies. . . .

The other nations of Europe have need of no such go-between for
their patriotism and national sentiment. Poles, Hungarians, Italians,
Spaniards, Frenchmen would under any or without any dynasty preserve their homogeneous national unity. The Teutonic stocks of the
north, the Swedes and the Danes, have shown themselves pretty free
from dynastic sentiment; and in England, though external respect
for the Crown is demanded by good society, and the formal maintenance of monarchy is held expedient by all parties that have hitherto
had any share in government, I do not anticipate the disruption of
the nation, or that such sentiments as were common in the time of
the Jacobites would attain to any practical form, if in the course of
its historical development the British people should come to deem a
change of dynasty or the transition to a republican form of government necessary or expedient. The preponderance of dynastic attachment, and the use of a dynasty as the indispensable cement to hold
together a definite portion of the nation calling itself by the name
of a dynasty is a specific peculiarity of the German Empire. . . .

Whatever may be the origin of this factitious union of Particularist elements, its result is that the individual German readily obeys the command of a dynasty to harry with fire and sword, and with his own hands to slaughter his German neighbors and kinsfolk as a result of quarrels unintelligible to himself. To examine whether this characteristic be capable of rational justification is not the problem of a German statesman, so long as it is strongly enough pronounced for him to reckon upon it. The difficulty of either abolishing or ignoring it, or making any advance in theory towards unity without regard to this practical limitation, has often proved fatal to the champions of unity; conspicuously so in the advantage taken of the favorable circumstances in the national movements of 1848–50. The attachment of the modern Guelf party to the old dynasty I fully understand, and to that party perhaps I should myself have belonged had I been born an Old-Hanoverian. But in that case I should never have been able to escape the influence of the national German sentiment, or be surprised if the *vis majeure* of the collective nationality were relentlessly to annul my dynastic liege-loyalty and personal predilection. How to fall with a good grace! solicitude to solve that problem accords in politics—and not merely in German politics—with other and better justified aspirations. . . . In the German national sentiment I see the preponderant force always elicited by the struggle with particularism; for particularism—Prussian particularism too—came into being only by resistance to the collective German community, to Emperor and Empire, in revolt from both, leaning first on papal, then on French, on all cases on foreign support, all alike damaging and dangerous to the German community. . . .

Dynastic interests are justified in Germany so far as they fit in with the common national imperial interests: the two may very well go hand in hand; and a duke loyal to the Empire in the old sense is in certain circumstances more serviceable to the community than would be direct relations between the Emperor and the duke's vassals. So far, however, as dynastic interests threaten us once more with national disintegration and impotence, they must be reduced to their proper measure.

The German people and its national life cannot be portioned out as private possessions of princely houses. It has always been clear to me that this reflection applies to the electoral house of Brandenburg as well as to the Bavarian, the Guelf, or other houses; I should have been weaponless against the Brandenburg princely house, if in dealing with it I had needed to reinforce my German national feeling by rupture and resistance; in the predestination of history, however, it so fell out that my courtier-talents sufficed to gain the King, and with him by consequence his army, for the national cause. I have had perhaps harder battles to fight against Prussian particularism than against the particularism of the other German states and dynasties, and my relation to the Emperor William I as his born subject made these battles all the harder for me. Yet in the end, despite the strongly dynastic policy of the Emperor, but thanks to his national policy which, dynastically justified, became ever stronger in critical moments, I always succeeded in gaining his countenance for the German side of our development, and that too when a more dynastic and particularist policy prevailed on all other hands. This, as I was situated at Nikolsburg, I was only able to effect with the help of the Crown Prince. The territorial sovereignty of the individual princes had in the course of German history reached an unnaturally high development; the individual dynasties, Prussia not excepted, had never a better historical right than under the Hohenstaufen and Charles V to partition the German people among them as their private property and claim the sovereign's share in its carcass.

The unlimited sovereignty of the dynasties, of the imperial orders, of the imperial cities, and imperial village communes was won by revolution at the cost of the nation and its unity. . . . That the dynasties have at all times been stronger than press and parliament is established by the fact that in 1866 countries belonging to the *Bund,* whose dynasties lay within the sphere of Austrian influence disregarded national policy and sided with Austria, those alone which lay under the Prussian guns throwing in their lot with Prussia. Hanover, Hesse, and Hanau were of course not in the latter category, since they thought Austria strong enough to refuse compliance with the Prussian demands, and conquer. In consequence they paid the reckoning, since it proved impossible to reconcile King William to the idea that Prussia at the head of the North German confederation hardly needed an accession of territory. Certain however it is that, as of old, so also in 1866, the material force of the confederate states followed the dynasties and not the parliaments, and that Saxon, Hanoverian, and Hessian blood was spilt, not to advance but to retard the unification of Germany.

THE SCHLESWIG-HOLSTEIN QUESTION [4]

The Schleswig-Holstein question was an extremely complicated international affair, intertwined with an equally complex succession question. Here, in retrospect, Bismarck deals with the difficulties caused by the adherence of the Prussian royal family and the liberals to the cause of Duke Frederick of Au-

[4] Ibid., 2: 9–15, 20–21, 23–25.

gustenburg, as the rightful duke of Schleswig-Holstein. Bismarck
takes the opportunity to discuss his view of public opinion and
German partisan strife.

The gradations which appeared attainable in the Danish question, every one of them meaning for the duchies an advance to something better than the existing conditions, culminated, in my judgment,
in the acquisition of the duchies by Prussia, a view which I expressed
in a council held immediately after the death of Frederick VII. I
reminded the King that every one of his immediate ancestors, not
even excepting his brother, had won an increment of territory for
the state . . . and I encouraged him to do likewise. This pronounce-
ment of mine did not appear in the protocol. As Geheimrath Coste-
noble, who had drawn up the protocol, explained to me, when I
asked him the reason of this, the King had opined that I should
prefer what I blurted out not to be embedded in protocols. His
Majesty seems to have imagined that I had spoken under the Bacchic
influences of a *déjeuner,* and would be glad to hear no more of it.
I insisted, however, upon the words being put in, and they were.
While I was speaking, the Crown Prince raised his hands to heaven
as if he doubted my sanity; my colleagues remained silent.

If the utmost we aimed at could not be realised, we might have, in
spite of all Augustenburg renunciations, have gone as far as the introduction of that dynasty, and the establishment of a new middle
state, provided the Prussian and German national interests had been
put on a sure footing—these interests to be protected by what was
the essential part of the subsequent February conditions—that is, a
military convention, Kiel as a harbor for the *Bund,* and the Baltic
and North Sea canal.

Even if, taking into consideration the European situation and the
wish of the King, this had not been attainable without the isolation
of Prussia from all the Great Powers, including Austria—the question
was in what way, whether under the form of a personal union or
under some other, a provisional settlement was attainable as regards
the duchies, which must in any case be an improvement in their
position. From the very beginning I kept annexation steadily before
my eyes, without losing sight of the other gradations. I considered
the situation set up in the public opinion of our opponents as our
programme to be the one which I believed must absolutely be avoided
—that is to say, to fight out Prussia's struggle and war for the erection
of a new grand duchy, at the head of the newspapers, the clubs, the
volunteers, and the states of the *Bund* (Austria excepted), and this
without the assurance that the Federal governments would carry the

affair through, despite every obstacle. Moreover, the public opinion that had developed in this direction . . . had a childlike confidence in the assistance England would render to isolated Prussia. The partnership of France would have been much more easy to obtain than that of England, had we been willing to pay the price which it might be foreseen it would cost us. I have never wavered in the conviction that Prussia, supported only by the arms and associates of 1848—and by these I mean public opinion, Diets, political clubs, volunteers, and the small contingents as they were then constituted—would have embarked upon a hopeless course and would have only found enemies in the Great Powers, in England also. I should have regarded as a humbug and a traitor any minister who had fallen back upon the erroneous policy of 1848, 1849, and 1850, which must have prepared a new Olmütz for us. Austria once with us, however, the possibility of a coalition of the other Powers against us disappeared.

Even though German unity could not be restored by means of resolutions of Diets, newspapers, and rifle-meetings, Liberalism nevertheless continued to exercise a pressure on the princes which made them more inclined to make concessions for the sake of the *Reich*. The mood of the Courts wavered between the wish to fortify the monarchial position and autocratic policy in view of the advance of the Liberals, and anxiety lest peace should be disturbed by violence at home or abroad. No German government allowed any doubt to remain as to its *German* sentiments; but as to the way in which the future of Germany was to be shaped, neither governments nor parties were agreed. It is not probable that the Emperor William as Regent, or subsequently as King, could ever have been brought so far by the road which he had first trodden, under the influence of his consort, at the beginning of the new era, to do what was necessary to bring about unity, namely, to renounce the *Bund,* and use the Prussian army in the German cause.

On the other hand, however, it is not probable that he could have been guided into the path that led to the Danish war, and consequently to that in Bohemia, but for his previous attempts and endeavors in the direction of Liberalism, and the obligations he had thereby incurred. Perhaps we should never have succeeded in holding him aloof from the Frankfort Congress of Princes in 1863 if his Liberal antecedents had not left behind in him a certain need of popularity in the Liberal direction, which before Olmütz would have been foreign to him, but since then was the natural psychological result of the desire to seek healing and satisfaction on the field of German policy, for the wounds inflicted upon his Prussian sense of honor on the same field. The Holstein question, the Danish war, Düppel and Alsen, the breach with Austria, and the decision of the

German question on the battlefield—all this was a system of adventures upon which he would, perhaps, not have entered but for the difficult position which the new era had brought him.

Even in 1864 it certainly cost us much trouble to loosen the threads by which the King, with the cooperation of the Liberalizing influence of his consort, remained attached to that camp. Without having investigated the complicated legal questions of the succession, he stuck to his motto: "I have no right to Holstein." My representation that the Duke of Augustenburg had no right to the Ducal and the Schaumburg portion; never had had, and has twice (in 1721 and 1852) renounced his claims to the Royal portion; that Denmark had as a rule voted with Prussia in the Federal Diet; that the Duke of Schleswig-Holstein, from fear of the preponderance of Prussia, would hold with Austria—produced no impression. Even though the acquisition of these provinces, washed by two seas, and my historical reminder in the cabinet council of December 1863, were not without effect on the dynastic sentiments of the King, on the other hand the realization of the disapproval which, if he threw over the Augustenburger, he would have to encounter at the hands of his consort, of the Crown Prince and Princess, of various dynasties, and of those who in his estimation at that time formed the public opinion of Germany, was not without effect.

Without doubt, public opinion in the cultured middle class of Germany was in favor of the Prince of Augustenburg, with the same want of judgment as at an earlier period palmed off "Polonism" as the German national interest, and at a later period the artificial enthusiasm for Battenbergian Bulgaria. The press was, in these two somewhat analogous cases, worked with distressing success, and public stupidity was as receptive as ever of its operation. Criticism of the government in 1864 had only reached the level of the phrase: "No, I don't like the new burgomaster." I do not know if there is anybody today who would consider it reasonable that, after the liberation of the duchies, a new grand duchy should be formed out of them, possessing the right of voting in the Federal Diet, and as an *ipso facto* result called to go in fear of Prussia and hold with her opponents. At that time, however, the acquisition of the duchies by Prussia was regarded as an act of profligacy by all those who, since 1848, had set up to play the part of representatives of national views. My respect for so-called public opinion—or, in other words, the clamor of orators and newspapers—has never been very great, but was still materially lowered as regards foreign policy in the two cases compared above. How strangely, up to this time, the King's way of looking at things was impregnated with vagabond Liberalism through the influence of his consort and of the pushing Bethmann-Hollweg

clique is evident from the tenacity with which he clung to the contradictory attitude in which the Austro-Frankfort-Augustenburg programme stood towards the Prussian efforts after National Unity. This
policy could not have recommended itself to the King on logical
grounds. He had taken it over, without making a previous chemical
analysis of its contents, as an appurtenance of the old Liberalism,
from the point of view of the earlier critical attitude of the heir to
the throne, and of the counsellors of the Queen. . . .

After the Gastein Convention and the occupation of Lauenburg,
the first addition made to the kingdom under King William, his
frame of mind, so far as I could observe, underwent a psychological
change; he developed a taste for conquest. This was nevertheless accompanied by a preponderating satisfaction that this increase—i.e.,
the harbor of Kiel, the military position in Schleswig, and right to
construct a canal through Holstein—had been won in peace and
amity with Austria.

I imagine that the right of absolute disposal of Kiel harbor had
more weight with his Majesty than the impression produced by the
newly won pleasant district of Ratzeburg and its lake. The German
fleet with Kiel harbor as the basis of its establishment had since 1848
been one of the enkindling thoughts around whose flame the German
endeavors for unity were wont to center and from which they drew
their warmth. At times, however, the hatred of my parliamentary
opponents for me had been stronger than their concern for the German fleet; and it seemed to me that the Party of Progress would
then rather have seen Prussia's newly won right to Kiel and the
prospect of our maritime future which was bound up with it, in the
hands of the auctioneer Hannibal Fischer than in those of the Bismarck ministry. The right of complaining and grumbling over this
government's annihilation of German hopes would have afforded the
deputies far more satisfaction than the progress already made on the
way to their fulfillment. . . .

In looking back upon this situation, we have lamentable proof of
the degree of dishonesty and cosmopolitanism to which political
parties with us attained when actuated by party hatred. Something
similar may have happened elsewhere; but I know of no other country where the universal national feeling and love for the whole
Fatherland offered so little resistance to the excesses of party passion
as with us. The expression, considered apocryphal, which Plutarch
puts into Caesar's mouth, namely, that he would rather be the first
man in a wretched mountain village than the second at Rome, has
always struck me as a genuinely German idea. Only too many among
us think thus in public life, and look about for the village; and when
they cannot find it on the map, look for the group, sub-group, or

coterie, as may be, in which they can be first. This state of mind which you may call egotism or independence—whichever you please—has found its realization throughout German history, from the rebellious dukes of the first imperial period, down to the innumerable princes, imperial cities, imperial villages, abbeys, knights, holding immediately of the Empire, with, as its result to the Empire, feebleness and defenselessness. At the moment it finds more vigorous expression in the party system, splitting up the nation, than in any disintegration by way of laws or dynasties. Parties diverge less in respect of programmes and principles than of the persons who stand as *condottieri* at the head of each, and seek to gain for themselves as large a following as possible of deputies and pushing publicists, who hope to arrive at power along with their leader or leaders. Differences of principle and programme whereby the groups might be forced into conflict and hostility with one another are not forthcoming in sufficient strength to supply a motive for the passionate encounters which the groups think it necessary to wage between themselves, flinging Conservatives and Free Conservatives into separate camps. Even within the Conservative party certainly many felt that they did not agree with the "Kreuzzeitung" and its hangers-on. But to fix precisely and express convincingly in a programme the line where principles divide would be a difficult task even for the leaders and their henchmen—just as denominational fanatics, and not laymen only, when you ask them to give the distinguishing characteristics of the various confessions and directions of belief, or to explain the harm they fear for their soul's welfare if they do not fiercely assault some divagation of the heterodox, as a rule turn the dilemma, or leave you still thirsting for information. So far as parties are not grouped simply according to economic interests, they fight in the interests of the rival leaders of their groups, and not according to their personal wishes and ambitions; the whole question is one of Cephas or Paul, not a difference of principle.

THE EVE OF VICTORY [5]

In this conversation with the Berlin correspondent of the Parisian newspaper Le Siècle *before the Seven Weeks' War was well underway, Bismarck speaks with great frankness. In the first of many interviews, he recognizes his unpopularity, explains his aims, and looks toward conciliating the liberals once victory is won. This contemporary account bears comparison with the views he expressed in his memoirs.*

[5] J. Vilbort, *L'Oeuvre de M. de Bismarck, 1863–1866* (Paris: Charpentier et Cie., 1869), pp. 210–16. Translated by the editor.

. . . This conversation of the statesman and the journalist took on . . . an especial interest because of this circumstance to which I direct the reader's attention. It is on the 4 June [1866] that all this was related to me by this strange and marvelous diplomat, the 4 June before the occupation of Holstein, before the invasion of Hanover and Saxony by the Prussians, before the rupture of diplomatic relations between Berlin and Vienna, even before Bismarck had launched this project of Confederation reform (10 June), by which he turned Austria out of the doors of Germany.

"Your Excellency," I said to him, "I have made it my business to inform . . . the French public of all that happens in Germany. Permit me, therefore, to speak to you with complete freedom. I will confess that today, in its foreign policy, Prussia appears to be tending toward goals eminently sympathetic to the French nation, to wit: Italy definitely freed from Austria; Germany constituted on the basis of universal suffrage. But is not the contradiction between your Prussian policy and your German policy flagrant? You proclaim a national parliament as the sole fountain-head from which Germany can emerge rejuvenated . . . , and, at the same time, you treat the second chamber at Berlin in the manner of Louis XIV, when he entered the parlement of Paris, whip in hand. We do not admit in France that the marriage between absolutism and democracy is possible. . . ."

"Well done!" Bismarck replied, "You get to the bottom of things. I know I enjoy the same unpopularity in France as I do in Germany. Everywhere I alone am held responsible for a situation I did not make, but which was imposed upon me as upon you. I am the scapegoat of public opinion, but I torment myself little about that. With a perfectly tranquil conscience, I pursue a goal which I believe useful to my country and to Germany. As for the means, for want of others, I make use of those that are offered to me. There are many things to say about the Prussian domestic situation. In order to judge it impartially, it is necessary to study and to know thoroughly the especial character of the men of this country. While today France and Italy each form a great social body animated by a common spirit and a common feeling, in Germany, on the contrary, it is individualism which dominates. Here each one lives apart in his little corner, with his own opinion, among his wife and children, always distrusting the government as well as his neighbor, judging everything from his personal point of view, but never from the viewpoint of all. The feeling of individualism and the need of contradiction are developed in the German to an inconceivable degree; show him an open door,—rather than going through it, he is bent upon wanting to open a hole in the wall beside it. Also, whatever it does, no government will ever be popular in Prussia. The greatest number will always parade the opposite opinion. It is condemned to be perpetually contradicted by the moderates and decried and spit upon by fanatics by the fact alone that it is the government and that it places itself as an authority opposed to the individual. That has been the common fate of all regimes which have followed one another since the commencement of the dynasty. Our politicians have given no more mercy to liberal ministers than to reactionary ministers. . . .

"They acclaimed," he added, "Frederick the Great's victories, but at his death they rubbed their hands joyfully at seeing themselves freed of this tyrant. Beside this antagonism, however, exists a profound attachment to the dynasty. No sovereign, no minister, no government can win the favor of Prussian individualism, but all cry from the bottom of their hearts: 'Long live the King!' and they obey when the King commands."

"There are those, however, Your Excellency, who say that discontent might approach rebellion."

"The government has never had to fear that, and it does not fear that. Our revolutionaries are not so terrible. Their hostility is especially vented in epithets against the Minister, but they respect the King. It is I alone who has done all the evil, and they bear a grudge against me alone for it. With a little more impartiality, perhaps they would realize that I would not have acted differently because I was not able to. In the present German situation and in face of Austria, we had to have an army before anything else. In Prussia, it is the only tractable force. . . .

"The Prussian who got his arm broken on a barricade . . . would re-enter his dwelling sheepishly, and would be treated as an idiot by his wife, but in the army he is an admirable soldier, and he fights like a lion for his country's honor. Evident though it is, a fault-finding politician does not wish at all to recognize this necessity of a great armed force, imposed by circumstances. As for me, I cannot hesitate; I am, in my family, in my education, the King's man before everything. Now the King holds to the military organization as to his crown, because he also judges it indispensable in his soul and his conscience. Therefore, no one is able to make him surrender or compromise that. At his age—he is seventy [sic]—and with his traditions, one becomes obstinate in ideas, especially in the case where one believes them good. Besides, on the subject of the army, I completely share his viewpoint.

"Sixteen years ago, I was living as a country gentleman when the sovereign's will designated me Prussian envoy to the Frankfort Diet. I had been raised in admiration—I could say the cult—of Austrian policy. I did not need a great deal of time to lose my youthful illusions with regard to Austria, and I became its declared enemy.

"The abasement of my country, Germany sacrificed to foreign interests, a cunning and perfidious policy—all that was not designed to please me. I did not know that the future would call upon me to play a role, but since that epoch I conceived the idea whose realization I pursue today, that of removing Germany from Austrian pressure, at least that part of Germany united to Prussian destinies in spirit, religion, customs, and interests,—North Germany. In the projects I have brought forward it is not a question of overturning thrones—of taking his duchy from this one or his little domain from that one. Besides, the King would not assist in that. And then there are family connections, cousins, a crowd of hostile influences with which I have had to keep up a fight at all times.

"All that, no more than the opposition with which I have had to struggle in Prussia, has been unable to prevent me from devoting my body and soul to this idea: North Germany constituted in its logical and natural form under the aegis of Prussia. In order to achieve that goal, I have braved everything: exile and even the scaffold. And I told the Crown Prince, who, in his education and inclinations, is by preference a man of parliamentary government: 'What does it matter if I am hanged, provided that my hangman's rope binds your throne solidly to Germany!' "

"May I also ask you, Your Excellency, how you intend to reconcile the free mission of a national parliament with the rigorous treatment which the Berlin chamber has suffered? How, above all, are you able to persuade the King, the representative of divine right, to accept universal suffrage, which is the democratic principle par excellence?"

Bismarck replied to me spiritedly:

"It is a victory won after four years of struggle! When the King summoned me four years ago the situation was most difficult. His Majesty placed a long list of liberal concessions before my eyes, but none of them to be expected in the military question. I said to the King: 'I accept, and the more the government can show itself to be liberal, the better it will be.' The Chamber was obstinate on the one hand and the crown on the other. In this conflict, I followed the King. My veneration for him, all my past, all my family traditions, made it my duty. But that I am, by nature or policy, the adversary of national representation, the born enemy of parliamentary government, is an entirely gratuitous assumption. I did not wish to disassociate myself from the King in fighting the Berlin chamber, at that time when the Berlin chamber placed itself athwart a policy which imposed itself on Prussia as a necessity of the first order. But no one has the right of directing to me that insult that I think of hoaxing Germany with my parliamentary project. The day when—my task complete—my duties toward my sovereign accord ill with my duties as a statesman, I will be able to take the course of effacing myself without it being necessary for me to disavow my labors."

THE EMS DISPATCH [6]

Great events lose nothing in their retelling. In one of the more famous—and inaccurate—passages from his memoirs, dictated in the early nineties, Bismarck relives the stirring days of 1870. He gives his own version of one of the most notorious editing jobs in history and its effect, though it has been argued that the French decision for war was reached before the publication of the Ems telegram had roused public opinion. Bismarck concludes by warning against military determination of political decisions and particularly attacks the idea of preventive war. In the last line, he takes a heartfelt jab at William II's leadership.

. . . I conversed with the Minister of War, von Roon: we had got our slap in the face from France, and had been reduced, by our complaisance, to look like seekers of a quarrel if we entered upon war, the only way in which we could wipe away the stain. My position was now untenable, solely because, during his course at the baths, the King under pressure of threats, had given audience to the French ambassador for four consecutive days, and had exposed his royal person to insolent treatment from this foreign agent without ministerial assistance. . . .

Having decided to resign, in spite of the remonstrances which Roon made against it, I invited him and Moltke to dine with me alone on the 13th, and communicated to them at table my views and prospects for doing so. Both were greatly depressed, and reproached me indirectly with selfishly availing myself of my greater facility for withdrawing from service. I maintained the position that I could not offer up my sense of honor to politics, that both of them, being professional soldiers and consequently without freedom of choice, need not take the same point of view as a responsible Foreign Minister. During our conversation, I was informed that a telegram from Ems, . . . was being deciphered. When the copy was handed to me it showed that Abeken had drawn up and signed the telegram at his Majesty's command, and I read it out to my guests, whose dejection was so great that they turned away from food and drink. On a repeated examination of the document I lingered upon the authorization of his Majesty, which included a command, immediately to communicate Benedetti's fresh demand and its rejection both to our ambassadors and to the press. I put a few questions to Moltke as to the extent of his confidence in the state of our preparations, especially as to the time they would still require in order to meet this sudden risk of war. He answered that if there was to be war he expected no advantage to us by deferring its outbreak; and even if we should not be strong enough at first to protect all the territories on the left bank of the Rhine against French invasion, our preparations would nevertheless soon overtake those of the French, while at a later period this advantage would be diminished; he regarded a rapid outbreak as, on the whole, more favorable to us than delay.

In view of the attitude of France, our national sense of honor compelled us, in my opinion, to go to war; and if we did not act according to the demands of this feeling, we should lose, when on the way to its completion, the entire impetus towards our national development won in 1866, while the German national feeling south of the Main, aroused by our military successes in 1866, and shown by the readiness of the southern states to enter the alliances, would have to grow cold again. . . .

In the same psychological train of thought in which during the Danish war in 1864 I desired, for political reasons, that precedence should be given not to the old Prussian, but to the Westphalian battalions, who so far had had no opportunity of proving their courage under Prussian leadership, and regretted that Prince Frederick Charles had acted contrary to my wish, did I feel convinced that the gulf, which diverse dynastic and family-influences and different habits of life had in the course of history created between the south and north of the Fatherland, could not be more effectually bridged over than by a joint national war against the neighbor who had been aggressive for many centuries. . . .

. . . All these considerations, conscious and unconscious, strengthened my opinion that war could be avoided only at the cost of the honor of Prussia and of the national confidence in it. Under this conviction I made use of the royal authorization communicated to me through Abeken, to publish the contents of the telegram; and in the presence of my two guests reduced the telegram by striking out words, but without adding or altering, to the following form: "After the news of the renunciation of the hereditary Prince of Hohenzollern had been officially communicated to the imperial government of France by the royal government of Spain, the French ambassador at Ems further demanded of his Majesty the King that he would authorize him to telegraph to Paris that his Majesty the

King bound himself for all future time never again to give his consent if the Hohenzollerns should renew their candidature. His Majesty the King thereupon decided not to receive the French ambassador again, and sent to tell him through the aide-de-camp on duty that his Majesty had nothing further to communicate to the ambassador." The difference in the effect of the abbreviated text of the Ems telegram as compared with that produced by the original was not the result of stronger words but of the form, which made this announcement appear decisive, while Abeken's version would only have been regarded as a fragment of a negotiation still pending, and to be continued at Berlin.

After I had read out the concentrated edition to my two guests, Moltke remarked: "Now it has a different ring; it sounded before like a parley; now it is like a flourish in answer to a challenge." I went on to explain: "If in execution of his Majesty's order I at once communicate this text, which contains no alteration in or addition to the telegram, not only to the newspapers, but also by telegraph to all our embassies, it will be known in Paris before midnight, and not only on account of the manner of its distribution, will have the effect of a red rag upon the Gallic bull. Fight we must if we do not want to act the part of the vanquished without a battle. Success, however, essentially depends upon the impression which the origination of the war makes upon us and others; it is important that we should be the party attacked, and this Gallic overweening and touchiness will make us if we announce in the face of Europe, so far as we can without the speaking-tube of the Reichstag, that we fearlessly meet the public threats of France."

This explanation brought about in the two generals a revulsion to a more joyous mood, the liveliness of which surprised me. They had suddenly recovered their pleasure in eating and drinking and spoke in a more cheerful vein. Roon said: "Our God of old lives still and will not let us perish in disgrace." Moltke so far relinquished his passive equanimity that, glancing up joyously toward the ceiling and abandoning his usual punctiliousness of speech, he smote his hand upon his breast and said: "If I may but live to lead our armies in such a war, then the devil may come directly afterwards and fetch away the 'old carcass'. . . ."

. . . His love of combat and delight in battles were a great support to me in carrying out the policy I regarded as necessary, in opposition to the intelligible and justifiable aversion in a most influential quarter. It proved inconvenient to me in 1867, in the Luxemburg question, and in 1875 and afterwards on the question whether it was desirable, as regards a war which we should probably have to face sooner or later, to bring it on *anticipando* before the adversary could improve his preparations. I have always opposed the theory which says "Yes"; not only at the Luxemburg period, but likewise subsequently for twenty years, in the conviction that even victorious wars cannot be justified unless they are forced upon one, and that one cannot see the cards of Providence far enough ahead to anticipate historical development according to one's own calculation. It is natural that in the staff of the army not only younger active officers, but likewise experienced strategists, should feel that need of turning to account the efficiency of the troops led by them, and their own capacity to lead, and of making them prominent in history. It would be a matter of regret if this effect of the military spirit did not exist in the army; the task of keeping its results within such limits as the nations' [sic] need of peace can justly claim is the duty of the political, not the military, heads of the state. That at the time of the Luxemburg question, during the crisis of 1875, invented by Gortchakoff and France, and even down to the most recent times, the staff and its leaders have allowed themselves to be led astray and to endanger peace, lies in the very spirit of the institution, which I would not forego. It only becomes dangerous under a monarch whose policy lacks sense of proportion and power to resist one-sided and constitutionally unjustifiable influences.

ALSACE-LORRAINE 7

The new German Reichstag met in 1871 in an atmosphere of cordiality and triumph; German unity was at last achieved. In one of the most genial of his speeches, Bismarck, after examining the various alternatives, defends the acquisition of Alsace-Lorraine, not, despite many conciliatory references to liberal ideas, on the basis of the principle of self-determination, but as a necessity for the defense of the German Empire. He makes no bones about the fact that acquisition was unacceptable to the indigenous population, but counsels patience and benevolence as solutions. This attitude did not last long, and he adopted a hostile policy toward the national minorities, especially the Alsatians and the Poles. Acquisition of Alsace-Lorraine apparently convinced Bismarck, as it did many others, that France would never accept the German Empire. He also takes a remarkably dispassionate attitude toward the Commune uprising, which later altered to total condemnation.

⁷ Bismarck's speech in the German Reichstag, 2 May 1871. In Kohl, *Die politischen Reden*, 5: 51–61. Translated by the editor.

. . . If we transport ourselves back a year—or, more exactly, ten months,—then we can say to ourselves that Germany was united in its love of peace; there was hardly any German who did not desire peace with France, as long as it could be maintained with honor. Those morbid exceptions, who perhaps wanted war in the hope that their own native country would be defeated, are not worthy of the name; I do not number them among the Germans! (*Bravo!*)

I insist the Germans unanimously wanted peace. But, if war were forced upon us, if we were forced to resist in our defense, if God should grant us victory in this war we had decided to wage valiantly, they were likewise unanimous in seeking for guarantees which would make repetition of a similar war more improbable and, if it should occur nevertheless, defense easier. Everyone remembers that, for three hundred years, there was really hardly one generation among our fathers which was not forced to draw its sword against France, and everyone said to himself, when at earlier opportunities, when Germany was among the victors over France, the possibility was missed to give Germany better protection to the west. This resulted from the fact that we gained the victory in common with allies, whose interests were simply not ours. When we now, depending independently and purely on our sword and our own right, gained the victory, everyone decided to work with complete seriousness for the goal of leaving behind an assured future for our children.

In the course of centuries, war with France, since it was almost always able to result in the dismemberment of Germany to our disadvantage, created a geographical-military boundary formation, which, in itself, was full of temptation for France and full of menace for Germany. I cannot more strikingly characterize the position in which we find ourselves, in which South Germany especially finds itself, than to relate a conversation with an intelligent South German sovereign when Germany was pressed to take the side of the western powers in the eastern war [in the Crimea], without it being his government's conviction that it had an independent interest in waging war. I can also name him; it was the late King William [I] of Würt-temberg. He said to me: "I share your view that we have no interest in meddling in this war, that no German interest is concerned there, which is worth the trouble of spilling German blood for it. But if we should fall out with the western powers over that, if it should go that far, count on my vote in the Diet until the time when war breaks out. Then the affair assumes another dimension. As well as any other, I am determined to maintain the obligations which I assume. But take care not to judge men other than they are. Give us Strasbourg, and we will be united for all eventualities, but as long as Strasbourg is a sally port for a power which is continuously armed, I must fear that my country will be inundated by foreign troops before the German Confederation comes to my assistance. I would not reflect an instant about eating the hard bread of an exile in your camp, but my subjects would write to me. They would be crushed by contributions to obtain an alteration of my decision. I don't know what I would do; I don't know whether all people would be firm enough. But the knot lies in Strasbourg, for as long as it is not German, it will always be a hindrance to South Germany giving itself, without reservation, to German unity, to a German-national policy. As long as Strasbourg is a sally port for an army of 100 to 150,000 men continually under arms, Germany remains in the position of not being able to intervene at the right time with equally strong forces on the upper Rhine—the French will always be there earlier."

I believe everything said in this case taken from life; I have nothing to add to it.

The wedge which the corner of Alsace at Wissembourg shoves into Germany separates South Germany more effectively from North Germany than the political line of the Main, and it takes a greater degree of decision, of national enthusiasm and devotion from our South German allies, disregarding this neighboring danger, which would arise with a skillful waging of the campaign by the French, not to hesitate an instant, to see in North Germany's danger its own and to take a vigorous role in order to march in common with us. (*Bravo!*) We have seen through the centuries that as soon as domestic conditions made a diversion abroad necessary, France was ready at any time to succumb to the temptation of this superior position, of this advanced bastion that Strasbourg forms toward Germany. (*Very true.*) It is known, that even on 6 August 1866, I was in the position to observe the French Ambassador make his appearance to see me in order, to put it succinctly, to present an ultimatum: to relinquish Mainz, or to expect an immediate declaration of war. (*Hear! Hear!*) Naturally I was not doubtful of the answer for a second. I answered him: "Good, then it's war!" (*Bravo!*) He traveled to Paris with this answer. A few days after one in Paris thought differently, and I was given to understand that this instruction had been torn from Emperor Napoleon during an illness. (*Laughter.*) The further attempts in relation to Luxemburg and further questions are known. I will not return to them. I believe I also do not need to prove that France did not always have the strength of character to resist the temptations which accompanied possession of Alsace.

The question how guarantees against that should be obtained—they must be of a territorial nature; guarantees of foreign powers could not help us much, for, to my regret, such guarantees have preserved, among other things, odd attenuating declarations. (*Laughter.*)

One would have believed that all Europe would feel the necessity of preventing the frequently recurring struggles of the two greatest cultural nations in the midst of European civilization, and that the insight was obvious that the simplest means of preventing them was the one of strengthening defense of the unquestionably peaceloving party. Nevertheless, I cannot say this idea was considered obvious everywhere. (*Laughter.*) Other expedients were sought. It was frequently proposed to us that we could be satisfied with war costs and the razing of French fortresses in Alsace and Lorraine. I have always resisted that, since I consider this expedient an impractical one in the interest of the maintenance of peace. It establishes an obligation on foreign ground and soil, a very oppressive and troublesome burden on the feelings of sovereignty, of independence, of those it concerns. Cession of fortresses would hardly be felt more severely than the foreign order not to be able to construct within the area of one's own sovereignty. The razing of the unimportant site of Hüningen has perhaps more often been used effectively to stir up French passion, than the loss of whatever territory France had to suffer after its conquest in 1815. For this reason, I put no value on this expedient, so much the less so, since, according to the geographical configuration of the projecting bastion, if I may so characterize it, the point of departure of French troops would still border on Stuttgart and Munich, the same as now. It was a matter of putting it further away.

Besides Metz is a place whose topographical configuration is such that the art of making it a strong fortress needs to do very little. Indeed, even if it were destroyed, anything that had already been done by the way of reconstruction could quickly be rebuilt, although, of course, it would be very expensive. I viewed this expedient, therefore, as inadequate.

Another expedient—and that was also advocated by the inhabitants of Alsace and Lorraine—would have been to establish in that place a neutral state, similar to Belgium and Switzerland. There would have been established a chain of neutral states from the North Sea to the Swiss Alps which would, of course, make it impossible for *us* to attack France by land, because we are accustomed to observe treaties and neutrality (*Very good!*), and because we would be separated from France by the intervening space. But France would, by no means, be prevented in the plan, actually projected but never implemented in the last war, of sending, at its convenience, its fleet with landing troops to our coasts, or of landing French troops at their allies and having them march on us. France would have gotten a protective zone against us, but, as long as our fleet is not equal to the French, we would not have been protected at sea. This was only a secondary reason. The primary reason is that generally neutrality is only tenable when the population decides to preserve an independent neutral position and, in case of necessity, to intervene with armed force for the maintenance of its neutrality. Belgium has done that, so has Switzerland; neither found it necessary against us. But both have actually protected their neutrality; both wish to remain independent neutral states. In the near future, this hypothesis would not be true for the new neutrals, Alsace and Lorraine, to be formed. But it is to be expected that the strong French elements, which will survive in the land for a long time and which adhere to France in their interests, sympathies, and memories, in this neutral state, which may always be sovereign, would certainly follow France again in a new Franco-German war. For us certainly neutrality would only be a dangerous phantom illusion, but a useful one for France. After that nothing else remained but to put this tract of land with its strong fortresses completely in Germany's power, in order to defend itself as a strong German glacis against France and in order to push back, by a number of days' marches, the point of departure of an eventual French attack, if France, either by her own strength or with allies, should again throw down the gauntlet to us.

The complexity of this idea of satisfying this imperative necessity of our security is in opposition, above all, to the disinclination of the inhabitants themselves to be separated from France. It is not my task here to investigate the reasons which made it possible for a thoroughly German population to become attached to this extent to a country with a foreign language and with a government that was not always benevolent and indulgent. Something truly lies in all those characteristics which distinguish Germans from Frenchmen and were incorporated to a high degree precisely in the Alsatian population, so that the population of this land forms in ability and love of order, I may truly say without exaggeration, a kind of aristocracy in France. It was more capable in office, more reliable in service. In a proportion far exceeding their ratio to the population, Alsatians and Lorrainers were deputies in the military, the gendarmerie, and to officials in state service. There were $1\frac{1}{2}$ million Germans, who had all the German merits in a population that had other advantages, but precisely not those they were in a position to make use of and actually made use of. Through their qualities they had a privileged position which made them forget many legal injustices. It is a German characteristic that every branch claims in some way or another a kind of superiority, especially over his closest neighbor. As long as it was France, Paris with its magnificence and France with its united greatness, which stood behind the Alsatians and Lorrainers, the German peasant was overcome with the feeling that: "Paris is mine," and he found there a source for a feeling of particularist superiority. I will not trace back the further reasons why everyone is more easily assimilated into a great state, which gives his capability full rein, than into a dismembered, if also kindred, nation, which this side of the Rhine earlier represented to the Alsatian. The fact is that this disinclination was present, and that it is our duty to overcome it by patience. In my opinion, we have many means to do that. Generally Germans have the habit of ruling more benevolently—if, among other things, somewhat more clumsily, but it is still correct in the long run—more benevolently and more humanely than French statesmen do. (*Laughter.*) It is a merit of the German nature which will become perceptible and soon remind the Alsatians' German hearts of home. Besides, we are in the position to grant the inhabitants a much greater measure of community and individual freedom than French arrangements and traditions really have the power to do. When we observe the present agitation in Paris, then it is unquestionable that, as with any movement that has a certain duration, there is also a rational core in its foundation next to all the irrational motives which adhere to it and determine its details; otherwise no agitation would have been able to reach even the amount of power which the Parisians have momentarily achieved. This rational core— I don't know how many people support it, but, in any case, the best and most intelligent of those who momentarily fight their fellow countrymen—, I can characterize it in a word; it is the German city ordinance; if the Commune had this, then the *best* of its adherents would be satisfied—I don't say all. We must consider how the matter is. The atrocity's militia consists preponderantly of people who have nothing to lose. In a city of two millions, there are a great number of so-called *repris de justice*, whom we would characterize as under police surveillance, people who spend the interval between two prison terms in Paris and who congregate in considerable numbers, people, who, above all, help themselves willingly where there is disorder and plundering. They are precisely those who have given the movement its threatening character for civilization; a character through which they occasionally distinguish themselves before investigating their theoretical goals, and one which has, I hope, been surmounted in the interests of mankind, but can, of course, easily suffer a relapse. Next to these scum, who are found so abundantly in that great city, is the militia, which I mentioned, which is made up of a number of adherents of a European international republic. Figures of the foreign nationalities who are involved there have been mentioned to me, of which I only recollect that nearly 8,000 Englishmen are supposed to be in Paris with the aim of working out their plans—I presuppose that a greater part are Irish Fenians, who are designated by the word "Englishmen"—, likewise a great number of Belgians, Poles, Garibaldians, and Italians. They are people who are pretty indifferent to the Commune and to French freedom, they strive for something else, and naturally I do not direct this argument at them, when I say: In every agitation, there is a rational core. (*Laughter.*) Such wishes, which are really very justifiable in the great communities in France when compared to the constitutional past, which left them only a very limited amount of agitation and, nevertheless, in the tradition of French statesmen, offered them the utmost that one could guarantee to community freedom, make themselves really more palpable to the German character of the Alsatians and Lorrainers, who strove more for individual and community freedom than did the French, and I am convinced that, without injury to the entire empire, we can, from the very beginning, leave for the Alsatians tolerably free elbow-room in the sphere of self-government, which will gradually be so extended that it will endeavor to reach the ideal that every individual and every small restricted district will possess the degree of freedom which is generally supportable in the entire state system. I consider it the task of rational statecraft to attain that, to come as near as possible to this goal, and it is much more attainable in the German system under which we live than it could ever be in France, with the character of the French and the unitary French constitution. On this account, with German patience and German benevolence, I believe that it will succeed in winning over the peasant there, perhaps in a shorter time than we now expect. But there will still survive elements, which are rooted in France in their entire personal past and which are yet too old to break loose from them, or which necessarily adhere to France through their material interests and which, either only later or not at all, can find compensation with us for breaking the tie that binds them to France. Therefore, we will not flatter ourselves that we can swiftly reach the goal in Alsace of the situation with regard to German feeling in Thuringia, but then, if we make good the time which is given men on the average, we, for our part, still should not despair of living to see the goal for which we strive.

Now how to approach this task? That is the question which now concerns you first, gentlemen, but still not in a decisive way which commits the future. I would like to ask you not to take the standpoint that you want to make something last for eternity, that now you already want to form a fixed idea of the shape of the future, as it perhaps should be after many years. In my opinion, no human foresight reaches that far. Relations are abnormal; they *must* be abnormal—our entire task was,—and they are not only abnormal in the way by which we acquired Alsace; the person of the winner is also abnormal. A confederation consisting of sovereign princes and free cities, which makes a conquest it must keep for the necessities of its defense and therefore finds it a possession *in common,* is a very unusual phenomenon in history and, if we subtract the several enterprises of the Swiss Cantons, which still did not intend to assimilate lands conquered in common by granting equal rights, but by managing them as provinces in common to the conquerors' advantage, then I scarcely believe anything similar is to be found in history. Therefore, precisely with this abnormal situation and abnormal task, I would like to believe that the admonition, not to overestimate the foresight of subtle politicians in human affairs, particularly concerns us. At least I do not feel that I am already in the position to say now with complete security how the situation will be in Alsace and in Lorraine in three years. That depends upon factors, whose development, whose behavior and good will, are not in our power at all and which cannot be controlled by us.

2

The Kulturkampf

The following two selections represent contrasting phases in the struggle with the Center party and the Catholic church. The first, an official attempt to secure advance agreement on the election of a new Pope, received no support. Here, at the beginning of the Kulturkampf, Bismarck emphasizes the hostile attitude of the papacy. In the second selection, Bismarck has embarked upon the policy of ending the struggle by modifying and repealing anticlerical legislation and blames the conflict not on the papacy, but on the Center party, not omitting sideswipes at other members of the opposition. He particularly defends his repressive policy toward the Poles. At the same time, he plays down his personal responsibility for the harshness of Kulturkampf legislation, while supporting greater freedom of education for priests.

THE DANGER FROM THE PAPACY [8]

According to all reports reaching us, Pope Pius IX's health is completely satisfactory, and no symptoms suggest an alteration soon. Nevertheless, a new papal election must occur either in a short or a long time; the moment lies beyond human calculation and foresight. The position of the head of the Catholic church is of such importance for all governments in those countries where this church has a recognized position that it seems imperative to present the consequences of a change in the person of the Pope promptly. It has already been recognized earlier that governments with Catholic subjects thereby also have a great and immediate interest in a papal election, as well as in the elected personality himself and also in the election being surrounded with all guarantees of formal and material relations which enable governments to recognize it as valid and to exclude all doubt for themselves too and on the part of the Catholic church in their countries. Because of that, before they actually concede the right of election of a constituted sovereign who is called

---

[8] Bismarck's confidential diplomatic circular to German representatives abroad, Berlin, 14 May 1872. In ibid., 5: 345–48. Translated by the editor.

upon to exercise far-reaching rights, which, in many circumstances, border closely upon sovereignty in their countries, they are obligated to consider conscientiously whether they can recognize the election. There can be, it seems to me, no doubt about that. A Pope, whose recognition all or a majority of European sovereigns believed they must refuse on formal or material grounds, would be as little conceivable as a bishop of a country exercising rights in any country without being recognized by the state government. This was already true in the earlier scheme of things when the position of bishops was still an independent one and governments only came into contact with the Pope on religious matters in unusual cases. The concordats already concluded at the beginning of the century produced direct and, to some extent, intimate relations between the Pope and governments, but, above all, the Vatican Council, and both its most important statements about infallibility and about the jurisdiction of the Pope, also entirely altered his position in relation to the governments. Their interest in the election of the Pope increased to the greatest degree—but with that their right to concern themselves with it was also given a much firmer basis. For, by these decisions, the Pope has come into the position of assuming episcopal rights in every single diocese and of substituting papal for episcopal power. Episcopal has merged into papal jurisdiction; the Pope no longer exercises, as heretofore, individual stipulated special privileges, but the entire plenitude of episcopal rights rests in his hands. In principle, he has taken the place of each individual bishop, and, in practice, at every single moment, it is up to him alone to put himself in the former's position in relation to the governments. Further the bishops are only his tools, his officials without real responsibility. In relation to the governments, they have become the officials of a foreign sovereign, and, to be sure, a sovereign who, by virtue of his infallibility, is a completely absolute one—more so than any absolute monarch in the world. Before the governments concede such a position to some new Pope and grant him the exercise of such rights, they must ask themselves whether the election and person chosen offer the guarantees they are justified in demanding against the misuse of such rights. Further related to that is that, precisely under present circumstances, it is not to be expected with certainty also that only the guarantees which formerly surrounded a conclave and which it itself offered in its forms and composition will be applied. The veto exercised by Roman Emperors, by Spain and by France has proved to be illusory often enough. The influence in the conclave which the different nations could exercise through cardinals of their nationality depends upon chance circumstances. Who wants to predict under what circumstances the next papal election will take place and whether it will not perhaps be held in an overhasty manner, so that earlier guarantees, even of form, are not assured?

For these reasons, it seems desirable to me that those European governments which are interested in the papal election by the ecclesiastical interests of their Catholic subjects and by the position of the Catholic church in their country should occupy themselves with this same question and, if possible, agree among themselves on the possible way they will conduct themselves toward it and on the conditions upon which eventual recognition of an election would depend.

A union of European governments in this sense would be of incalculable weight and would perhaps be in the position to prevent severe and critical complications beforehand.

I, therefore, most respectfully request Your Excellency confidentially to ask the government to which you have the honor of being accredited whether it would be inclined to offer us a helping hand in an exchange of ideas and in an eventual understanding with us on this question. If we are previously assured of readiness, the form in which this could take place could then be easily found.

I empower Your Excellency to read this dispatch aloud, but I ask you not to let it out of your hands just now and generally to handle the matter with discretion.

THE ENDING OF THE KULTURKAMPF [9]

. . . Generally I really have to struggle with the disadvantage that my opponents know how to blame me for all possible evils of the world and exaggerate by far my influence and my power in secular matters. As a result, their advantage with gullible people increases by saying at every unfortunate occurrence that the guilt for that is principally mine. I did not share in the initiation of these laws as the departmental minister, not even once as Minister President, but actually as a member of the Ministry of State. Count v. Roon was Minister President at the time when the laws first originated. Also afterwards I was in the position of delegating my authority in domestic matters, because foreign affairs occupied my activity entirely, . . . until a subsequent period to which I'll return later. Nevertheless, I do not gain the right from that to free myself from responsibility; I will only delimit my responsibility in that regard to the fact that I completely share the responsibility for the aim and tendency of the May Laws as conflict legislation, still support them today, and

---

[9] Bismarck's speech in the Prussian Chamber of Peers, 12 April 1886. In ibid., 12: 77–86, 89–91, 92, 93. Translated by the editor.

answer that it is necessary and useful to give the laws this aim. The responsibility for all details of these laws is something else, which concerns departmental lawyers, for all the arabesques, for this technically perfect building, whose corners I do not know even today, and which demands exact study by an expert and more time than I have for it. But I must still categorically oppose an interpretation of this entire legislation which is spread abroad today in the public press. There it is represented as if the May Laws were not a regrettable necessity—when I say "May Laws" I know very well that not all originated in May, but it is, as things are, the usual expression—but that one has to honor in them the palladium of the Prussian state, which may not be moved under any circumstances, if one does not wish to injure the state's honor.

Now, gentlemen, I must say that a question of honor is not concerned here in any way. It is brought in with I don't know how much time and energy and especially attempted from the direction of what one can characterize in the ecclesiastical struggle as *tertius gaudens duobus litigantibus,* in the Progressive party press. It is of tremendous importance whether there is war or peace between the state and the church, and the Progressive party must defend itself with hands and feet even against only the blunting or moderation in any way of the struggle between the two in which the third finds its pleasure, its satisfaction, its domination, its support and its prop. . . .

In my position on the matter, I am, I can truly say, really strengthened by the vehement and untrue attacks, which the possibility of concessions to the Roman Church has suffered in the Progressive press. In my long term in office, I have always found that I am on the right track when the Progressive newspapers attack me and that, as a rule I am doing well if, when if I myself cannot form a definite opinion, I do the opposite of what is in the Progressive newspapers. (*Laughter. Bravo!*)

It is one of the most extreme absurdities, proof of what one can imagine about the readers of these newspapers, when one makes a question of honor of this matter. In domestic conflicts, among fellow countrymen, the government's honor consists in its peaceableness, not, however, in its picking quarrels. It is really something else in conflicts with foreigners. Fifteen years ago when we did not have ecclesiastical legislation, were we perhaps a people without honor? Do we only feel honorable since we've had them, and must we view their loss as the loss of our honor? Yes, if the Pope stood on our borders in the French army's suite or a Polish army at the Pope's disposition threatened us simultaneously from the east, then one could talk about points of honor, then it would be permissible to fight to the last man and drop of blood against the power which Prussian legislation is supposed to offer violence to. But the power here which Prussian legislation offers violence to originates solely from the personal necessity of His Majesty the King to come into closer contact with his Catholic subjects; I do not wish to say: to be just to them, for I would not admit that this has not been the case heretofore, but to offer the hand of reconciliation. Herewith I believe I have disposed of the harassments which refer to the point of honor; I can only show opponents who strike this note that precisely their anger has marked out the right path in this matter more clearly.

As already mentioned, the May Laws were conflict laws, by which it is rather obviously stated that a lasting institution, which would dominate the Prussian state with constitutional authority, was not meant to be created by them. They were just means of battle to achieve peace. At that time, in the middle of the struggle, it was not envisaged with complete clarity how this peace would be achieved. I permit myself to cite passages out of my speeches at the time as proof that we envisaged, however, the idea of peace originally from the initiation of the May Laws. . . . Immediately with the first one I offer, I must again emphasize that I initially entered this struggle not from sectarian considerations, but from political ones—as you will see from an aphorism in a speech of 9 February [1872], given in the Chamber of Deputies. It is the first manifestation of my participation in the struggle that I have been able to find. At the time I said to the gentlemen of the Center:

> You will obtain peace with the state more easily if you forsake Guelf leadership and if you do not take into your midst Guelf Protestants who have nothing in common with you, but actually need conflict to occur in our peaceful country, for Guelf hopes can only succeed when conflict and revolt dominate. . . . I come herewith to the third ally who needs this struggle and conflict, that is the Polish nobles' exertions. The fact is that, generally, the Catholic priesthood —also the German-speaking ones—favor the Polish nobles' exertions to free themselves from the German Empire and the Prussian monarchy and to re-establish old Poland in its former boundaries and treat them benevolently, and that is one of the most sensitive points at which the struggle on the part of the Catholic Church first began and where every Minister who knows his responsibility must see to it that the state is protected from that in the future. . . .
>
> The complaint which we have against the ecclesiastical school inspectors in the Polish-speaking provinces is that they do not permit the German language its legal rights, but work to the end that the German language is neglected and not learned, that the teachers whose pupils have made progress in the German language do not receive a favorable report from the priest.

In its context, this belongs to a different discussion than that which will really occupy this chamber soon. I cite it here only in order to bring to mind again the pretext which brought me at least into the so-called Kulturkampf. Next to that, there also existed the pretext of comradeship with other colleagues. As long as one is assembled with a ministry, he is unable to criticize each of the dots over an i and the remote roots of his colleagues' decisions. . . .

. . . But, first of all, I may still remark that I am in complete agreement . . . that the millennial struggle of the priesthood with the kingdom will not allow itself to be changed into a definitive peace by some resolutions of some chambers; if we say, the peace, not only between a German emperor and the Catholic Church, but between king and priests, will always remain the squaring of the circle, which one can approach but which one cannot achieve completely. In the year 1873 [on May 10], I said in this chamber: "The struggle of the priesthood with the kingdom, the struggle in this case of the Pope with the German Emperor, as we have already seen it in the Middle Ages, is to be judged like every struggle; it has its alliances, it has its conclusions of peace, it has its truces, it has its armistices. There have been peaceful Popes; there have been bellicose and conquering ones."

There you also see, therefore, a glance directed to the future in which one hopes to come to an understanding. The thought is expressed still more distinctly in the utterance of the year 1875, where one was still already battling with a rather considerable anger but with an eye, nevertheless, fixed steadily on peace. At that time [16 May], I said in the Chamber of Deputies:

> My relations are restricted to the shrewd, as stated, but unfortunately powerless Cardinal Antonelli. Nevertheless I keep hoping that papal influence on the Center will be maintained.
>
> For as the history of bellicose, pacific, combative, and spiritual Popes shows us, I hope that the succession will still also go once again after this to a peaceloving Pope, who is ready to let other people live in their way and will let peace be concluded with him. My hope is directed at that, and then I hope to find an Antonelli again, who is intelligent enough to meet the secular power halfway in peace.

Generally, at that time also in the most violent struggle, this pointing to peace, and therefore the nature of the May Laws as conflict legislation, was never lost from sight. And yet I am now reproached—in the newspapers I've read—that never since Olmütz has anything more unworthy been expected from the state. "Canossa" is the third term I'm reproached with. The same speech [of 14 May 1872] in which I said: "We are not going to Canossa," a promise which I also still repeat today, shows how this Canossa is to be understood, what bearing it has. I said at the time:

> The German Imperial Government seeks diligently, seeks with the great care that it owes its Catholic as well as its evangelical subjects, the means to proceed from the present situation to a more agreeable one in a manner as little startling as possible to the empire's sectarian relations. . . .
>
> The government is obligated to Catholic fellow subjects not to become tired of seeking the way in which the determination of the boundary between ecclesiastical and secular power, which we absolutely require in the interests of domestic peace, can be found in the most considered and least discordant manner to the sects.

Approximately three years after the last utterance [of 1875], the hope that a Pope inclined to peace would come to power was fulfilled. I refer here to one of the first pronouncements of Pope Leo XIII, soon after he came to the throne in 1878. This says: "So, in the midst of all sorts of obstacles, we will continue to work for the German nation, for our soul can never find rest as long as clerical peace in Germany is not restored."

I believe, gentlemen, these selections suffice to invalidate the idea that, at the time, we viewed the ecclesiastical conflict laws as a basis for the lasting future of the empire or Prussia. In the sense of what has been said, as soon as the present Pope assumed power, I also formed connections which are *publici juris*. We have had negotiations in Kissingen [from 31 July to 31 August 1878] with the Nuncio Masella, which promised all expectations of success until the moment when the Cardinal Secretary of State Franchi died suddenly and the negotiations were put off. [On 15 to 19 September 1879,] I negotiated with the present Cardinal Secretary of State Jacobini in Gastein; we have negotiated in Vienna. Therefore, without the real heating of tempers perchance on both sides, we have worked untiringly and continuously for peace. We made little progress in view of the resolution of so many parties which as *tertii gaudentes* stood close to the combatants. It therefore occurred to me to try to do what we could unilaterally to meet the King's Catholic subjects halfway; in other words, what we could do *gratis* and without compensation by way of legislation. As a result of studying this question, I have also been induced to come into closer contact with the details than had generally been possible for me as a result of my other occupations in my restricted administrative province. Examining the *status quo* the struggle had reached, I convinced myself that we, as really always happens in conflicts, had occupied many portions of enemy territory, which, when examined closely, were really largely worthless to us.

I have sought to test their value in order to establish in my inner judgment the precise line up to the point I believed the King of Prussia could make voluntary uncompensated concessions to his Catholic subjects without injuring his own authority and state security and rights. With that there was also the consideration that a struggle with domestic foes has quite different rules than one with external ones. When one fights with external enemies, then one says: "It's too bad when any blow misses!" In domestic disputes, one must always also question how every injury which one does to the opponent stands in relation to other injuries one wishes to ward off; in other words: what use will the opposing party make of that? In all domestic struggles the chief minister, at least, should never leave out of consideration the whole, the consequences for all, and even more difficult domestic struggles than this, in the struggles which preceded this, I have never failed in that. I have never been a party man; I have always been the man of the state and of the King.

Among the stipulations which I, in my personal judgment, consider of inferior value for the state are particularly a great part of those which apply to the education and appointment of priests— . . . inspection of educational institutions, rights of the state toward the priest in his jurisdiction—in brief, the entire competition, which the state seeks in the ecclesiastical laws, with the Roman Curia in regard to the control and appointment of Catholic priests. In my private conviction, a greater part of all these stipulations fall for me in the category—at this moment I don't know any adequate German expression for that—of what the English call a "wild goose chase". . . . From the moment he is a priest, the Catholic priest is the regimented officer of the Pope; he is supposed to be pressed to the wall and be destroyed if he remains a priest and, in the meantime, fight against the Pope and against his superiors. I consider it an endeavour without the slightest chance of success. . . .

. . . My entire position on the question cannot be a sectarian one; it is purely political. In my position I cannot adopt the viewpoint of any sect or any party. I must so stand in relation to that, even if I were a believing Catholic, I, as His Majesty the King's Minister President, would be able to propose the same thing I now propose. My last predecessor in office, the late Prince von Hohenzollern, was a Catholic, and the same task could have been his just as easily. . . .

In these deliberations, in conjunction with my colleague the Minister of Religions [von Gossler], I got definite proposals in the Ministry of State, whose result you finally see in the governmental bill before you. We would advance the uncompensated established line envisaged therein still further, if it had been possible to make a legislative distinction between the German and Polish parts of the country. Regard for the fact that the Polish priesthood has unfortunately exploited its clerical freedom to a high degree in order to further and to favor Polish national goals—in our sense revolutionary goals—has made it appear impossible for us to approve much in the Polish-speaking parts of the country, which would have caused no offense to us in the German-speaking ones. In this connection, I am also inclined to make room, not for the present bill, but for another interpretation in a look at the future. If we succeed in battling Polonism in the way we have recently attempted [through the government subsidizing German peasant purchases of Polish land], then it gives us a substitute for many means of conflict which we could not dispense with in the clerical field, and I believe it a milder substitute, which is less similar to a battle in that we seek to do with Mammon, what was not done by force of law. Therefore, this consideration, the prospect of help from another quarter against Polonism, makes me inclined to go further on many points than was possible when the governmental bill was initiated.

After we had reached an understanding over the governmental bill and had received His Majesty the King's approval of it, it was a question . . . of offering a correct understanding of the government's view to His Majesty the King's Catholic subjects. There were two ways: one, that of simple ordinary legislation, then that of prior negotiation with the Roman Curia. For many reasons I preferred the latter; not that I sought or conducted a two-sided negotiation, but I considered it useful to bring to His Holiness the Pope's knowledge the bill we envisaged introducing into the Prussian Landtag and to hear his opinion on it, without promising we would change our decision according to the opinion. I gave this way priority because I had the impression that I would find more benevolence and more interest in strengthening the German Empire and for the Prussian state's welfare from Pope Leo XIII than I would have found at this time in the majority of the German Reichstag. (*Hear!*)

I consider the Pope more friendly to Germany than the Center. The Pope is certainly a wise, moderate, and peace-loving sovereign. I express no opinion whether that can be said of all members of the Reichstag majority. (*Laughter.*)

Besides the Pope is not a Guelf, he is not a Pole, and he is not a German Left Liberal either. (*Laughter.*)

He also has no inclinations to Social Democracy. In short, all the influences which falsify the situation in parliament are not permitted in Rome. The Pope is a pure Catholic and nothing but a Catholic. The fact that he is really gives rise to a number of difficulties in themselves, but the difficulties are not compounded by the necessity of approaching and receiving and rewarding the favors of other parties. The Pope is free and represents the free Catholic Church; the Center represents the Catholic Church in the service of parliamentarianism and electioneering practices. . . .

To complete the government's declaration I have only to add further that the revision of the May Laws, upon which the last Roman note [on 4 April 1886] made dependent the granting of the complete obligation [of the Church] to inform the government [of ecclesiastical appointments], can, I am convinced, be approved by the government without difficulty (*Hear! Hear!*), since such a revision has always been intended by the government. . . .

It will be up to, not public opinion, but, the expression of popular feeling, which has the opportunity of making itself known officially in both Chambers of the Landtag, to determine the limit to which the state government gladly and willingly will go.

3

A Prussian or German Administration?

As the swing to a new economic policy and new taxes gained momentum, friction with the freetraders in the Reichstag increased. As a counterweight, Bismarck put more emphasis on the Bundesrat and wished to see more able men participate in it. He was also concerned that the imperial administration was not functioning effectively and proposed reorganization to the emperor. He desired a more rational system which would be more responsive to his policies and less of a potential challenge to his authority than the Imperial Chancellery under Delbrück. To clear the way for new sources of imperial revenue, he expresses here his objections to the Prussian finance minister Camphausen, whose laissez-faire policies he found repugnant. The friction between Prussian and imperial agencies emerges clearly here, where Bismarck is groping for an institutional solution to his problems.[10] This friction was to become more and more aggravated as the Prussian Chamber of Deputies, elected by an electorate weighted toward the wealthy, became more and more conservative and thus presented different problems to the Prussian government than the Reichstag, chosen by universal suffrage, put to the imperial government. Often, as time went on, the inclination of the government was to back Prussia against the empire. The Prussian-German conflict was to last throughout Bismarck's chancellorship and beyond.

Previously prevented by illness, it is only today that I am able to report on the reform of the organization of imperial agencies. . . .

In comparison with today, the volume of imperial business that demanded the Chancellor's action was much more restricted at the foundation of the North German Confederation. At that time, it was obvious and also expedient to have all the business, which, in 1867,

[10] Letter from Bismarck to William I, Varzin, 22 January 1878. In Hans Goldschmidt, *Das Reich und Preussen im Kampf um die Führung* (Berlin: Carl Heymann Verlag, 1931), pp. 223–28. Translated by the editor.

52

was incumbent on the Imperial Chancellor, be handled, under his direction, by a unitary authority, the Imperial Chancellery. The latter was . . . conceived of as an office relatively circumscribed in activity and closely allied to Your Majesty's Prussian ministry. The circumstance that the presidency of this office was assumed by such a considerable personality as Minister Delbrück actually led from year to year more to the strengthening of its preponderance as opposed to the other cooperating elements, especially the Prussian ministers. The eminent activity of the first President of the Imperial Chancellery contributed no less than the continual development of all imperial institutions to enlarge the Imperial Chancellery's sphere of activity far beyond the extent previously envisaged. The combination of all imperial business under Minister Delbrück's experienced direction substantially promoted the establishment of the development of organic imperial institutions, guaranteed the nursery in which the education of the individual higher imperial offices and their personnel was made possible and was, I admit, simultaneously, as long as it went on, the means to retain the creative activity, which was demanded for the foundation and schooling of the imperial organs, of Minister Delbrück's powers which are difficult to replace. But for years I could not conceal the conviction that this phase in the continued development of imperial institutions through a unitary and central Imperial Chancellery would, considering the existing situation in the German Empire, reach a limit beyond which it would be replaced by another system. There is no place in our German situation for such a mighty central agency as a permanent Imperial Chancellery would become, concurrent with, or superior to, our state governments, especially the Prussian. Thus an Imperial Chancellery including all imperial state business could only have a future if it were possible to win a statutory position for it constitutionally *over* the general state governments. But that existed neither in the original idea of the confederation nor in German imperial arrangements nor do I consider it really practical. Such an imperial ministry organized as a central agency would as the superior authority be supposed to issue orders in regular current business to the Prussian, Bavarian, and Saxon Ministries of State; this would hardly be an acceptable arrangement for the smallest among the allied states. But if the Imperial Chancellery were to operate as a central imperial ministry not superior to but concurrent with the ministries of the large states, as has been partially and nearly the case lately, then, to the very involved gears of the German imperial machine, it would add only one more cog, which worked at cross-purposes with all others, increasing friction by that, and making the conduct of business more difficult.

The Imperial Chancellery, in the form of a centralized imperial ministry with the imperative aim of exercising and strengthening its influence on state governments not subordinate to it, has, already up to the present, periodically had the effect, in a very palpable way, that the ministers of the large states, and especially Your Majesty's Prussian ministers, participate in the Bundesrat's labors only rarely and cautiously. They have abstained from that through a not unnatural repugnance to subordinate themselves to the chairmanship and leadership of those young colleagues who possess the direction of business in the Imperial Chancellery, the committees, and the Bundesrat. . . . Your Majesty's Prussian ministers have preferred to concentrate their energy in their own departmental sphere which they dominate with complete independence and, as I find humanly explicable, to adopt a more defensive demeanor toward the empire in order to maintain their own Prussian department; in other words, a particularist demeanor diverted from strengthening the empire. As a new state organization which is still not deep-rooted, does not possess its own governmental power, and, moreover, is opposed by general particularistic elements, the empire suffers from that; the empire is without resources and substantially, to be sure, because Your Majesty's *empire* is not usually supported by Your Majesty's *Royal* Government and is often checked by active and passive resistance. I need only recall the railway question. It is not thereby my intention to bring an accusation against Your Majesty's Prussian Ministers. I find the guilt much more in the condition of imperial institutions, which should be so constituted that struggles with existing and legal particularist authorities would decrease, but the one with the Prussian Ministry of State would be done away with if possible. For that, in my opinion, a return to the closer relations, which originally existed after the introduction of the constitution of the North German Confederation, of the imperial authorities to Your Majesty's Prussian ministry is necessary. This miscarried in the battle between the concept of separate imperial ministerial power on the one hand and, on the other, the established possession of power by the Prussian Ministry of State. Instead of working together, both state organizations finally have sought to be rivals in power, to gain influence, and to block one another. This struggle will last as long as, apart from smaller agencies, there exist side by side in the German Empire two *great* ministerial authorities, of which one, the Prussian, is in real and complete possession of the government of 25 million Germans, while the other is the theoretical government of 40 million Germans and seeks to gain possession from the existing Prussian government. Considering our ministerial traditions and customs, the attempt to dominate will never become extinct in the Imperial Chancellery, as long as in its name and its organization it retains a central imperial ministry and the pretensions tied to that. These pretensions may slumber at times, but as soon as a personality suited to their execution becomes President of the Imperial Chancellery, they will always awake. In my opinion, the solution lies only in the complete dissolution of this office into separate imperial agencies. . . .

The separate imperial agencies, like the General Post Office, the Imperial Justice Office, and the like do not oppose the state governments with the demands of a ministerial and central state government. In observing their departmental business, they are more accessible to state governments and more given to an understanding with them than one of the sections of a general imperial ministry can be which has no other communication with the outside than through the mediation of the President of the Imperial Chancellery, who, for his part, as one of our ministers, naturally strives to repel outside influences from his sphere of power. The bond, which, in the highest leadership structure, the imperial agencies maintain for the Chancellor, who is responsible for all of them, is really of a different nature. As a rule, he does not concern himself with the imperial agencies' current course of business. The totality of imperial offices subordinate to the Chancellor does not form one compact authority, whose single sections are only accessible through a common chief. The Imperial Chancellor's control over the imperial agencies does not prohibit them from looking after their business by themselves and in conjunction with the relevant Prussian department. The Imperial Chancellor can never have the task, which suggests itself to each President of the Imperial Chancellery, of representing and considering as particularly his own single departments in their struggle for power and influence. The Imperial Chancellor—and for this reason it is advisable that he be simultaneously Prussian Minister-President —should belong to all departments equally and should never form his decisions according to departmental interests, but according to general political considerations. . . .

. . . I say that the Imperial Chancellery and the impetus Minister Delbrück inspired in it, formed a necessary and indispensable channel for the development of imperial institutions, but that this office, and particularly even its name which gives rise to misunderstandings, should presently disappear from among imperial institutions and make way for two new independent imperial offices: an Imperial Treasury Office for finance and [an Imperial Office of the Interior], an administrative office for other business. The imperial administrative office would have allotted to it the sphere of business which is answered for, in Prussia, by the department of the Ministry of Interior, before the Religious, Commerce, and Agricultural Ministries were separated from it. Whether later a special commerce office should come out of that can be reserved for further deliberation.

At present I see as the most important necessity the establishment of a separate imperial financial administration in the form of the Imperial Treasury Office, so that this agency will be put in the position, by its independence of the organs of the Imperial Chancellery, of maintaining lasting and regular communication with Your Majesty's Prussian Minister of Finance. . . . The Empire does not possess its own customs and tax administration; they are much more in the Prussian Finance Minister's hands. We need . . . , in my opinion, a basic reform of our customs and tax system and, above all, very great revenues from the latter. In this regard we have remained behind all other great powers. No other place save only Your Majesty's Finance Ministry contains the necessary technical assistance to prepare these reforms. Therefore, it alone can provide the necessary preliminary studies and drafts, and, if this does not happen, justice demands that the place, in which this does not happen, bear the responsibility for this not happening to Your Majesty and the Empire. Previously this lay formally with the Chancellor. But, if Minister Camphausen does not make up his mind to undertake urgent reform of the financial situation in a more inclusive and energetic way than hitherto, I would not be able to continue in this situation which is becoming increasingly difficult without a public statement of the actual conditions to the Reichstag. The timid beginning which the slight increase of the tobacco tax has made on the road to reform is insufficient, if it does not form precisely this transition to a great, systematically prepared reform. Considering earlier Reichstag debates, it is not improbable that a great reform system, which had an eye on a surplus at least in excess of 100 million marks, would have more chance than the moderate bill now intended, which I only agreed to in the opinion that slight progress is better than none.

4

The Socialists and the Workingman

Bismarck's approach to the problem of the growing Social Democratic party and the misery of the workers are explained in the following selections. The first records conversations with the indefatigable Moritz Busch, who wrote press articles for the chancellor and functioned as an inferior Boswell. Here the tax system is tied in with social reform, and the opposition of the liberals is stressed. In the second selection, Bismarck publicly defends both the repressive anti-Socialist law and "preventive measures," emphasizing the limits of statecraft. He attributes the continued growth of the socialists not to failures of the government but to oppositional agitation, particularly by the Left Liberals. He also directly attacks the Social Democrat Bebel and the Centrist Windthorst, while implying, by his favorite maneuver of identifying himself with the emperor, that they are traitors as well.

STATE SOCIALISM [11]

I went to the Chancellor's palace at the appointed time [1:00 P.M., 21 January 1881], and I remained with him for an hour and a half. . . . He said: "So you have come for material, but there is not much to give you. One thing occurs to me, however. I should be very thankful to you if you would discuss my working-class insurance scheme in a friendly spirit. The Liberals do not show much disposition to take it up and their newspapers attack my proposals. The Government should not interfere in such matters—*laisser aller*. The question must be raised, however, and the present proposal is only the beginning. I have more in view. I grant that here may be room for improvement in many respects, and that some portions of the scheme are perhaps unpractical, and should therefore be dropped. But a beginning must be made with the task of reconciling the labor-

[11] Moritz Busch, *Bismarck: Some Secret Pages of His History* 3 vols. (London: Macmillan, 1898), 2: 450–52, 483.

ing classes with the State. Whoever has a pension assured to him for his old age is much more contented and easier to manage than the man who has no such prospect. Compare a servant in a private house and one attached to a Government office or to the Court; the latter, because he looks forward to a pension, will put up with a great deal more and show much more zeal than the former. In France all sensible members of the poorer classes, when they are in a position to lay by anything, make a provision for the future by investing in securities. Something of the kind should be arranged for our workers. People call this State Socialism, and having done so think they have disposed of the question. What then are the present provisions for municipal assistance to the poor? Municipal Socialism?"

He paused for a moment, and then continued: "Large sums of money would be required for carrying such schemes into execution, at least a hundred million marks, or more probably two hundred. But I should not be frightened by even three hundred millions. Means must be provided to enable the State to act generously towards the poor. The contentment of the disinherited, of all those who have no possessions, is not too dearly purchased even at a very high figure. They must learn that the State benefits them also, that it not only demands, but also bestows. If the question is taken up by the State, which does not want to make any profit, or to secure dividends, the thing can be done."

He reflected again for a few seconds, and then said: "The tobacco monopoly might be applied in that way. The monopoly would thus permit of the creation of an entailed estate for the poor. You need not emphasise that point however. The monopoly is only the last resource, the highest trump. You might say it would be possible to relieve the poor of their anxiety for the future, and to provide them with a small inheritance by taxing luxuries such as tobacco, beer, and brandy. The English, the Americans, and even the Russians have no monopoly, and yet they raise large sums through a heavy tax upon these articles of luxury. We, as the country which is most lightly taxed in this respect, can bear a considerable increase, and if the sums thus acquired are used for securing the future of our working population, uncertainty as to which is the chief cause of their hatred to the State, we thereby at the same time secure our own future, and that is a good investment for our money. We should thus avert a revolution, which might break out fifty or perhaps ten years hence, and which, even if it were only successful for a few months, would swallow up very much larger sums, both directly and indirectly, through disturbance of trade, than our preventive measures would cost. The Liberals recognise the reasonableness of the proposals—in their hearts; but they grudge the credit of them to the man who initiated them, and would like to take up the question themselves, and so win popularity. They will, perhaps, try to bury the scheme in Committee, as they have done other Bills. Something must, however, be done speedily, and possibly they may approve of the general lines of the scheme, as they are already thinking of the elections. The worst of the lot are the Progressists and the Freetraders —the one party wants to manage things its own way, and the other is opposed to all State control, and wishes to let everything take its own course. . . ."

I then inquired [on 4 May 1881] how he expected the next elections to turn out. He said: "The moderate parties will be weakened, while the Progressists will probably increase their numbers, the Conservatives, however, doing the same. This time, however, we will not stand by and see our plans wrecked. We shall dissolve if we cannot carry our State Socialism—our practical Christianity! At present it is not worthwhile for the sake of three months."

"Practical Christianity?" I asked. "Did I rightly understand your Serene Highness?"

"Certainly," he replied. "Compassion, a helping hand in distress. The State which can raise money with the least trouble must take the matter in hand. Not as alms, but as a right to maintenance, where not the readiness but the power to work fails. Why should only those who have in battle become incapable of earning a livelihood be entitled to a pension, and not also the rank and file of the army of labor? This question will force its way; it has a future. It is possible that our policy may be reversed at some future time when I am dead; but State Socialism will make its way. Whoever takes up this idea again will come to power. And we have the means, as, for instance, out of a heavier tobacco tax."

THE STICK AND THE CARROT [12]

. . . I would like to oppose the overly high estimate of many Catholics I have encountered that, particularly, it is precisely their belief which is stronger against Social Democratic aberrations, that it is a more certain and firmer shield against them than other Christian sects. Look at the history of nations, and you will find the odd phenomenon that it is precisely the Catholics . . . who have not distinguished themselves by their internal unity, domestic order, and internal peace. Take the Poles, take the Irish, take the Latin peoples, and all-Christian France, they have been torn apart by domestic conflicts. . . .

[12] Bismarck's speech in the German Reichstag, 20 March 1884. In Kohl, *Die politischen Reden*, 10: 70, 71–78, 81–86. Translated by the editor.

When here the first speaker [Bebel] frequently and even Deputy Windthorst have again laid weight upon our only demanding a two-year extension [of the Anti-Socialist Law], and the conclusion is drawn that in two years we hope to have made distinct progress in the healing of the disease, then I still permit myself to draw the Reichstag's attention to the fact that this time stipulation fundamentally has nothing whatever to do with the idea that this extraordinarily difficult and huge task will let itself be solved in the foreseeable future, but that it is the result solely of the Reichstag majority's expression of distrust in the way in which the government has employed its full powers. Every two years you have wished to convince yourself whether some acid drops or other from the acidity of the interference with Social Democracy could not also splash off on the Progressive party or elsewhere. You have limited us to two years in order to be able to control us; it has no other basis at all. . . .

I have never had the remotest thought that we could achieve something in two years. I appeal to the fact—I believe it was in the closing statement in the October 1878 session—that I had already at that time expressed myself for $2\frac{1}{2}$ years and added that no one could believe that we flattered ourselves with the hope of doing something to heal this evil in this short period. To deprive the agitators of part of their territory by means of reform—we did not let ourselves dream we could deprive them of all of it; we did not have this hope; but still to lessen the evil—, the positive efforts began really only in the year 1880 or 1881—I don't know exactly—with the imperial message of that time [17 November 1881], which lies before me here, in which His Majesty said: "Already in February of this year, we have expressed our conviction that the healing of social ills is not to be sought exclusively by means of repression of Social Democratic excesses, but equally in the positive promotion of the workers' welfare. . . ."

In consequence of this, first of all, the insurance law against accidents was submitted to the allied governments.

And then it reads further: "But those who have, through age or disability, become incapable of working have a confirmed claim on all for a higher degree of state care than could have been their share heretofore."

You see that there the application of means, which we promise ourselves will improve, is still only spoken as something in the far distant future and that we are widely separated from such sanguine and optimistic hopes that we could be rid of such a deep-rooted state of disease in so short a time. If I have correctly understood Deputy Windthorst, then he has blamed the government that in its efforts it has set foot in socialist territory and approaches socialistic goals very closely. . . . With Deputy Bebel I am not in doubt. He has made me welcome in the element entrusted to him and says in this sphere I would be his pupil and he the master. Now, gentlemen, I fear this master will not derive very much pleasure from his pupil. (*Laughter.*) I would also ask the deputies to reflect that, if I want to concern myself with legislative means to combat evil, I would have to approach the carrier of this evil in one way or another, and that my duty still remains to investigate whether I consider correct a part of the grievances overlying the sickness, whether I can remedy it and to what extent. In this sense, I have approached every opponent; in this sense, circumstances permitting, I have approached not only the socialists but also the Progressive party, yes, even foreign opponents, as one approaches an illness, to see how one can heal it. Deputy Bebel has really no right to go through my rather agitated political life in the manner as though I had once desired this and then again something very much different. I have often declared already that in each period of my life I have worked and striven for what I consider most necessary for my native land and for God. It was not the same thing in each period. It is impossible to explain the reasons for that; they are closely connected with high—I mean to say, foreign—policy. Really until the years 1876 and 1877, I did not have the time to concern myself with other matters, but had to leave them in the hands of Him to whom they are entrusted. You will admit to me that in most countries, in most great national states, and especially in those which lie in the center of Europe and which are, as history proves, more exposed to coalitions and attacks of others than any other, the burden of foreign affairs alone is sufficient to absorb one man's activity completely and that not much time is left over for domestic affairs. Subsequently I have been able to manage domestic affairs, insofar as I had the time for them; still I did not do much testing for defects, which could perhaps be hidden in our social and economic system. I have always had to concern myself with the most necessary new organizations. In brief, approximately seven years ago I first got *the* leisure from other business which seemed more important to me; then I could really familiarize myself with economic questions. You will not deny me the acknowledgment that, since I have declared I have time for that, I have occupied myself uninterruptedly with the improvement of economic conditions in some way or other.

The first urgency in this regard lay for me, on the one hand, in the danger of the agitating tumult in 1878, which Social Democracy had gained possession of and which threatened our quiet, and, on the other side, in the crimes which had been committed against His Majesty the King's sacred head and which formed the initial starting point of the legislation which occupies us today and is still in force. If the gentlemen are convinced, if you have full security, that the like will not be repeated, then with a good conscience you will also express yourself in opposition to the extension of this moderate protection and will toss away this thin shield against the return of such occurrences. But, even beyond that, you cannot delude yourself that you are not thereby assuming a weighty responsibility for yourselves, which perhaps will not be justified by success. (*Very true! From the right.*) This could be all the more so, since up to now, thanks to His Majesty's policy, we move in peaceful and calm relations. Suppose that, instead, dangers of war, of domestic unrest, in short, unemployment and starvation appeared among us—dangers which we were quite near to in the time of bloodlessness, of anemia, in 1877, and which, for the moment, I certainly may view as a position happily overcome. Suppose that unemployment occurs and that, with less real complaints, many grounds for hunger and lack of work appear. Are you quite certain that the government, which would be at the rudder, would be in the position to offer resistance and recapture the reins which you now take from our hands? . . .

. . . Where such great objects and such great interests for the domestic peace of the great German nation are at stake, as in this, I still consider preventive measures, if they are as inexpensive as the one under consideration, are necessary, and I do not want to wait until the matter assumes greater dimensions.

Deputy Windthorst has not closed his eyes to the perception that, in comparison with previous times, the danger has increased. . . . He has more courage than we others. He sees foes coming, he sees Social Democracy growing, but he does not fear himself. He will wait until they open fire, possibly with dynamite or petroleum, and only then intervene. With my feeling of conscientiousness and impartiality, I still consider that unbearable. . . .

Now when, despite this law, the number of Social Democrats increases, if the organization has become more cautious, if, as Deputy Bebel apparently supposes, under the aegis of this law a kind of Eldorado has commenced for the Social Democratic efforts, which will never prosper better than in the hothouse of this special law, then he should still be satisfied; then, I hope, he himself will vote for it, so that the Social Democratic advantages will not be lost. I hope he does that. If he doesn't do it, then I cannot reconcile his conduct with his speech.

If, despite, I will not say the crippling, but, the weakening of its agitation, which it suffers under this law's administration, Social Democracy continually finds itself growing, if the number of the dissatisfied grows, then it is not a matter of the law's operation, but the agitating efforts of other parties that still stand at Social Democracy's side, the Progressive agitation against the government, the accusations against the government in the Progressive press, the casting of suspicion on the government, which produces mistrust of the government, yes, even of His Majesty's intentions as they are expressed in the message. All that must increase the number of the dissatisfied, the number of those who expect nothing of their government, who have no trust in it and in the Emperor. But without awakening trust in the workers, it is impossible for us to do something for them with the efforts at reform. . . .

The plan of reform which we adhere to according to the will of the Emperor and of the allied governments cannot be implemented in a short time; it needs a period of years for its accomplishment. We have bestirred ourselves to improve the laborers' position in three directions. One, at a time when opportunity for work is slight and wages have become low, we have taken the necessary steps to protect work in our native land against competition; in other words, we have introduced protective tariffs to protect domestic labor. As a result of these measures, a real improvement of wages and a diminution of unemployment has taken place. Since then, work has reappeared more and more, and you trouble yourself in vain in seeking other grounds for that. On the contrary, I believe this event must have a considerable effect in the quietening down of socialist efforts. The person who still remembers the period from 1877 and 1878 and the conditions at the time will not deny that even in foreign writings the hope of connecting their revolutionary plans to the workers' dissatisfaction has declined to some degree. Therefore, this protective tariff system has usefulness for the goal.

A second plan, which is in the government's mind, is the improvement of tax conditions, in that a fit division of them is sought, by which particularly oppressive sales for taxes on account of small amounts are, if not eliminated, then, at least, decreased, which perhaps will lead to a further decrease. Sales for taxes have earlier destroyed and broken down many small individuals in the working class and the few groschen which they brought in taxes at the stipulated time also often were the reason why a family, which did not stand right on the lowest rung of affluence, was thrown back into want. You now say what we have given with one hand we take back with the other; we have imposed much more on the workers in indirect taxes than in direct ones. That is a false calculation, an untruth. . . . If you compute for the worker what he must pay now in import duties on oil, petroleum, and grain, and for bacon and who knows what, you always keep silent that neither bread nor petroleum has become a penny dearer. On the contrary, they are still cheaper than before, despite the earlier, I can truly say, crop failures. This proves that the calculation is not correct when you say 60 marks is specially imposed upon the worker, but even if a price raise had occurred because of that, it is quite certain that the worker did not pay it in the last instance. Perhaps he paid it the first time, but the shifting of this sum to the employer and from the employer to the consumer is really completely certain. The so-called iron law of wages, that an unskilled laborer can never earn more than he needs for necessary upkeep and for the defrayal of his necessary means of existence has a certain truth, but is still to be taken *cum grano salis*. This truth changes according to time and place. What a worker needs differs according to the time. Those of us who can think back fifty years know that the entire condition of a worker's life, the nourishment he took, the dwelling, the clothing which he and his children wore, are better today than at that time and that today what the laborer needs of necessity is better clothing, better nourishment, and a better dwelling than at that time. Likewise, in place. I employ workers in Holstein and in Pomerania. In Holstein the daily wage is about 50 per cent higher than in Pomerania, because that is the custom of the country, not that money is worth less there. Generally it does not consist in variation in the falling value of money, but in the fact that the Holstein laborer is used to having a higher degree of luxury than is necessary for his value; and what remains for me as an employer other than satisfying this necessity? It is, therefore, the clearest proof that what the laborer has needed and is necessary for the means of existence has also shifted onto the employer, and that the iron law of wages is quite certainly not correct in regard to the wage level. It is quite impossible for a business, whose workers do not get what they need for their usual and customary existence, to continue permanently, for if they do not get it, they simply give up this branch of business or emigrate to America, which is really very easy. They must be guaranteed an increase in wages which is adequate to an increase in prices. . . . Therefore [there] exists the great fallacy told to the workers, the fallacy that the relief they got through the abolition of the class tax must be paid many times over through taxes on the most necessary means of existence, whose prices are inequitable to the worker. I only wish it were possible to let a different relief be introduced, also in community taxes, and, in Prussia, especially in the immoderate demands placed upon communities for educational goals. But that is only possible if state funds could be transferred and in order to be able to transfer them, they would have to be covered by contributions from other quarters. But we have hitherto found, to express myself in English, an "obstruction," an obstruction to this contribution from other quarters—of indirect taxes on luxury items; we have been denied the tobacco tax and the license tax [on brandy] and we can help here only if you grant us the money, for we ourselves cannot create it.

The third branch of reforms, which we strive for, lies in direct provision for the workers. The question of labor time and wage increases is extraordinarily difficult to solve through state intervention, through legislation at all; for in any settlement that one makes, one runs the danger of interfering very considerably and unnecessarily in the personal freedom of getting value for one's services; for when one butchers the milk-giving cow or an egg-laying hen at a single time, then this industry perishes, because it cannot bear the burden laid upon it of short work for high wages. Then the worker suffers from that as well as the entrepreneur. That therefore is the governing borderline, and every legislative intervention must stop before that. I have also heard only sporadic local complaints about that. The workers' real sore point is the insecurity of his existence. He is not always sure he will always have work. He is not sure he will always be healthy, and he foresees some day he will be old and incapable of work. But also if he falls into poverty as a result of long illness, he is completely helpless with his own powers, and society hitherto does not recognize a real obligation to him beyond ordinary poor relief, even when he has worked ever so faithfully and diligently before. But ordinary poor relief leaves much to be desired, especially in the great cities where it is extraordinarily much worse than in the country. When we read in Berlin newspapers of suicide because of difficulty in making both ends meet, of people who died from direct hunger and have hanged themselves because they have nothing to eat, of people who announce in the paper they were tossed out homeless and have no income, they are clearly things which we do not know and understand in the country. There the county councillor and the police would appear immediately and re-install the nearly evicted person and help the hungry by paying for food and drink. There worries about food are not possible at all. Now it seems that those privy conciliar agencies which have authority in Berlin do not act with the same acuteness as do the others in the provinces. Meanwhile, for the worker it is always a fact that falling into poverty and onto poor relief in a great city is synonymous with misery, and this insecurity makes him hostile and mistrustful of society. That is humanly not unnatural, and as long as the state does not meet him halfway, just as long will this trust in the state's honesty be taken from him by accusations against the government, which he will find where he wills; always running back again to the socialist quacks . . . and, without great reflection, letting himself be promised things, which will not be fulfilled. On this account, I believe that accident insurance, with which we show the way, especially as soon as it covers agriculture completely, the construction industry above all, and all trades, will still work amelioratingly on the anxieties and ill-feeling of the working class. The sickness is not entirely curable, but through suppression of its external symptoms by coercive legislation we only arrest it and drive it inward. I cannot have anything to do with that alone. . . .

. . . I have, of course, said: We derive our right to let the exceptional law continue from duty and from the fulfillment of the duty of Christian legislation. On the Progressive side, you call it "socialist legislation"; I prefer the term "Christian." At the time of the Apostles, socialism went very much further still. If perhaps you will read the Bible once, you will find out various things about it in the Acts of the Apostles. I don't go as far in our own times. But I get the courage for repressive measures only from my good intention of working to the end that, so far as a Christian-minded state society may do it, the real grievances, the real hardships of fate, about which the workers have to complain, will be alleviated and will be redressed. How far? That, indeed, is a matter of implementation, but the duty of doing what one recognizes to be a duty is not annulled by the difficulty of implementation, and . . . our action is completely independent of success.

5
Imperial Foreign Policy

The history of the chancellor's foreign policy is essentially the history of European diplomacy from 1871 to 1890. Here, a few key questions are considered.

DEFEATED FRANCE [13]

In this official dispatch to the German ambassador in Paris, Count Harry von Arnim, the chancellor rebukes him for attempting to pursue a policy independent from his own. The ambitious and sometimes shrewd Arnim believed that a monarchical France would benefit Germany and attempted to win Bismarck over to his side, not neglecting to use persuasion with William I. Bismarck, on the other hand, felt that the provisional republican government of Thiers would pay off the war indemnity, permitting the complete evacuation of France by German troops, and would, above all, keep France divided internally and incapable of making foreign alliances. While today, whatever the practice, the principle is generally established that an ambassador is the agent of policy not its initiator, it was by no means clear at the time. Bismarck, at the Frankfort Diet and in St. Petersburg, certainly was not reluctant in attempting to control policy-making. But as the man in charge, fearing the scheming Arnim as a potential successor, he felt very differently and even eventually secured Arnim's conviction for treason. This was perhaps the most dramatic example of Bismarck's draconian policy toward rivals for power.

Doubtless the position of French affairs is such that it is a difficult if not an impossible task for anyone, even the shrewdest diplomat, to form a *trustworthy* judgment about the country's condition, the im-

---

[13] Dispatch from Bismarck to Count Harry von Arnim, Berlin, 20 December 1872. In J. Lepsius, A. Mendelssohn Bartholdy, and F. Thimme, eds., *Die grosse politik der europäischer Kabinette, 1871–1914* 40 vols. (Berlin: Deutsche Verlagsgesellschaft für Politik, 1922), 1: 157–62. Translated by the editor.

portance of individual political parties and persons and especially the probabilities of the near future. This difficulty is increased by the incalculable passion which is peculiar to the French character and from which even the most mature French statesmen are less free than the majority of Germans or English. At the same time, however, just as great as the difficulty of judgment is the importance for the German Imperial Government of not arriving at an incorrect judgment of the state of affairs in France and their consequences, of not accepting false premises as correct or as secure bases of one's own policy. In my opinion, in such a situation, it is the task of the official representative of the German Empire to subject the impressions he receives to a very scrupulous examination and analysis before he reports them. For with the fatal importance which each of His Majesty's foreign policy decisions could have for the future of the German Empire and Europe, it would be a great danger for both if essential suppositions behind royal decisions proved wrong, although they were viewed and reported as certain from the Imperial Embassy. If Your Excellency would have the goodness to subject to a comparative examination your reports from your first return to Paris until now and the opinions you have given in them about the situation and the near future, about the position and importance of individual statesmen and about the problems of our policy, then I believe you yourself will estimate the magnitude of the difficulties there are in forming an opinion, in such a country and in such a situation, which one can express in official documents with that assurance His Majesty the King demands in such weighty questions.

My official position gives me the duty of notifying His Majesty's representatives when I have the impression that their reporting rests upon erroneous assumptions and of establishing the truth either through common discussion or in cases which concern calculations of future probability and an understanding is not reached concerning them, to establish the philosophy which is the basis on which I advise His Majesty and before which an Ambassador's diverging opinion must bow as long as His Majesty the Emperor and King has entrusted me with the conduct of Germany's foreign policy. No department can stand a double management less than the Foreign Office; such an event would lie for me in the same category of danger, possible in war, of a brigadier and his divisional commander acting according to opposing operational plans. Knowledge of this danger places the obligation on me of saying to Your Excellency that I consider the confidential conviction expressed by you that our outstanding demands are unconditionally guaranteed by *every* French government an erroneous one and every assurance Your Excellency gives concerning that as very risky.—You assume for yourself an assurance which no one can give and which on this account should not be given in an official report on the basis of which His Majesty could make decisions. I consider it probable that the payments [of the war indemnity] will follow, if Thiers holds on to office or even with governmental conditions following a regular legal development. On the other hand, if a republic with another breed of leaders came into power by a violent revolution, I fear we would have to draw our sword again to satisfy our demands. Already because of this possibility it is in our interest, for our part, at least not to weaken the present government nor to contribute to its fall. If one of the monarchical pretenders took power before the payments and evacuation, the situation I am anxious about would develop differently, but still not in a manner desired by us. Then we would be asked in a friendly way to promote the success of the young monarchical sprout by making concessions on the payments and evacuations which we had refused the republic. We could certainly reject that, but I fear that this would not be expedient—not to speak of *other* cabinets, and especially those closely befriending us, also more or less pressingly recommending consideration of the monarchical element in France. If one is also too intelligent in London, Petersburg, and Vienna to believe that a monarchical France is less dangerous to us than the incidental domination of republican factions in France, then the assertion of having such an opinion is certainly too useful a cloak for the pursuit of other goals that, under this mask, one would not give expression to the ill-feeling about our position, because of the transfer of billions from France to Germany, uncomfortable, of course, to all except us. In this way, within a short time, a rather uncomfortable European grouping could form out of that, which would exert a friendly pressure on us at first in order to induce us to renounce part of the advantage won. Moreover, analogous phenomena would perhaps be wanting later, but *our* task is certainly not to make France powerful and capable of making alliances with our friends until now, by consolidation of its domestic condition and by restoration of an orderly monarchy. France's hostility compels us to wish that it be weak, and we act unselfishly indeed, if, as long as the Peace of Frankfort is not completely implemented, we do not oppose ourselves with decision and force to the restoration of consolidated monarchical institutions. But if our foreign policy consciously assisted the enemy with whom we have to fear the next war, by strengthening its internal unity and making it *capable of concluding alliances*, then one could not conceal such a transaction carefully enough, if one would not provoke a just and angry dissatisfaction in all of Germany, which even might want to see a criminal proceeding taken against the responsible minister who pursued a policy so antagonistic to the country.

These considerations are connected to another error, already indicated, which leads Your Excellency to incorrect political conclusions. Your Excellency believes, and has also expressed this verbally to His Majesty the Emperor, that the temporary continuance of republican institutions in France is dangerous to monarchical institutions in Germany. I presume that Your Excellency would not have arrived at this fear if, in the last years, foreign conditions, of necessity, had not preponderantly claimed your attention, and if a long residence in Germany and in the center of German affairs had put you in the position to form an expert opinion. In your most recent reports, Your Excellency alleges that connections of French democracy with South Germany occur. This observation can be as little a novel one for Your Excellency as it is for us here; for forty years the archives of all domestic and foreign agencies, especially, I may take for granted, the existing one at the Parisian Embassy at Your Excellency's disposal, have contained voluminous and regrettable disclosures about that. Since the July Revolution and longer, connections of French democracy have existed not only with South Germany, but much more strongly . . . with Switzerland and Belgium, with England and Italy, Spain, Denmark and Hungary and especially Poland. Generally its intensity has kept rather exact pace with France's authority in Europe, for no monarchical government in France, even when it prosecuted French democracy with the greatest vigor, disdained to keep this lever in operation against other states and particularly Germany. Here is the same ploy always repeated, as with suppressing Protestants in France and supporting them in Germany and the friendly policy toward the Turks of the All-Christian King Louis XIV. If God ordained the misery of republican anarchy for *us*, I am convinced that the thought would occur to no Frenchman of helping *us* to the benefits of a monarchy again. Participation in that sort of benevolent interest in the destiny of hostile neighboring countries is a fundamental German characteristic. But His Majesty the Emperor's government has all the less occasion to make allowance for this impractical inclination when it can escape no careful observer how strong and enormous the conversion has been in Germany, and still is, from red to moderate liberals, from moderate liberals to conservative opinions, from doctrinaire opposition to the feeling of interest in the state and responsibility for it, since the *experimentum in corpore vili* which took place before the eyes of Europe with the Commune. France serves usefully as a horrible example. If France staged another act of the interrupted drama of the Commune before Europe, which I would not desire for humanitarian reasons, then it would only contribute the more strongly to make clear the benefits of the monarchical constitution and the adherence in Germany to monarchical institutions.

Our necessity is to be left alone by France and, if France does not keep at peace with us, to prevent it finding allies. As long as it does not have any, France is not dangerous to us, and, as long as the great European monarchies stick together, no republic is dangerous to them. But, on the other hand, a French republic would find a monarchical ally against us with great difficulty. This, my conviction, makes it impossible for me to advise His Majesty the King to encourage the monarchical right in France which would simultaneously involve strengthening the Ultramontane elements hostile to us.

Since I strongly regret the differences of opinion, over such fundamental principles of our policy, in which I find myself with Your Excellency, I could surely not evade the duty of candidly bringing them to your attention. I am convinced that the differences of opinion between us would be substantially diminished if Your Excellency would accede to the request, expressed in my prefatorial remarks, to subject the admissibility of your impressions of Franco-German relations to a conscientious and extended examination before you incorporate them in an official report which I have to submit to His Majesty and which also must be used, circumstances permitting, as a *pièce justificative* of our policy in parliament or to other cabinets. Also in this way an assured agreement of your reporting within itself would be introduced insofar as it is necessary for me to obtain a firm and lasting impression of the entire contents of Your Excellency's reporting and proposals for the purpose of my reports to His Majesty the King.

I permit myself further, and more from formal considerations, to make the following remark. You mention in your report of the 16th of this month that "one" believes in direct connections between the German Government and Gambetta. If Your Excellency realizes that in the first instance the German Government is directed by His Majesty the Emperor, then Your Excellency is adequately aware of our most gracious master's train of thought not to be in doubt that such an assertion contains a grievous insult to His Majesty the Emperor personally. But if, in the interest of the service, you believe you must incorporate such a thing in your official reports then, in my opinion, it is advisable to substantiate the source of such an opinion somewhat more exactly than by the indeterminate pronoun "one" and make good the professional necessity of such an insinuation more nearly than happened here. Certainly, and with justice, Your Excellency yourself would not consider it proper, if I, in an official dispatch, wanted to impart rumors, without demonstrable motive and under the anonymous reference of the pronoun "one," which could perhaps exist concerning the connections of the Imperial Embassy in Paris in an analogous way to the rumor alleged by you of a connection of the

Imperial Government with Gambetta. Before I could consider it correct to make intimations like that in an official dispatch, it certainly must be very believable, with the authority who made it given by name, and serve an evident goal of the service.

BETWEEN AUSTRIA AND RUSSIA [14]

In these conversations with P. A. Saburov, the Russian ambassador in Berlin, the chancellor pushes the idea of the advantages to Russia and Europe of the revival of the League of Three Emperors. He shows his concern at the Russo-Austrian rivalry in the Balkans and stresses Germany's disinterested attitude.

Conference of 20 January 1880

"Believe me," he [Bismarck] said, "it is not in your [Russia's] interest to try and embroil Austria and Germany. You too often lose sight of the importance of being one of *three* on the European chessboard. That is the invariable objective of all the Cabinets, and mine above all. Nobody wishes to be in a minority. All politics reduces itself to this formula: to try to be one of three, so long as the world is governed by the unstable equilibrium of five Great Powers. That also is the true preservative against coalitions. There was a time when Prince Gortchakov entertained the illusion of a close Entente with England. I wished then to enter it as a third, and Austria would not have been necessary to me if that combination had been achieved. But I soon realised that it was a chimera. There is still too much antagonism between you in the East; you will need a great 'Königgrätz' one day in order to settle this great Asiatic dispute. Further, since that time, my favorite idea has been the Triple Entente with Austria. The first attempt miscarried, and I had to begin this work again by making the Entente between two of the parties stronger, in order to return afterwards to the Triple Entente with you, if you are sincerely disposed towards it. . . ."

Conference of 24 January 1880

In devoting himself to an analysis of the points on which an entente might be established, Prince Bismarck returned anew to the advantages of a *triple* arrangement. The objectives of Russia are the follow-

[14] J. Y. Simpson, ed., *The Saburov Memoirs* (New York: Macmillan, 1929), pp. 111, 118–20, 122–23, 173–74, 175–77. Reprinted by permission of the publisher.

ing: She desires to protect herself against coalitions. She wishes also to strengthen the principle of the closing of the Straits. Now both objects will be more surely attained as one of three rather than one of two. So far as *coalitions* are concerned, Germany alone will be able to do as follows: She will be able to undertake *in writing* to prevent France from taking sides. But she will not able to make an engagement in similar form against Austria, not that she would tolerate an attack on Russia by Austria, but because a stipulation *in writing* against Austria would make that country once again distrustful of Germany and throw her again into the arms of the Western Powers. Should it so happen, it is more than probable that Germany would have sufficient influence at Vienna to hold Austria back, just as we save from suicide an individual whose existence is necessary to us. Thus Russia will have the moral certainty of being sheltered from coalitions in mutually securing herself with Germany against France, without whom no coalition is possible. Italy is of no account as a Great Power. There are countries extinct like certain heavenly bodies, which do not return to life a second time. Today Italy is nearly a republic, and her unity will not hold out against it.

So, for a treaty between two, Germany will only be able to bind herself against France. That will be sufficient to provide the moral certainty that a coalition will no longer be possible, but the mathematical certainty will only be secured by attracting Austria into this system. Forming a permanent coalition ourselves, we shall have no fear of one against us.

It is the same with the closing of the Straits. What will Germany be able to do by herself to prevent the violation of them? She can protest, write notes, but her army will not be able to swim to London, nor pass over the body of Austria to go to fight in the Straits. The question changes in aspect if one can interest Austria in it. She is in a better position to threaten Turkey, and compel her, in concert with Russia, to fulfill her obligations of neutrality. By means of a Triple Treaty, a real and effective guarantee will be secured. . . .

Conference of 26 January, 1880

In the witty definition of the Chancellor, the object of this Treaty will be to protect the "flabby parts" of the Three Empires.

Towards the end of the conversation he returned to the necessity for conducting these negotiations with extreme prudence. "Nobody," he said, "will have occasion to rejoice over an intimate rapprochement between us; neither England, who only dreams of isolating you, nor France naturally, nor even Austria up to a certain point. Austria would like to have a monopoly of alliance with Germany, but she would also like to preserve her own freedom of action. Even at the present time she probably does not tell us all that she thinks. That certainly cannot suit us, and I shall not be sorry to put her sincerity once more to the test by this proposal of an accord between three. But an untimely indiscretion can spoil everything. All the hostile elements in Europe will exert themselves to wreck this project. . . ."

Friedrichsruh, 27 and 28 November, 1880

The Prince answered . . . with a certain animation: "Austria would be much mistaken, if she thought herself completely protected by us. I can assure you that this is not the case. Our interest orders us not to let Austria be *destroyed*, but she is not guaranteed against an attack. A war between Russia and Austria would place us, it is true, in a most embarrassing position, but our attitude in such a circumstance will be dictated by our own interest and not by engagements which do not exist. Our interest demands that neither Russia nor Austria should be *completely* crippled. Their existence as Great Powers is equally necessary to us. That is what will guide our conduct in such an event. . . ."

The second question which I [Saburov] put to the Prince was to learn whether a treaty on the projected bases could remain secret, and whether at Vienna and at Berlin it would be possible to avoid the communication of it to Parliament.

As far as Germany was concerned, the Prince was very categorically of the affirmative opinion. The Treaty of Alliance with Italy in 1866 had not been submitted to the Houses. The article in the Constitution is very elastic on this matter. It requires the presentation to the Houses of treaty which would lay any "burdens" on the nation. This word leaves a large margin of interpretation.

As for Austria, the Prince thinks he remembers that the article of the law in question is framed in the same sense. . . .

This talk led us to touch on future eventualities, and to ask how far the arrangement now planned will facilitate the future settlement of the Eastern problem. The Prince, far from evading this subject, was, on the contrary, quite open-hearted. He said that if there were really perspicacious statesmen at Vienna, he would not have hesitated to undertake to draw on the map of Turkey a line of demarcation between the interests of Austria and ours, and that to the satisfaction of both parties. But the Austrian Ministers are the most timid in Europe; they are afraid of every question which is not a question of present interest, and one would not arrive at any result with them by a premature discussion. He went on: "To-day we must be satisfied with the projected arrangement which gives us the great advantage of keeping Austria better under control, and of forcing her, should occasion arise, into an entente. When that arrangement has become an accomplished fact, suppose a situation like that which brought about the Crimean War. If Austria were tempted to join England against Russia, would she dare to do so without asking us if we shall remain neutral? Our reply will be dictated by the present understanding, and Austria will not be able to think of budging. Suppose then that a fortunate campaign takes you to the Bosporus. I flatter myself on having been the first, in Europe, to break with that old tradition with which the Western Powers have inoculated all the Cabinets, namely, that Constantinople in the hands of Russia would be a European danger. I consider that a false idea, and I do not see why an English interest must become a European interest. As for the interests of Germany, they will decidedly not be affected by that eventuality, and I believe, on the contrary, that the Russian nation will become more seriously converted to the cause of peace when their ambitions at last have reached their goal, and when, having attained possession of Constantinople, they are convinced *von der Nichtigkeit aller irdischen Dinge*—as I am," he added, with a sad smile.

THE COLONIAL QUESTION [15]

One of the most important sources on Bismarck are the memoirs of Robert Lucius, Prussian minister of agriculture from 1879 to 1891. Here Lucius relates Bismarck's statements in the Prussian Ministry of State. The chancellor reveals his pique at Great Britain for failing to support German expansion in Southwest Africa and his intention of making difficulties for the British government in Egypt. He also refers to his policy of letting the flag follow commercial settlements.

22 July 1884

In today's ministerial council Bismarck gave a very exhaustive exposé of the Egyptian conference proposals and of his colonizing ideas which are tied up with the Angra Pequena question. As in all foreign questions he approaches this one very seriously and cautiously —but in grand style. The intimacy between England and France is highly suspect to him. England gives into France everywhere and

[15] Robert, Freiherr Lucius von Ballhausen, *Bismarck-Erinnerungen* (Stuttgart and Berlin: J. G. Cotta'schen Buchhandlung Nachfolger, 1920), pp. 296–98. Translated by the editor.

leaves it a free hand, while it turns a deaf ear to German wishes and interest. Bismarck read many long dispatches about the conversations Count Herbert [Bismarck] had with Granville. He reproached him rather clearly with a "conveniently short memory" and with quotations from earlier statements which proved his anti-German attitude. Earlier they had recognized that Angra lay outside the English sphere of interests, while now they developed a sort of Monroe Doctrine with respect to Africa.

Bismarck will not bring about a conference in agreement with Vienna and Rome, before the foundation for it is established in the English Parliament.

He does not want to make the decisions of a European conference depend upon later parliamentary decisions. Obviously he's preparing some embarrassments for Gladstone with that. Finally he wants to bring home to the English government that one cannot expect services from a government which has been badly run for years. It is too late to undo the conference. Enough, he now settles accounts sharply with England; he spoke seriously and farseeingly as he always does when it concerns European questions. He used this opportunity to emphasize sharply and play variations on the sentence: "We are the friend of our friends and the enemy of our enemies. . . ."

The colonization question, rich for the future, is to be fostered. Not that one could colonize with non-commissioned officers with warranted claims on a post in the civil service, but one had to protect commercial settlements and follow them. I wish he would repeat his performance before the entire Reichstag or in committee; it would cause a sensation, and he would emerge in creative second bloom.

THE BASES OF FOREIGN POLICY [16]

> *In this dispatch to the German ambassador in London, Count Paul von Hatzfeldt, whom he often referred to as the "best horse in my diplomatic stable," Bismarck develops his idea of France's threat to European peace and the desirability of all powers combining to meet it.*

. . . I am unable to formulate a reply, or still at most only in general, to Lord Salisbury's question whether an English approach to Russia appears advisable to me. In general, I can answer yes. A good understanding between England and Russia can only be desir-

---

[16] Secret dispatch from Bismarck to Count Paul von Hatzfeldt, Varzin, 8 August 1887. In *Die grosse Politik*, 4:338–42. Translated by the editor.

able to us, since we do not expect that either power would exploit its understanding with the other against us. Neither of them has interests which could impose an anti-German policy on it. We are friendly with both and wish to remain so; also we do not fear that their love for each other will be stronger than that of each of them for us. Whether such an understanding will be useful is entirely dependent upon the price England is willing to pay for Russian friendship. If it involves abandonment of Austria, then by that Austrian policy possibly would be compelled to compete for Russia's favor with England. Likewise, not only Austrian supervision of the condition of things in the east, but also, as a consequence thereof, any calculation of the development of Turkish power in the service of England would definitely be lost to England. Turkey would become dependent upon England alone or on an Austro-Russian combination and would lose the ability to join with England.

In any case we have even fewer interests than England in the Turkish east and cannot risk the German Empire's peace and power for expansionist Austrian plans in this direction. But if Austria can count on our support only on the defensive and not on England's at all, because of friendship with Russia, if perhaps it also lost the security of existing Italian support as a result of England's Russian policy, then Austria would scarcely have any other choice than to reach a direct understanding with Russia in the sense of its policy in the preceding century and to accept what profit there is in that for Austria. We would also have no interest in opposing this development of affairs, insofar as it was completed against Austria without force. Only a new Three Emperors' League on another basis would result from it, strengthened by the necessity of the solidarity of the three imperial *monarchies* against the progress of social and political democracy and guarding against the domination, impractical for great nations, of their foreign policy by changing parliamentary majorities and the press, on the model of France and, I may also truly say, recently England.

If a possibility offers of reaching an understanding not only between England and Russia, but between England, Russia, and Austria, then I would very gladly offer my assistance to prepare the way and to accomplish such a thing. We would not participate in an understanding between England and Russia *at the expense* of, and in opposition to, Austria.

If England initiates it, I do not consider an agreement in this sense impossible. On this basis, I also consider Italy's inclusion attainable. The key to the solution of this problem lies in the Bulgarian question. Heretofore *we* have not succeeded in uniting Austria and Russia in a delimitation of their interests, but, as the guide of *German* policy, we adhere to the line which we proposed for an Austro-Russian under-standing, *i.e.*, we vote with Russia in the Bulgarian question, with Austria in the Serbian, just as we do with England in the Egyptian one. Hitherto we have not felt the need to form firm views of these three points. Regarding these three separate eastern questions which have become a matter of practical politics, we have made no secret of our interpretation and our decision to act accordingly either to the Russian cabinet respecting Serbia and Egypt, nor to Austria re-specting Bulgaria.

For England, the path to an understanding with the Russian Em-peror will be more easily found in Bulgaria than in Asia. Just now Russia would be especially grateful for any assistance in the badly confused Bulgarian question. If England agreed to Russian wishes in respect to Bulgaria, *i.e.*, on the removal of the present regency and the installation of a Russian general, perhaps Ernroth, as governor or regent, then I believe English and German representations would succeed in Vienna even in getting Austria's consent to this concession, which is not easy because of the mood of Hungarian politics, so that in this way, if England consented to Russian plans in Bulgaria, an understanding between the three emperors and England would per-haps be achieved. If it was implemented without its knowledge and consent, such a combination could exercise a hazardous reaction on Italian policy. In this way, Italy, through wounded sensitivity with the strengthening of republican forces in the country, could be driven into the arms of France. A means to disinterest Italy and to draw it into understanding with the powers perhaps could lie in the Abyssin-ian question, and, circumstances permitting, also could be found in other directions. I do not consider the task in this connection hopeless.

If an agreement between the three emperors, England, and Italy, with the exclusion of France, which would do away temporarily with danger to peace among these five powers, were successfully brought about, then thereby the danger of war, which threatens Europe from the side of France, because of the incalculability of possible explosions there, would be ended.

France is the European state most eager for war, and European peace is assured with France's isolation.

I believe with Your Excellency that the chief instigation for Lord Salisbury's suggestion was the requirement of his *domestic* policy. . . . Earlier I have often expressed my opinion to the effect that my English colleague possessed no means by which he would be in the position to influence his country's domestic policy more conclusively than by the initiation of an action abroad by which England's do-mestic policy could be taken into tow. This action does not need to be a warlike one; it can remain a diplomatic one and would react, all the more on English policy, the more *an initiative of the English cabinet* in European policy was perceptible to it. If Lord Salisbury agrees to the idea, I would be ready for my part to help such an action with advice and cooperation and realize the pattern according to which Lord Salisbury, on his own initiative, would take occasion from the situation of the Bulgarian question to direct a communication to the interested courts, which would be so constituted that it would guarantee the expectations of Russian plans respecting Bulgaria. I would prefer it, if such an English plan was directed, first of all, only to the powers interested *primo loco* in the east, *i.e.*, to Russia, the Porte, Austria, and Italy, so that we and France would remain temporarily *ex nexu*. Then France could not complain of its isolation, and we thereby would still be in the position to come into close contact with the development as a midwife. If, from the beginning, Lord Salisbury prefers to direct his opening to all powers including Germany and France, our cooperation for the strengthening of European peace in this manner would, however, be assured to the same degree. In this pattern of procedure, as soon as the good understanding between England and Russia formed the basis of the operation, France's isolation would still remain the result. I believe that such an initiative of Lord Salisbury would not only promote peace and calm France, but would also re-invigorate the feeling in the English nation that it had the influence on European policy it was entitled to. A conference in London, which strove for and achieved the security of peace, would be more useful to the government in English public opinion than one interpretation or another of Irish laws.

. . . I remark further that I also believe Russia will refrain from action, until the Franco-German war breaks out. But perhaps Russia is not the only power which admits this eventuality in order to take a position, and the prudent section of the French again awaits also the outbreak of a Russo-German war in order to attack Germany after that.

There is not the slightest prospect and occasion for a Russo-German war today; it has been the same for a century. I consider our peace with Russia assured, and there is not even a propensity to a Russian war against Austria at the present, especially with Emperor Alexander. Personally the Emperor is peaceloving, and *no* Russian Emperor, who does not act under the pressure of a revolution or fear of it, would seize the first opportunity for a war with Germany, because there would be no prize even with a Russian victory, but in an unlucky result it would be dangerous for the dynasty. Germany, however, quite certainly would attack Russia even less than France, and, if France attacks us, then we must rely completely on God, if we are not equal to it.

I certainly do not believe that France would have Russian support in such an attack. In the case of a Franco-German war, I am convinced that, with a German victory, Russia would desire pledges about the nature of our peacemaking, but, if we gave such pledges, I am just as firmly convinced that French aggression would not have the slightest prospect of Russian support. But even if the opposite occurred, we would still be in no desperate position, with, quite apart from Austrian support, a million good troops under good officers on *each* of both our boundaries. Meanwhile, I repeat to Your Excellency the expression of my firm conviction that a Franco-Russian alliance against us lies quite outside our calculations, and that we will not attack France, but will await with calm assurance a one-sided French attack against us, which can be a consequence of political movements and convulsions.

Under these circumstances, the combination which I leave to the discretion of Your Excellency to give to Lord Salisbury in connection with the Bulgarian question has no further interest for us than our wish to maintain Europe's peace and welfare, not only for Germany, but also for the powers friendly to us, by my confidential proposal to Lord Salisbury to gain the credit in England as well as in Europe for bringing about their mutual understanding.

If he finds it interesting, Your Excellency will confidentially read or translate this communication to Lord Salisbury. I presuppose having his word as a nobleman that he will keep quiet about it, if he does not deem it in his position to agree to it.

6

The Jews

If it were not for the abominations of the Germans under Hitler, Bismarck's attitude toward the Jews probably could be passed over in silence. In this interview of July 1892, reproduced by Heinrich von Poschinger, the contemporary compiler of much voluminous Bismarckiana, the chancellor expresses his distaste for the anti-Semites and his friendly feeling toward the Jews.[17] While he shared a general aristocratic and rural distaste for Jews as philistines and opposed Jewish emancipation during the revolutions of 1848, he came to be associated with many Jews in his parliamentary career and with Jewish bankers and doctors. He brought about complete Jewish emancipation in Germany and used pressure on the Rumanian government to halt persecution. At the same time, when his break with liberal laissez-faire policies came about and his concern with poor economic conditions grew, he coquetted temporarily with the anti-Semites for political support. He was encouraged to take this stance because many liberal leaders were Jewish. Later, in 1887, he rebuked the later William II for associating with anti-Semites, an incident that may have led to their eventual estrangement. This interview after his dismissal may be considered as representing his final thoughts on the subject.

Bismarck considered that a combination of the Jewish and German elements was useful. There was something in the Jews that the German did not possess. They imparted to the population, especially of large towns, a *mousseux* that otherwise would be wanting, as well as impulses and emotions, which would hardly exist to the same degree under other circumstances. Apart from all considerations of justice and humanity, he did not see any way by which the aims of the Anti-Semites might be realized. If one questioned them about the practical execution of their plans, they became like the Social

---

[17] Bismarck's conversation at Kissingen, July 1892 (published January 1898) with the *Wiener Neue Freie Presse*. In Heinrich von Poschinger, S. Whitman, ed., *Conversations with Prince Bismarck* (New York and London: Harper and Brothers, 1900), pp. 163–66.

Democrats; they were unable to propose anything that could be practically carried out; their recipes were not applicable to the organism of the State of to-day. Moreover, what could one do? Measures like Bartholomew's Eve or the Sicilian Vespers could hardly be proposed even by the Anti-Semites themselves. Nor could the Jews be expelled without grave injury to the national welfare. Any measures by which the Jews would be excluded from judicial and other positions in the State would only increase the evil which the Anti-Semites thought they had to do away with. For then the same Jewish intelligence, to which public careers would be closed, would embrace those fields in which the over-weight of the Jews is already said by the Anti-Semites to be intolerable, i.e., of commerce.

The Prince then stated his opinion that the Jewish movement sprang less from religious and social instincts than from economic reasons. He mentioned as a fact that the Jews are greatly superior to the other elements of the population in making money. Their superiority rests on qualities which, whether they are pleasing or not, cannot be removed by measures of State. The Jews, by reason of their natural dispositions, were generally more clever and skillful than Christians. They were also, at any rate as long as they had not made the fortunes, if perhaps not more industrious at least more frugal and saving than their Christian competitors. To this must be added the fact that the Jew would risk something more readily once in a way in order to gain a commercial advantage, and in applying his methods to gain his object, would also act more kind-heartedly than his Christian competitor. All this gives him an advantage in commerce which could not legally be taken away. Even the Anti-Semites had up till then been unable to suggest anything which might paralyze this advantage and its effect on the economic life of the nation. Their proposals had hitherto been impracticable, and no government would be found able to carry them out. It was also inadvisable for the State to put obstacles in the way of the pursuit of gain and fortune, for the other elements of the population would thereby suffer equally, and the national wealth would decrease.

It is not necessary on that account to allow the Jews to dominate, or to make one's self dependent on them financially, as is the case in some states. In his own dealings, as a minister, with the *haute finance,* he had always placed them under an obligation to him.

He considered the Jews to be useful members of the State of to-day, and thought it unwise to molest them. The rich Jew especially was generally a regular taxpayer and a good subject.

Finally the Prince spoke about his personal relations with Jews, and remarked *inter alia* that he had really reaped ingratitude at their hands. No statesman had done more for their emancipation than he had; yet, in spite of this, it was just the Progressive and Radical papers, in the hands of the Jews, which attacked him most violently. But he did not take that too much to heart; the reason was, probably, that the owners of the papers considered it due to their Liberal or Radical spirit not to allow the memory of that, for which they as Jews had to thank him, to influence the attitude of their papers with regard to him and his policy. On the other hand, he had witnessed many a trait of Jewish gratitude. Whilst he was farming his Pomeranian estate he, like the other landowners there, often employed a local Jew. One day the Jew became bankrupt, and came to him with the entreaty not to lodge a claim that he had against him, because then he would be able to get off unpunished. Bismarck consented, and allowed his claim to lapse. The old man showed his gratitude later on, by making payments every year, which he was not legally bound to do, and continued to do so until the Prince moved away from the neighborhood, and said to him, "That's enough; let us wipe out the remainder."

PART TWO

THE WORLD LOOKS AT BISMARCK

The gamut of contemporary opinions on Bismarck ranged from the most fulsome praise to the strongest condemnation. Many of the comments presented here hinge on the rigid nature of German partisan politics. German parties were not loose coalitions on the British and American models of the day, but were narrowly organized along class and ideological lines. Thus, Left Liberal leaders tended to be urban, middle class, and laissez-faire, while Conservatives were rural landowners, in favor of state subsidies. Other observations are greatly influenced by nationality; the French tended to see, and stress, the darker side of Bismarck.

LUDWIG BAMBERGER: MINISTER OF CONFLICT [1]

Ludwig Bamberger, of Jewish religion, revolutionary of 1848, and Paris banker, was to become one of the most influential parliamentary leaders. As a National Liberal, he advised the chancellor on the French war indemnity, the founding of the Imperial Bank, and monetary reform. He became a Left Liberal and a strong opponent of Bismarck's protectionist and social welfare legislation, as well as colonial expansion. During the ninety-nine days in 1888, he secretly advised the Empress Victoria. In this sketch of 1868, published in French, he examines the responsibility of the Prussian minister president in the constitutional conflict.

We would risk fatiguing the reader if we asked him to follow us through all the events of that long and painful struggle which, for three and a half years, excited the indignation of the public opinion of the civilized world. Now that we have witnessed the fifth act of this drama and know the causes of the chief action, we are perhaps tempted to judge the enormities to which the Minister

---

[1] Ludwig Bamberger, "Monsieur de Bismarck," in *Gesammelte Schriften* 5 vols. (Berlin: Rosenbaum and Hart, 1894–98), 3: 391–97. Translated by the editor.

let himself be impelled a little less severely. Obliged to hide his cards not only from his principal enemy, but also from his chief ally, one must grant that he found himself in a terribly embarrassing situation. One must perhaps even take into consideration that, entirely filled with his dominant idea, convinced that, in the end, it was justified, he was provoked wrongly, but in good faith, against a resistance which seemed to him the result of blindness.

But even if it was, history will never be able to vote him the bill of indemnity he obtained from the national representation. It had to yield to the necessity of placing itself on the ground of accomplished fact and the future; its vote was only a compromise between the faults of yesterday and the interest of tomorrow. History has a contrary duty; . . . it pronounces judgments, but does not render services. And even when the largest share is given to circumstances, when the necessity in which Bismarck found himself of concealing projects of great utility under an unpopular exterior is admitted up to a certain point, one must nevertheless still examine whether the aristocratic sentiment and disdain for legality which engendered all these events do not belong too much to the essence of his personality for him to be able to throw the responsibility for that upon a concatenation of external circumstances. He displayed too much natural animation in an odious role, he showed too much talent in the art of making a mockery of public morality to persuade us that his way of thinking did not anticipate the excessive actions which could have been imposed upon him by the situation.

. . . He and his apologists have said that upon entering the ministry on 24 September 1862, he seriously trusted in the power of conciliating the liberal opinion of the country and of acting in accordance with it. Those who support this version even add that in refusing a portfolio at first, he would have acted solely under the impression that the conflict born of the military law would not be of too long a duration and that in the interest of his great projects, he would have done better to enter the ministry only after the removal of this difficulty and with the prospect of assuring himself of the Chamber's goodwill. In no way would the Progressives' attitude have warranted him in this hope. To wish to make them share the idea of propaganda by armed force was to be singularly mistaken about the basis of their thought. It could not even be said that they recoiled in horror at the idea; no, they were not yet at that point, because they did not suspect anyone of having conceived it, so it appeared impossible, monstrous, to them. They still belonged to the tradition of moral conquests adopted by the Regent; they had the firm conviction that Prussia, identifying herself with the liberal cause, would be irresistible and that Austria as well as the princelings would capitulate without firing a cartridge. They did not despair of seeing the chief of the Hohenzollerns embrace knowingly and openly the cause of the German people. In all that Bismarck was of an absolutely contrary opinion; despite all his perspicacity, it is not inadmissible to say that he surrendered to the illusion of making his conviction enter into the spirit of the opposition party. For he is not exempt from that common law which permits the most striking contradictions to be found united in the same individual. He had astonished the world as much by his frankness as by his guile. He has been seen now to prepare events from afar with refinement of caution, now to brave them with perfect swiftness. To Bismarck the difficulties he might encounter in parliament, in the constitution, in public opinion were only an incident, a simple detail, one of those domestic questions with which, through a lack of natural vocation he did not concern himself at all. On this basis he was thus exposed to being dangerously mistaken.

He did not reflect any longer that he had come to power in circumstances and with a reputation made for frightening public opinion and that instead of counting upon a favorable mood, he would have had to do the impossible to reassure it. Reports of intimacy which lately existed between him and high personages placed the capstone on his unpopularity, which was already so great. He was openly accused of having cemented, at Paris, an agreement of feudal royalism with modern Caesarism. Certain allusions which fell from his lips and shortly spread made him not only appear the instigator of an obscure plot hatched against progressive ideas, but further as a docile student of the science of adulterating the democratic principle. There was nothing up to universal suffrage which he was not suspected of wishing to make a weapon against liberty. Instead of understanding all that was legitimate in their suspicions, Bismarck lost patience at the first resistance he encountered. He understood all the slowness and all the care it was necessary to employ with royalty; he did not consider the precautions to use in accosting public opinion. From this instant he threw himself headlong into the arms of the feudal party, whose nothingness he had recognized perfectly in lucid moments. Naturally this party asked nothing better than to regain possession of its old favorite.

It was the military law that was almost always responsible for conflict with parliament. The Chamber was dissolved two times. Another time it was simply dismissed with the declaration that it would be dispensed with in determining the budget. All challenges and all insults were thrown before the country. Bismarck and his principal colleague, Roon, the War Minister, had moments of cynical audacity. One day an orator having stated very grave suspicions about the ministers and Virchow having demanded that they be invited to be present at the debates so that they could reply, Bismarck nonchalantly emerged from a room close by the meeting hall and tossed some disdainful words at the assembly, declaring that it was useless to recapitulate, since in the place he had been he had understood what had passed between the gentlemen sufficiently. Another time he said in the midst of the sitting, before the deputies: "When we make up our minds to wage war, we will wage it with or without your approval." One day when the President wished to stop the War Minister in an anti-parliamentary tirade, he cried out that the President did not have the right to interrupt; a minister was above the rules of the house and presidential control. From that was born a long conflict which bordered on an open violation of constitutional principle; the King sent the Chambers a message lacking the signature of any minister. At the same time the Chambers were dissolved (27 May 1863). The press ordinances appeared some days later. The system of warnings and confiscations, which were obviously imported from abroad, were applied to the newspapers. Violent pressure was openly put on officials. Whosoever had the courage not to submit was persecuted with a vengeance, disciplined, and sent to the depths of a province. The cry of general indignation reached such a pitch that the Crown Prince himself was unable to avoid the common emotion. In a public meeting at Danzig, he declared that the ordinances had been issued without his knowledge and that he disapproved of them. He came to the point of writing the King, his father, in order to protest against a government, which, he said, put his rights to the crown in jeopardy. His letter resulted in sending him away from court for a while. Then the cup was filled to the brim with the notorious judgments of the court of appeals in Berlin, expressly created for the needs of the case in imitation of those tribunals which under James II were called a "packed jury." Set aside were the acquittals rendered in the first and second instances regarding the deputies persecuted for having attacked the ministers in their speeches; parliamentary immunity, expressly sanctioned by an article of the constitution, was suppressed by penal means. These judges whose incorruptibility had become proverbial—perhaps too easily; those officials, who, although pedantic and caviling, had preserved a sort of rigidity even in servility,—in short, all who were concerned closely or distantly in the official sphere seemed to submit to a treatment of systematic demoralization. Traffic with consciences came into full bloom. A new word characterized young employees who made a rapid fortune without any merit beyond being ready to do anything for a little preferment. They were termed "careerists". . . . It seemed that the moment when the pessimists triumphed in their predictions had come; one was going to see all the abuses of the old regime combined with all the trickery of modern despotism; the prejudices of orthodoxy would be joined to the laxity of frivolous realism. A very moderate scholar [Adolph Schmidt] expressed himself thus: *"With a people less cold than ours, a single one of the numerous measures of this time would have sufficed to make a revolution break out."*

If all these measures were not Bismarck's personal work, if precisely the most odious of them was perhaps prepared without him by his colleague [Lippe] in the Justice Ministry, a pure feudalist, personally dear to the King, the prime minister does bear the responsibility before the world for all that has happened and by virtue of his recognized superiority; that is only justice. At least he let it happen, where he did not act himself.

VICTOR CHERBULIEZ: THE OPPORTUNIST [2]

Victor Cherbuliez, French popular novelist, minor critic, and commentator on German affairs, describes his view of Bismarck before the Franco-German War. Cherbuliez traces much of his foreign and domestic policy to observation of the France of Napoleon III, stressing Bismarck's freedom from principle and refusal to back any single party. He concludes that the North German chancellor is essentially an opportunist.

The victory [of Königgrätz] completely surpassed all that one dared hope,—a well-merited victory, if one considers not only the army's bravery, but Bismarck's political ingenuity, the exactness and firmness of his glance, the energy of his action, the rapidity which he knows how to imprint on all his actions. . . . How was the victory going to be used? It may be supposed that Bismarck foresaw all the possible risks. Diverse combinations must have presented themselves to so inventive and so fertile a spirit. This man with the iron will is not a man with his mind made up. He has a pliant imagination; he knows how to reverse himself.

While striding along one of the avenues of the Thiergarten with us one day, a Prussian liberal-conservative told us: "It is impossible for you to understand our *premier.* Such a man could only have been born in Prussia; he could only have grown up on the pavements of

[2] Victor Cherbuliez, *L'Allemagne Politique depuis la paix de Prague* (Paris: Librairie Hachette, 1870), pp. 28–31, 32–33, 34–35, 83–84, 183–87, 381–82, 401–2, 404. Translated by the editor.

Berlin. He contains within himself the university student, the Junker, the guard lieutenant, the diplomat, the despot, the revolutionary; all that set off by a sort of ironic fantasy which makes him an artist— almost a poet. He is an aristocrat to the core, not that he has preju- dices and respect for traditions, but by temperament, taste and talent for command, by his immense scorn for *liberal twaddle*. He is sceptic in the depths of his soul; he believes only in human stupidity and never in his life has he mistaken green cheese for the moon. He crumbles it without pity. Alas! He no longer respects our poor little liberal moons; he maliciously blows on their smoky light. With that, radical in his soul, radical in his method—by his lack of repugnance for violent and summary means, by his taste for cutting to the quick. . . ."

"No," continued our speaker, "this sceptical and radical aristocrat is not a common type; he is not a whole man, I know, but he is a very complex man. His audacity is admired; his genial and Me- phistophelean insolence is also admired. And be assured that more than once Prussia has been delighted at being represented in the world by an insolent person; it still feels the blow of Olmütz on its cheek. But Bismarck's insolence doesn't have the inflexibility of the narrow and arrogant spirit of the doctrinaire at all; it is a manner, a means of government. Nothing is more antipathetic to him than doctrinair- ism, and in that he is a true Prussian. Prussian policy characteristically turns up its nose at ideas as well as sentiments, at doctrines as well as traditions. Essentially it is a policy of the *free hand*, which is always ready to play all possible games, without ever pledging the future. In this respect, Bismarck is the paragon of the Prussian states- man. No man is more emancipated from all pedantry and all con- servative prudery. If necessary, he is ready to join hands with revo- lution; he feels himself strong enough to make it pull his chestnuts out of the fire and to devour them under its nose. It is not only Bismarck; it is the astonishing liberty and marvelous frankness of his language. He scorns little dissimulations; he has initiated a new type of diplomacy, which consists of winning by showing his cards. He talks; he talks a great deal; he tells the universe of his projects, and it doesn't believe a thing. He says: 'On such a day I'll do that'— and he does it. . . . Also for a long time one refused to take him seriously; he was treated as a braggart, a wrong-headed fellow. At Paris he was compared to a pike which stirred up the fish, and they said: 'We are the ones who will get the catch'. . . . Often a splendid means of domination for a statesman is to possess the qualities most opposed to the temperament of the nation he governs. In a country as taciturn, formal, grave, and reserved as Prussia, what advantages have not been given to Bismarck, in this marvelous abandon which characterizes him, this supreme ease in conduct and language, which reveals the perfect liberty of a spirit abounding in ideas, rich in ingenuity, who, sure of his goal, is always ready to change direction, enslaved by no system, seizing opportunity for flight, living from day to day, and, as it were, inventing the means proportionately—a great virtuoso whose political career is a perpetual improvisation! . . ." "Be assured," our speaker told us by way of conclusion, "be assured, that at Königgrätz our *premier* carried many plans in his head. His lively imagination foresaw the different projects that one could extract from the victory, and, if he had been let alone, perhaps events would have taken another turn. An Austrian indiscretion informs us that the idea which triumphed at Nikolsburg was the King's idea, for the King had one idea and only one. This idea was to take, to take a great deal, to take all there was to take. . . ."

On one point there was no hesitation: Austria must leave Germany. It was the first fruit of victory and literally it was for that that the war had been waged. By Austria's expulsion two aims were gained: simultaneously satisfaction was given to the interests of Prussia's greatness and to German national sentiment, tired of dualism and its anxieties. . . .

The first step was ousting Austria from Germany. That done, two systems of conduct, two policies were possible: one difficult perhaps, but generous, endeavoring to settle the German question, to reorganize Germany under Prussian hegemony; the other easier, with more obvious profit, more palpable, but leading perhaps to less lasting results, a policy of aggrandizement and conquest. The choice lay between annexions and the presidency of a new German confederation including Germany, and all Germany reconstituted under Prussian auspices. There was no probability of claiming to reconcile the two things. Any true confederation demanded a certain equilibrium of forces among the states that composed it—such as existed before 1866 when Prussian greatness was already an obstacle and a danger to a German federal organization. To enlarge it further was to prove clearly . . . that in the name of an alliance an empire was intended and that by empire absorption was meant. Since Prussia took Hanover, the secondary states know what awaits them, and it is because of this that German unity is not yet an accomplished fact, that Bavaria and Württemberg persist in what, at Berlin, is called particularism. . . .

It is sad that Bismarck is a complex, but incomplete man. A superior intelligence, a strongly tempered character, a man of enterprise and an incomparable diplomat, he does not possess the qualities which make a great minister the arbiter of parties. He has known how to create for himself an eloquence which is his alone, laborious eloquence, which seeks for words, but always finds the happy, exact, and, sometimes, charming one. His speeches, full of energy, humor, and ideas which are original and plausible (though often contradictory) are always events. And there is no oratorical talent which Europe is more curious about than his, but he understands nothing of that so delicate art of handling assemblies. Be it arrogance, be it nervous impatience, he has not found the skillful temperament which reconciles disagreements nor the decisive thrusts which astonish, and dissolve, a refractory majority. It is easier for him to make compliments than concessions, and his method is to carry off men with a high hand; resistance disgusts and embitters him. "Bismarck," said a politician who possesses everything that is lacking in the Prussian minister, "is a man of powerful imagination and stupendous character, who was not born a statesman, who has become one by a singular combination of circumstances, who has succeeded and who enjoys his success. More is needed, less is needed," he added, "to make a minister. The first point is not to be a fool; the second is not to fear details." A detail is next to nothing, but sometimes it is everything; politics, like life, depends upon it. Bismarck is a buoyant and resilient spirit, quick-witted, fertile in ideas and witticisms, but his career was a bit disconnected. He did not rise by the accustomed ropes; he had neither the time nor the opportunity to acquire learning, which he disdains and which instinct never provides. He scorns pedants, doctrinaires, and little men; he also scorns small matters, and small matters take their revenge. . . .

Although he has never broken with his old [Conservative] friends, who, in necessity, he knows how to regain and how to anesthetize discontents by agreeable attentions, by enticing promises, Bismarck has often dismayed them by the faithlessness of his memory, by the ingratitude of his genius. . . . He has an arrogant unconcern which holds cheap all that a Junker has most at heart; within him is a doubter who jeers at relics and dogmas, a utilitarian to whom all means are advantageous to reach his goal, a radical whose irreverence, whose fearless imagination frightens the fervent worshipper of the past. On his good-humored days, Bismarck has a youthfulness, a gaiety, and whims and sarcasms that make all the Berlin bonzeries shudder. He plays without ceremony with the fetishes and grotesque figures, and what is even more disagreeable to them, he explains them. . . . When he puts his rash hands on the ark of the Lord, when altars tremble at the jerky clamor of his voice and his laugh, they begin to quake. Today all gods have become so fragile! If the reports are evidence, this astonishing man was not afraid to declare one day to the entire Ministry of State that the union of church and state was a source of grave embarrassment for a government, that it is a heritage of the past which has had its day, that absolute freedom of denominations is suited to modern society, that America has it good, that Europe has a great deal to learn from her. And another day, he exclaimed to himself: "If the porter at the Orpheum comes to me with a good idea, a good financial expedient, I don't see any harm in confiding the Finance Ministry to him."

Like all great spirits, Bismarck is in secret correspondence, in tactiturn communication with his century; he belongs to it in part, and the prejudices of old fogies cause him nervous restlessness. He knows very well what time he lives in; he asks nothing better than to make certain concessions to the modern spirit, to revolution itself. He greatly astonished the Reichstag by assuring it that he gladly accepted the rights of man like those that had been proclaimed in France in 1789. It is true that he believes somewhat less in Prussian rights, but a little democracy does not frighten him at all. If he served his apprenticeship at St. Petersburg, he also studies at Paris. He is convinced that democracy is more manageable than is believed; that universal suffrage is an instrument which one learns to play very quickly. Since 1861 he has regretted that, as a result of Conservative prudery, Germany was not given at all a great elective parliament which could effect the civil and economic reforms desired by the nation. In industrial freedom, Prussia was twenty-four years behind its Western neighbors; it had preserved entire a system of fetters, of prohibitions and monopolies, the very beautiful remains of the antiquated regime of masters and wardens. The Conservative party would never have been gotten to take a hand in sacrificing these Gothic traditions. Behind the back of the Chamber of Peers, Bismarck had them swept away by his young federal parliament, and, uncontestably, it was a precious service he rendered to Prussia.

Bismarck is ready to understand everything, to support everything, to love everything, except liberalism. If he is of his century in political economy, if he comes to terms with democracy on such and such a point, he never gives anything at all to the parliamentarians. His ideal is an enlightened, intelligent government which executes by itself all the desirable reforms without having to impose on itself the fatigue of reasoning with an assembly. Unhappily, assemblies exist, and he is not able to suppress them. In incurable cases, a palliative certainly has its price. Bismarck has discovered that the surest means of weakening parliaments is to multiply them; this gives rise to conflict that a skillful government can exploit. When he longed for a great elective parliament for Germany, he made the shrewd observation that it could be used to serve to hold in check the individual state parliaments. The creation of the Northern Confederation permitted him to apply this principle. The Prussian parliament had to be stripped of part of its powers to the profit of the federal parliament; it no longer concentrated in its hands the voting of all laws and of the complete budget; its credit and its importance were lessened. What is true in arithmetic is not true of parliaments; two halves of a parliament do not equal one parliament. Add that the Prussian Chamber has to deal with royalty represented by a responsible minister. The federal chamber which henceforth supplants the Prussian one in part of its duties and rights finds itself in the presence of an anonymous and irresponsible body, a sort of royalty without a king, a ministry without ministers. When one speaks to that body, when one questions it, often there is no one to reply— which shortens dialogue in an amazing fashion. What diverse uses the Northern Confederation has! Besides the services Bismarck can expect in the regulation of the German question, he has reaped the precious advantage of mediatising, not Prussia,—Good God!—but the Prussian constitution.

Decidedly the publicist was not wrong who lauded the new charter to the skies, the new political machine invented by Bismarck's fertile genius. To manufacture something which resembles a confederation and which greatly differs from it, something which seems to be Germany in miniature and is only Prussia enlarged, a constitution which, viewed at a distance, has I don't know what liberal and democrat appearances and, seen close up, does quite the contrary. The task was not slight; it requires a profound knowledge of linear and aerial perspective applied to politics and of all the optical illusions of the theater. . . .

It was France which took upon itself to declare that it considered that the treaties of Vienna had lapsed. It was the first to proclaim what it called the new law. When, after the Italian war, it paid itself for its expenditure of men and money by an increase in territory, it employed all the forms old and new. No conquest was correct any longer: one could employ voluntary cession of the possessor, a proper transfer of property, the principle of nationalities and unity of language, the vote of populations. The French government's offence was to wish to replace the Vienna treaties by a dogma which was still poorly fathomed and all of whose consequences were not foreseen. It publicly professed its new law; it prided itself on teaching it to Europe. . . . Among the auditors that France indoctrinated, there was one with an accomplished ear, a shrewd and cunning intellect. . . . His intelligent docility led him to marvelous results. He did not apply the new maxims at random; he accommodated them to his convenience. He carefully distinguished between cases. In the name of the principle of national will, he denied Europe the right of preventing the Southern Germans from giving themselves to him, but he put himself to no trouble to consult the Hanoverians and Hessians before taking them. He only wished to possess them by the right of conquest. Is it quite certain that Hanover and Electoral Hesse had a will? It is true that in return he promised a vote to the Schleswigers, but the treaties having stipulated nothing about the voting method, he was not put to the trouble of finding it. Is it certain that voting proves something after all? . . .

. . . Today Prussia is one man. And it is known that this man has good reasons for being peaceful, but it is also known that if he makes up his mind to it he is going to keep his secret and that he cannot reply to those who ask him whether liberty or Germany: "You will have neither the one nor the other." Some of his enemies are pleased to say that his sack is empty, that he has dared all he is capable of daring. Impudent and loose talk! Bismarck recently observed in the Reichstag that men of this century are ready to censure others, but they fear action and giving an account, that fear of responsibility is the great malady of our critical and impotent epoch. Certainly it is a contagion that he has not had to suffer. There are few men in history, who have taken so much upon themselves, who have consented to be held to account for so many things to their contemporaries and posterity, but his audacity has a counterweight in his marvelous political intelligence. He sees situations clearly, he knows everything they permit, and the result has justified his apparent recklessness. One can apply to him Polonius' words: he has a method in his madness. Sadowa proves that. . . .

To borrow a word which the [Vatican] Council put into circulation, Bismarck is an "opportunist". . . .

GUSTAV FREYTAG: THE FAILURE [3]

Gustav Freytag was one of the most distinguished dramatists and novelists of his epoch, and a pioneer of realism in literature. A fervent liberal nationalist and later admirer of Bismarck, he served as a National Liberal in the North German Reichstag. His journal, Die Grenzboten, *published in Saxony, was the most influential liberal journal of the years of unification. Here he voices his doubts of the chancellor's national policy and its effect on South Germany, just before the outbreak of the Franco-German War.*

[3] Letter from Gustav Freytag to Duke Ernest II of Saxe-Coburg-Gotha, Siebleben, 1 July 1870. In E. Tempeltey, ed., *Gustav Freytag und Herzog Ernst von Coburg im Briefwechsel: 1853 bis 1893* (Leipzig: Verlag von S. Hirzel, 1904), p. 244. Translated by the editor.

Thank God that politics has traveled to the spas. That was a hard winter with legislative paragraphs. And the dear Northern Confederation has provoked people. The exclusion of South Germany in the year 1866, which most approved and which I have always considered Bismarck's most mistaken measure, begins to reveal its dark consequences. It is not true that the southern states have gradually come closer to us; of necessity they will become more estranged from us the further the legislative organization in the north progresses. Even the Badensers doubt if they can hold firm past the next elections to their diet. And what then? Division into two parts *in sempiternum;* there will gradually be an alienation.

It seems to me that Bismarck finds the bitterness of his mistakes more threatening in quiet than in the patriotic public. The speculation about a violent act, the searching out of the old idea of the Emperor for the Hohenzollers, occurred as a result. This is the point where the joke ends. The stale idea of an Emperor of 48 would, if realized now, have none of the consequences Berlin hopes for. But it would experience a generally cool aversion from the people even in Prussia and, what would be worse, would bring us all at once a complete deluge of new pretensions, princely courts, combinations, and new intruders in the path which the new Emperor would find it much more difficult to accommodate himself to in the time which still may be necessary. For, despite all the weaknesses of liberals, the near future still belongs to liberalism. Emperor! The unlucky prince in Mexico should still disgust every honorable prince with this pretentious twisting of his gold circlet.

HANS DELBRÜCK: VICTOR IN THE KULTURKAMPF [4]

Hans Delbrück, a cousin of Rudolf Delbrück, was a pioneer military historian, professor of history at the University of Berlin, and a prominent publicist. Editor of the influential Preussiche Jahrbücher, *he served as a Free Conservative in both the Prussian Chamber of Deputies and the Reichstag. In this article of 1897, he takes a novel stand on the Kulturkampf. He sees it as a triumph of Bismarck's national policy, for the chancellor won over first the National Liberals and then the Center party.*

If I correctly judge Prince Bismarck, he is very far removed from conceding that the Kulturkampf ended with a simple defeat of the

[4] Hans Delbrück, "Deutschland und Ultramontanismus," in *Erinnerungen, Aufsätze und Reden,* 3rd ed. (Berlin: Verlag von Georg Stilke, 1905), pp. 415–19. Reprinted, and translated by the editor, by permission of the publisher.

Prussian state, for the reason that he never surrendered to the illusion that he could have imbued German Catholics with a new spirit by legislative pressure. Never was the battle anything else to him but a political encounter. It was not a question to him of influencing the ecclesiastical-religious feeling of German Catholics in any way, but it was a question to him of giving battle to them as enemies of the new imperial structure under Prussian leadership. When he had succeeded in toppling Herr von Mühler and was looking around for a new Minister of Religions, then he wanted a "boarhound for wild boars." He was indifferent about how this battle was conducted in detail; he only desired severity and greater and greater severity from the Ministry of Religions. These Catholics had worked against the half-formed empire; well and good. They should feel what it meant to be "an enemy of the empire."

From the modern standpoint, it was, under all circumstances, a mistake that it was not restricted to the suppression and prevention of ecclesiastical means of domination, but that it also interfered in the heartfelt region of religious conviction. But this reproach is easier to make than to avoid. With the possible exception of some cases, it was by no means admitted at that time that one oppressed or wished to oppress consciences at all. When it happened, so it was said, that was not the fault of laws of the state, but of the Catholic hierarchy, which did not wish to submit to these laws, but rebelled against them, and thereby hindered the ordinary cure of souls. It was not the state which disturbed religion, but the church which occupied itself with politics.

But really is religion to be divorced from the church and the church from politics? . . .

In what way . . . was this struggle a success? First of all in welding together an effective Reichstag majority. Since 1866 the government was really on a compromise footing with the National Liberals. But this party had by no means yet overcome or completely abandoned the old bad political habits of liberalism. One did not immediately desire to dispense completely with the comfortable feeling of being in opposition; to many liberalism and opposition seemed identical concepts! There was a very heated fight over whether the death penalty should be abolished in the new penal code. The National Liberal party was not to be brought further than a provisional solution of the basic question of the new state structure: the securing of the stability of the army, and even today we drag wearily from one septennate stage to the next. Despite all the opposition to the rump Progressive party, which persisted in die-hard opposition, one could not decide to renounce the idea of a great all-inclusive liberal party. It was only in the Kulturkampf that, despite everything, the National

Liberal party manifested itself as an effective governmental party. The unconditional necessity of joining with the government in the battle against Catholic obscurantism also made the party accommodating in other areas of public life. Since, in the battle against the Catholic Church, even the Progressive party now felt friendly impulses toward the govenment—it was Virchow who coined the term "Kulturkampf"—and the Conservatives as orthodox Protestants considered themselves obligated to follow, the Reichstag assembled not, of course, an entirely firm, but an available, majority. What do people miss today when they speak of the stagnation of party life? What they miss is the great opponent, against whom they flew into a passion, against whom they banded together, whom they could attack courageously. One of the first principles of Bismarckian statecraft was always to have a regular opponent, first the liberals, then the Ultramontanes, then the Social Democrats; finally he put the Poles to the test. When he returned from war in 1871, he lit upon the newly-formed Center. He could not wish for anything better. Passion for battle against the Center produced the combat-ready parliamentary army for him.

But even greater was his success with the Center itself. Doubtless when it was founded, the Center was "an enemy of the empire." Today this term has as good as disappeared. . . . [This] result is to no other credit than that of Prince Bismarck and the Kulturkampf. The first Chancellor's sharp sword pursued the party in this struggle long enough for it to be driven onto imperial soil. There was no other means to get out of the Kulturkampf except to give the empire support worthy of gratitude in a great task of national policy. This first happened with the customs legislation of the year 1879. Since then the Center has advanced step by step and has become a party with which one can come to terms. . . .

In this political context, the defeat which the state is supposed to have suffered in the Kulturkampf disappears, and the entire encounter appears a series of triumphs of Bismarckian statesmanship. For the most part, he had, in return, to abandon the laws he had sought to impose upon the Catholic Church; no doubt, but to him these laws were a means, not an end. The complaisance he showed was in his eyes as little a defeat as the Indemnity Law and the complaisance he showed after 1866 to the liberals, with whom he had fought so terribly in the time of conflict. At one time it was Lasker, at another Windthorst, with whom he negotiated; in his eyes it did not make the slightest difference. Only the catastrophe of March, 1890 prevented the strategist of the Kulturkampf from entering into even a much closer relationship with his old opponent [Windthorst].

EUGEN RICHTER: THE TURN FROM LAISSEZ-FAIRE [5]

*"As the Imperial Chancellor has just said," was the frequent
starting point of Eugen Richter's attacks on Bismarck, who
stalked out of the hall as the Progressive, and later Left Liberal,
orator began to speak. Richter's knowledge of the budget and
dialectical skill aroused even the admiration of military officials.
This doctrinaire supporter of classical economics was also a
prominent journalist, editing the* Freisinnige Zeitung. *In his
memoirs, Richter sees Bismarck's shift from laissez-faire and the
National Liberals beginning as early as 1874.*

Prince Bismarck's reversal of the entire direction of domestic
policy began to be prepared in the course of the year 1874 and, indeed, soon after the compromise over the military law, through
whose conclusion Bennigsen believed he had assured the binding of
even the Chancellor to his [National Liberal] friends and a calm continued development of legislation. All that Prince Bismarck with
the liberals' aid had created in imperial economic legislation since
1867 was henceforth to be converted into its opposite.

Of course, it was years before these plans reached a definite form;
they were to be undertaken cautiously and gradually; no direct sign
of them appeared externally to the public in the year 1874.

Poschinger . . . has Bismarck say to the deputies who enjoyed his
personal confidence, explaining his reversal: I am bored, the great
things are done, the German empire is established. *No longer do I
have any desire to hunt hares badly.* I am too tired for that. Of
course, if it were a question of slaying a *large and powerful boar* . . .
then I would be there. . . . Then Prince Bismarck's later financial
plans were characterized in their intricacy as an attractive hunts-
man's bag. Since the existing adviser [Delbrück] moved in deepened
ruts and had no creative ideas, the Chancellor himself was designated
to formulate reform plans and for their execution to take tools
wherever he found them.

. . . Just as little—though it has frequently been attempted—can
a basis be found in the alleged poor experiences with the new imperial legislation. Experiences in the area of establishing railways,
which stood at the time in the forefront of public interest, could
already in no way have on this account relation to imperial legislation,
because the Prussian railway law of 1838 . . . remained in force un-

[5] Eugen Richter, *Im alten Reichstag: Erinnerungen* 2 vols. (Berlin: Verlag
Fortschritt, 1894–96), 1: 98–100. Translated by the editor.

altered. . . . Allusions to freedom of trade and movement are just as little to the point, for, in both cases, imperial legislation had only generalized and codified what had already long before been in force in the separate areas of Germany, in part in law, in part in fact. Unfavorable working conditions stand out at the time merely in consequence of a strong demand for workers—a consequence of the extensive military orders after the war and the soaring of the spirit of enterprise after the conclusion of peace.

Of course, this great soaring of the entire acquisitive life after the conclusion of peace in 1871 was followed by a great set-back in May, 1873, brought forth by overproduction and overspeculation in many branches of economic life instigated by the events of the war, which was not even increased by imperial legislation; on the contrary, the increased possibility of free movement was adapted to the end that the consequences of them could be softened and it eased the transition to other productive opportunities.

But Prince Bismarck had never been a liberal man at all and had never had liberal views. After the war of 1866, when he faced a threatening new war, Prince Bismarck believed a certain notice of the liberals was indicated. Also he needed their support in order to give greater meaning to imperial power itself through imperial legislation.

Also from 1871 to 1874 Prince Bismarck could not yet dispense with liberal support in the battle with the Vatican. But now in 1874 he began gradually to perceive that there were no longer any particular laurels to be won in these struggles and that he had led Falk . . . at a false pace.

Now Prince Bismarck again became reactionary proportionately as his practical political interest ceased proportionately to be, and to appear, liberal. Of course, at the time he faced a Reichstag which after the elections appeared to bear more of a liberal stamp than its predecessors. This Reichstag had already deeply humbled itself in the military question and, with suitable treatment, gave expectation of further pliancy. First of all,—as soon became apparent—it occurred to Prince Bismarck to split the decisive party of the National Liberals. For the future, new elections could be prepared through which the liberal element was generally weakened and old Conservative friends would again increase.

Prince Bismarck henceforth began to excogitate on the prescription for this in Varzin.

BEAUCHAMP WALKER: BISMARCK'S EASTERN POLICY [6]

As the war clouds gathered in the Balkans in 1877, Major General Beauchamp Walker, British military attaché in Berlin, recorded his view of Bismarck's foreign policy. He notes the emperor's pro-Russian predilections and the chancellor's fear of French action.

The Hermit of Varzin [Bismarck] is to me an undefinable quantity, as the mathematicians saw, and him I never pretend to fathom. Further than this his stomach is very much out of order which is, in my opinion, quite sufficient to account for any vagaries, political or personal. He is a huge feeder and takes no exercise, lives in an atmosphere like that of a forcing house, and smokes powerful tobacco. One's only wonder is that he does not blow up altogether, instead of only blowing up his subordinates. To me he is as inscrutable as the other Sphinx, and I look upon him with much the same awe and wonderment, not a little thankful that no roll of the ball can ever bring me into the position of being required to read this human riddle.

. . . Far less am I able to judge his conduct during the present crisis [Russo-Turkish War]. I learn that Lord Odo Russell thinks that he has been sincerely desirous of acting with England, and, as I have no other means of judging at present than what I hear from Lord Odo, I do not like to form any opinion at variance with that which I derive from him. I have not seen Bismarck to speak to for more than a year. The one opinion however which I hold in regard to his general line of action whenever Russia is concerned is this—the only point on which he dare not openly differ from the Emperor is Russia. Need I say more. . . .

Russia will have to fight someone and that someone is either England or Germany. Now Germany will put off the fight with all the means available because—war with Russia means an attempt on the part of France to recover the lost provinces. And this I think is the clue to Bismarck's policy throughout. He always sees France before his eyes, and would be glad to see Russia weaken herself in a contest with some power other than Germany. . . .

. . . The Germans are very fit, always fit, but the Germans have

[6] Letter from Beauchamp Walker to Major General Sir Henry Ponsonby, Berlin, 15 January 1877. In Arthur Ponsonby, *Henry Ponsonby: Queen Victoria's Private Secretary* (London: Macmillan, 1942), pp. 321–23. Reprinted by permission of the publisher.

as much idea of going to war on the Eastern question as they have of meddling with the moon. They have quite enough to occupy them at home, and have no intention of giving France the hoped-for chance at present. . . .

AUGUST BEBEL: VANQUISHED BY THE SOCIALISTS [7]

A workingman, a founder of the German Social Democratic party, and one of the chancellor's most hated parliamentary opponents, August Bebel here presents his view of Bismarck. He sees the chancellor not only as failing to crush the socialists, but also as being at fault in his many coercive measures.

Bismarck knew his Liberals [of the sixties] when he said of them, "More than they hate me they dread a revolution." He, indeed, took his instruments where he found them. He took many former Democrats of 1848 into his service; he tried to enlist Liebknecht, who was then in London; he did enlist Lothar Bucher, who in turn tried to secure Karl Marx as a contributor to the Prussian Government Gazette. These methods were those of Louis Napoleon, who in a masterly way exploited class antagonisms so as to prop up his system, even at the price of universal suffrage. It soon became obvious that Bismarck intended to exploit the Labor movement as against the Liberal bourgeoisie. . . .

A Bill was before the Reichstag [in 1875] to amend the criminal law. Fourteen fresh offences were placed in the category of criminal offences. Bismarck was always a man of wrath, eager to crush and abolish any tendency to the times which he found inconvenient or disagreeable, by the application of coercive measures. He applied such measures to the Roman Catholic Church, the Polish nationalist movement and to Social Democracy. And he was never converted from this standpoint, although at the end of his life it was plain as the day that it had been a mistake. He was the vanquished, not the victor. . . .

. . . The autumn of 1878: at which time, after the two attempts on the life of the Emperor William, Prince Bismarck thought it expedient to force a strong Coercion Bill through the Reichstag: a measure which, directed against the Social-Democratic party, after remaining in force for twelve years (until 1891 [*sic*]), proved utterly ineffectual, and cost the Chancellor his office.

Prince Bismarck had hoped by his Coercion Bill, if not to suppress,

[7] August Bebel, *My Life* (London: T. Fisher Unwin, 1912), pp. 8, 47–48, 288–89.

at least to retard the development of the party. Yet he was to see this party, after the suppression of its Press and organisation, increase the number of its votes from 312,000 in 1881 to 1,427,000 in 1890, by which time it had become the strongest party in Germany. This increase of power conclusively demonstrated that his coercive legislation was ineffectual and superfluous. Not Social-Democracy but Bismarck was vanquished, and his defeat was sealed by his dismissal.

CHLODWIG HOHENLOHE: THE AUSTRIAN ALLIANCE [8]

Among the most distinguished of Bismarck's collaborators was Chlodwig, Prince Hohenlohe-Schillingsfürst. He worked for national goals as Bavarian minister president in the sixties, as a Free Conservative backed the chancellor in the Reichstag, was ambassador in Paris, an envoy at the Congress of Berlin, acting secretary of state for foreign affairs, and governor of Alsace-Lorraine. Later he was to be the third German chancellor. Here he describes Bismarck's conclusion of the Dual Alliance with Austria, which resulted in one of the most serious conflicts the chancellor had with his monarch. It is perhaps characteristic of Bismarck's relations with his subordinates that Hohenlohe speedily came round to the chancellor's way of thinking.

Gastein, September 14, 1879

. . . Holstein received me, and told me very serious matters were in question, and the Chancellor wanted to consult me.

The situation is as follows. The Chancellor, who does not trust Russia, has come here to conclude a defensive alliance with Austria *within* the League of the three Emperors. Andrássy thought at first that it was not meant seriously; but when he saw that it was he "jumped right up to the ceiling" for joy, because Austria cannot stand alone and must look out for alliances. But when the Emperor received the Chancellor's proposition, Alexandrovo and the meeting with the Czar of Russia [on 3 and 4 September] had intervened, and now he will no longer consent to the project.

The Chancellor, on the other hand, means to resign if the Emperor does not assent. Holstein has proposed that I should talk him over. To this Prince Bismarck has agreed. I have talked to Holstein this evening, and told him that so far I do not approve of the project.

[8] F. Curtius, ed., *Memoirs of Prince Chlodwig of Hohenlohe-Schillingsfürst* 2 vols. (New York: Macmillan, 1906), 2: 252–56.

In the first place, I do not trust Austria, and, in the second, I do not regard Russia as seriously hostile. Lastly, I believe an alliance with Austria would result in one between Russia and France. And then there would be war, while Bismarck believes his treaty would ensure peace. . . .

August 16 [sic]

Yesterday read the documents and talked it over with the Prince. Bismarck, after all, convinced me of the necessity of the compact with Austria. He says the latter cannot remain isolated in face of the menace of Russia. She will look about her for an ally, either Russia or France. In either case we are exposed to the danger of isolation. My telegram touching the Russian overtures in Paris came very opportunely for Bismarck. Now, however, the Kaiser is unapproachable, thanks to the disastrous meeting at Alexandrovo, and will not agree to the alliance, in which he sees an act of treachery towards his nephew. Bismarck, on his part, has so far committed himself with Andrássy and is so convinced of the Russian danger, that he will not take the responsibility, and threatens to retire if things turn out so. The Emperor, on the other hand, threatens to abdicate. He is in a great state of perplexity as to what to do. Bismarck seems to be determined if the Emperor does not give way. . . .

[Strassburg,] September 22 (evening)

. . . On taking leave the Emperor commanded me to come at eight o'clock.

He received me at that hour in his study. To begin with, he inquired where I came from, and so on. Then he asked me if I had seen the Chancellor. I replied: "Yes, at Gastein," The Emperor: "He is very much annoyed, I suppose?" "No," said I, "but uneasy." Then he recounted the whole course of the matter—the Emperor Alexander's letter, the reply, the meeting at Alexandrovo, his interviews with Alexander, with Miljutin and Giers. Suddenly, after the most friendly assurances had been exchanged, the Chancellor, probably in order to revenge himself for Alexander's letter, made the proposal to conclude a treaty with Austria against Russia. That, he said, he could not do. He had acquired the impression that Bismarck was planning a coalition of Austria, Germany, France, and England. I refuted this. If now, while Andrássy is at the helm, such a treaty was not concluded, the Conservative party in Austria would come to an understanding with Russia at our expense. In that case France would not also be left in the cold. As regards France in particular,

Waddington was against Russia and in favor of England. But within three months he might fall. It was possible that then creatures of Gambetta's would take the helm, and these would open relations with the Russian revolutionary elements, and in concert with them conjure up a war in order to throw all Europe into revolution. Hence a double service would be rendered to Russia by the alliance with Austria—firstly, holding revolution in check, and, secondly, making Austria stable and keeping her from joining a coalition against Germany or Russia. That seemed to open his eyes. . . .

Memorandum of September 22, 1879

Russia is embittered against Austria, which upsets her plans in the East. Russia will and must declare war against her if her plans are to be carried through. Russia will then ask us what we mean to do. If we side with Russia and remain neutral, Austria will ally herself with France and England. Then we and Russia will stand opposed to France, Austria, and England. If we do nothing at all now, Austria may come to an understanding with Russia. Then if France is strong enough she will go to war with us, in which Russia and Austria will look on as unfriendly neutrals. We shall thus be isolated, or perhaps have to face a coalition of Austria, Russia, and France against us. But if we bind Austria by a treaty England will always be on this side of the Continental Alliance, and then we can look on with the others at the enmity of Russia and France.

In Russia the revolutionary current is so strong that one does not know to what lengths the government allows itself to be carried. It is very possible that the Constitutional Reform party wishes for war in order to achieve its reforms. In any case, there is no relying on the friendship of such a distracted country.

The Panslavic party will suffer a check by reason of the Austro-German alliance, and this will make it possible to afford support to the Conservative element in Russia.

JOSEPH ARCHER CROWE: THE SHIFT TO PROTECTION [9]

Joseph Archer Crowe married into German liberal circles and fathered the anti-German, Sir Eyre Crowe. By profession a journalist, by avocation an art critic, Joseph Archer Crowe served as commercial adviser on continental affairs to the British govern-

---

[9] Confidential letter from Joseph Archer Crowe to Lord Odo Russell, Berlin, 28 May 1880. In P. Knaplund, ed., "Letters from the Berlin Embassy, 1871–74, 1880–85," *Annual Report of the American Historical Association for the Year 1942* (Washington, D.C.: U.S. Government Printing Office, 1944), 2: 176–80.

ment. He reviews here the trading conditions that gave rise to Bismarck's shift from free trade to protection and notes the beginnings of Anglo-German commercial rivalry.

Prince Bismarck's commercial policy in the last few years has been dependent at different periods on foreign policy, party politics and the necessities of the Treasury. When Prince Bismarck signed the treaty of Frankfort (May 10, 1871), in which he conceded the most favored nation treatment to France for ever (Art. XI) he was, if anything, a free trader. When he negotiated for an Austro-German commercial treaty in 1877, his chief object was to find means to counteract the concessions made at an earlier period to France. In 1873 he foresaw future deficits and endeavoured to raise revenue, by charges on articles of consumption; his plan being to reduce the number of customs duties to a minimum and tax heavily, after the English fashion, tobacco and other goods of *prime necessity.* Hopes were entertained at that time that the German tariff would be brought into easy contrast as regards simplicity with that of Great Britain. But Prince Bismarck was aware when he made this proposal that the liberal party might ask for constitutional guarantees before granting large finance duties, whilst he was equally assured of mingled hostility and opposition "from the 25 governments and various interests and parliaments with which he would have to deal in carrying out his labors of Hercules."

The failure to carry a bill for the taxation of tobacco in 1873 produced the conviction in his mind that a different system might lead to more rapid results. To this period no doubt we may trace the germ of his determination to substitute the system of universal moderate custom, for that of duties numerically small but proportionally high.

Meanwhile the commercial prosperity of Germany, which had been gradually disappearing under a depression common to most European States, gave way. The ordinary sources of revenue failed to yield the usual supply. Direct taxation was doubled and trebled throughout the German Empire without covering the chasm of deficit, and the necessities of the Treasury created a natural demand for immediate relief.

Under similar circumstances and with similar symptoms Austria in 1876–1877 had begun to discuss the question of tariffs and international commercial relations. She denounced her treaty with England, opened negotiations with Germany and simultaneously began the reform of her customs legislation. She refused to treat with England, which "had nothing to concede." She hoped—with a normal

tàriff imbodying high duties as a weapon in hand—to force concessions from Germany.

But Prince Bismarck was quite aware of the object which Austria
had in view. He negotiated during the whole summer of 1877 without
any fixed intention as yet formulated in respect of the general tariff
of Germany, but with the obvious tendency to keep certain duties
in reserve for the purpose of negotiations with European powers.
He parleyed at Vienna for liberty as regards the imposition of import duties on the import into the Zollverein—of wine, corn, cattle
and other articles, probably with the view to use the wine duties as
a lever against France whilst Austria on her part strove to obtain
concessions for her manufactures and claimed at the same time to
keep her own duties on such a level as would exclude the competition
of England.

It was a question under these circumstances which would prevail,—
a system of moderate duties more or less protectionist, excluding
treaties and founded irrevocably on "autonomous" tariffs [sic]. The
game of interests became so intricate at Vienna and Berlin that far-
sighted persons foresaw the failure of negotiations; and, *de facto,* the
two powers are still negotiating after incessant renewals of treaties,
and are as far from an agreement as ever.

The first interruption of Austro-German negotiations in 1877 produced much ill blood. Naturally enough selfish motives were assigned
by public opinion to each of the powers. But German free trade
organs in the press committed the mistake of taking up a tone of
indignation and Austria was threatened with the prospect of a duty
of 25 p.c. on Hungarian corn and wine, and heavier duties on Austrian beer, spirits, hides, skins and fruit and vegetables.

Whoever it was that showed the way, Prince Bismarck came out
of the first negotiations with Austria a determined protectionist. There
were clear political advantages to be gained. The Prince might hope
to win the votes of the conservative landlords of Central and South
Germany by proposing to enact a corn law and barter this concession
for a reenactment of the iron duties that would give him the support
of the manufacturers of the Rhenish provinces and Silesia. He might
thus counterbalance the national liberal party whose claim to constitutional guarantees would be neutralized.

The failure of negotiations with Austria was attributed by the official organ of the German government (*Provinzial Correspondenz* of
Nov. 7, 1877) to the desire of Germany to obtain an extension of the
alleviations of duty conceded by Austria in the Austro-German treaty
of 1868, and a wish to equalize the duties in the tariffs on both sides
the Austrian tariff having been till then higher than the German. Austria was charged with claiming still higher dues claiming too to impose

a duty on German goods originally sent unfinished—so free of customs' charges—into her territory on their return over her frontier into Germany (*Appretur Zoll*). Her resolution to take payment of customs in gold ought, it was said, to have made her desist from other demands.

These, though they were not *all* the reasons for the failure were accepted as such by the German public. But business men and manufacturers felt that a crisis was at hand. . . . Prince Bismarck (Dec. 7) ordered the suspension of a concession hitherto made to Austria on the strength of old treaty obligations, and forbade the further importation of unbleached linen over the frontier of Silesia between Leabschütz and Seidenberg. In order to test the state of parties he laid a bill before the Bundesrath (Jan. 18—78) increasing the duty and excise on tobacco and raising taxes on stamps and playing cards. There was at this time a deficiency of 70 million in Imperial revenue to make up. Shortly after (Feb. 20) he submitted to the Bundesrath a resolution for appointing a commission to inquire into the state of the iron trade on the understanding that it was proper to reimpose the iron duties abolished in 1876.

Upon this the constitutional question came to the surface. The Reichstag in due course threw out the tobacco and other money bills [.]—A ministerial crisis ensued (Feb., 1878) and a breach was created between the national liberal party and the Prince Chancellor which has never since been healed.

The history of the gradual development of protectionism in Germany since 1878 need not be given in detail. Broadly stated the course pursued was this. By clever management, the protectionist element was judiciously favored and brought into prominence; and the principle of levying duties on everything was consistently carried out. During a debate in the Reichstag in February, 1878 Prince Bismarck took occasion to observe that political friendship should never be dependent on commercial questions and he roundly asserted that the tendency of Russia to keep up barriers against Germany could only be put down by raising duties on the import into Germany of Russian produce. In April the *Provinzial Correspondenz* was made to declare that free trade without reciprocity was illogical and *per se* injurious and, if only for the sake of finance duties, it was desirable that Germany should return to protection. On the same day a motion was made in the Bundesrath for a commission of inquiry into the cotton and woolen trades. A few weeks later the Reichstag was dissolved on the question of free trade or protection and a majority of protectionists was elected by the nation.

Then Prince Bismarck came forward with a complete scheme of financial and commercial reform. He called a conference of ministers of the German States at Heidelberg (Aug. 5–7) and there he not only submitted a proposal for revising the tariff [sic] which was approved, but he carried resolutions recommending indirect as against direct taxation and advocating measures for raising 230 millions of additional revenue by duties of excise and customs on tobacco, beer, sugar, brandy, coffee, petroleum, tea, colonial wares and wine.

On the 12th of November, 1878 the Prince addressed a first letter to the Bundesrath moving for the appointment of an imperial commission to revise the tariff, advocating indirect taxation, calling on the governments to defend the home markets of Germany from the attacks of foreigners and claiming increased protection for manufacturers as well as higher duties on articles of consumption. The Prince did not forget to state that it was desirable to gather together materials for the exercise of future pressure upon the commercial legislation of foreign countries.

A longer dispatch was addressed to the same body by the Prince on the appointment of the commission on the 15th of December, 1878 the gist of the paper being that increased protection was not only desirable in itself but peculiarly suitable for the occasion, and that the true principle to be applied was the principle of imposing duties on all articles crossing the frontier into Germany. With studied moderation the Chancellor put the rate of increase on customs at 5 to 10 percent *ad valorem*, urging that such an increase would scarcely influence home prices at all events at a short distance from the frontier. On the very morning of the publication of this state paper (Dec. 16) a temporary treaty was signed between Germany and Austria, putting an end to the conventional tariff [sic] in which Great Britain, in common with the other powers, had till then had a share. In the course of the same month, such treaties as embodied conventional tariffs between Germany and foreign powers were denounced. . . . Other treaties of commerce were placed on such a footing as to be terminable at a very short notice.

The tariff which the Bundesrath commission elaborated in 1879 was discussed by the parliamentary committee and by the Reichstag and passed on the 15th of July of that year. It came into force partly on the day of its passing, partly on the 1st of October and partly on the 1st of January, 1880. It almost completely realized the ideal proclaimed by Prince Bismarck and taxes almost everything from articles of prime necessity to articles of the most subtle manufacture. It imposes duties on many articles of consumption and on materials for finished manufacture as well as on the finished manufacture itself. But the whole tariff was voted by large majorities; and there is no reason to think that the nation at large has yet protested against it, although since its passing, the flax duty has been abolished. Papers recently presented to parliament show the increase of the duties imposed on articles already comprised in the Zollverein tariff, and they give the duties on articles hitherto free of those burdens. They enable us to discern that many of the manufactures of Great Britain have been made a special object of attack; and this is peculiarly the case as regards yarns, cotton and woolens and iron. In some cases, for instance in the case of the cheap woolens of Dewsbury and Leeds, the German market has been closed entirely against us. But the prospect of a change in the legislation which brought about this result is most hopeless; and all the movements which the authorities take, prove a steadfast action in the direction of protection; and as such I need only point to a bill lately presented to the Reichstag for controlling the German coasting trade and to a bill for altering the water frontier of the Elbe, both of which, though shelved for the present may become law at a future time.

The efforts made by Prince Bismarck to raise revenue by excise have not been so successful as was anticipated . . . ; and we still await proposals for taxing afresh beer, spirits and sugar. But the plans, though postponed, are not given up. . . .

CHRISTOPH VON TIEDEMANN: BISMARCK'S DECISIVENESS AND SELF-CONFIDENCE [10]

As chief of the chancellor's secretariat, the imperial chancery, from 1878 to 1881, Christoph von Tiedemann had a unique opportunity to observe Bismarck in action. Tiedemann also served as a Free Conservative in both the Prussian Chamber of Deputies and the German Reichstag. Here he sums up his experiences touching upon commercial relations with Austria, the summoning of the Berlin Congress, the Kulturkampf, and Bismarck's attitude to colleagues and public opinion.

Prince Bismarck's powers of judgment were developed in unusual harmony and uniformity. The ability to comprehend, the capacity to associate ideas, powers of decision, and memory counterbalanced one another; together they formed a complex which was capable of the most sublime performances. With marvelous assurance, he seized upon the core of the matter in every question—even the most complicated and intricate. At first glance he knew how to distinguish the essential from the superfluous. In reports he desired a "sustained

[10] Christoph von Tiedemann, *Aus sieben Jahrzehnten* 2 vols. (Leipzig: Verlag von S. Hirzel, 1906), 2: 468–71, 476–79. Translated by the editor.

extract," as he put it. Gradually one accustomed oneself to speak in
a lapidary style, and, at the last, I could report in ten minutes on
drafts of laws of more than a hundred paragraphs. Of course, the
preparation for such a report often took hours.

To a really unique and unrivalled degree, he was granted the
gifts of deciding swiftly and giving everything the most precise form.
As soon as a report ended, he gave his instructions without reflecting
an instant. Only when something did not interest him at all was
he accustomed to say: "Do what you will."

One day Justice Minister Friedberg was in Varzin on a visit and
took part in our common breakfast, while I, as usual reported on
matters which had arrived that morning. At that time negotiations
were pending with Austria-Hungary concerning renewal of the treaty
of commerce. The Austrian negotiators refused to make the concess-
sions we demanded. On the contrary, for their part they desired concessions which far exceeded the stipulations of the hitherto existing
treaty of commerce. Under discussion were seven or eight points of
difference upon which no agreement could be reached. The negotiations threatened to miscarry. The German Ambassador in Vienna
had reported concerning the state of affairs, and the Prussian Ministry
of State had deliberated exhaustively in a long session without being
able to make up its mind. Now the Prince's decision was called for.
After I had detailed the points of difference one by one, the Prince,
breaking open an egg with the greastest composure, said, without
reflecting an instant: "Answer: to 1, I will approve the concession in
a pinch; to 2, that doesn't please me at all; to 3, that must remain
reserved for later agreement; etc." The decision of the various points
came as though fired from a pistol.

Afterwards Friedberg took me aside and said: "What a man! We
debated that for six hours in Berlin and came to no decision. And
here the business was settled in six minutes at breakfast!"

A second example. European complications threatened after the
Preliminary Peace of San Stephano, which ended the last Russo-
Turkish War. Count Peter Schuvalov, then Russian Ambassador in
London . . . , saw the only way out of the dead-lock, in which
Russia and England had gotten because of the overzealousness of
some Russian diplomats, as the summoning of a congress of the great
powers, under, of course, the presidency of Prince Bismarck. Schuvalov traveled to Petersburg and was successful there in winning
over the Russian Emperor to his idea. . . . With the Emperor's consent in his pocket, he set about his return. From some intervening
station or other he telegraphed to Prince Bismarck that he would
arrive in Friedrichsruh that evening. . . . After lunch they both went
into the Prince's workroom. . . . I can no longer remember exactly

how long the conversation between the Prince and Schuvalov lasted, but certainly no longer than twenty to thirty minutes. Then the Prince appeared in the doorway, a sheet of paper in his hand upon which the entire program of the Congress . . . was written down. He dictated . . . this program, as well as the invitations to the powers and an instruction to our ambassadors which were to be forwarded in coded dispatches the same evening. The program was accepted shortly by all the great powers in its complete wording; only a single word was changed at England's behest, if I remember correctly. . . .

Prince Bismarck's self-confidence matched the power of his intellect. It was the most conspicuous trait of his being. He . . . never admitted having done something wrong. *"Nunquam retrorsum"* he called to me, once in parliament when I admitted to an error. That went against his grain. His criticisms by name about his ministerial colleagues' performance frequently lacked objectivity. In every great political action he was accustomed to ascribe success to himself, while he placed the burden of failure on the departmental minister concerned with it. At the time of the Kulturkampf he repeatedly complained that he could not move Falk forward; that he had to give the impulse to every law of the struggle; when peace with Rome was concluded, he flatly disavowed many of the laws of the struggle and maintained that they had been drafted without his previous consent, yes, even partially without his knowledge.

Every business transaction with colleagues was uncongenial to his Coriolanus-like nature. "If I want to drink a spoonful of soup, I must first ask eight jackasses for permission!" That was the upshot of a mood which frequently struck him after ministerial deliberations. Even if he began to stroke his eyebrows now and then, he always maintained a courteous demeanor during such sessions. But when the ministers had left the council chamber, it was difficult for him to suppress mocking remarks, even though they only referred to externals—for example, Leonhardt's protuberant lower lip or Puttkamer's long, well-groomed beard. . . .

In a similar manner to Frederick the Great and Napoleon, his self-confidence was coupled with a strong dose of cynicism and this not seldom tempted him to underestimate friend and foe. He saw in friends then only spineless tools of his plans, chess pieces which he liked to shift here and there on his political board and could also sacrifice if this suited the play; in his enemies he saw only scoundrels and blockheads. Friends were only useful to him when they completely identified themselves with him. He looked upon them with mistrust as soon as they permitted themselves to have another opinion than his or took a position that did not correspond to his expectations. I never found that he could give an opponent his complete due. He was too passionate for that, too impetuous, too pugnacious. In this, as in many other relations, he is comparable to Luther. Every attack, even the slightest, provoked him to resistance, and he was always ready to repay a pin prick with a swordthrust; it cannot be denied that now and then in his joy in battle he broke butterflies on the wheel. Some Further Pomeranian or Hanoverian hick rag which fell into his hands in Varzin or Friedrichsruh at times gave occasion for a violent polemical article in the *Norddeutsche Allgemeine Zeitung.*

Even if his self-confidence was developed to the highest degree, he was completely free of the fault of vanity. He was accustomed to designate vanity as a mortgaged burden of man, whose amount limited his value. . . . Rarely has there been a human being to whom externals were so indifferent, who laid so little value on rank, precedence, and etiquette. He coveted neither recognition from above nor applause from below. He bore nothing more lightly than the feeling of being the best hated man in Germany during the time of conflict. And, when after the war with Austria, waves of enthusiasm lifted him high above his fellow men in popular opinion, that too left him cold.

PAUL VASILI: THE AGING TYRANT [11]

Paul Vasili was the pseudonym used by the author of La Societé de Berlin, a work that showed too much knowledge of life in the German capital for the comfort of those named in it. It has been variously ascribed. One name often mentioned is that of August Gérard, a French diplomat, who had been a reader to the Empress. Probably, however, the author is Madame Juliette Adam, in whose salon the French revanchists gathered and who spread her views through La Nouvelle Revue. Here the chancellor is pictured as an aging tyrant, seeking only to enhance his own power and acting from opportunistic motives. The danger to the German state of his domination is under-scored.

. . . The Prince is still an enigma to all who would wish to gain a true idea of his character. Even the people who have been closest to him have not been able to penetrate the secrets of that multiple nature: great in intelligence, dangerous in genius, superior

---

[11] Comte Paul Vasili, *La Societé de Berlin*, 9th ed. (Paris: La Nouvelle Revue, 1884), pp. 67–73, 99. Translated by the editor.

to Machiavelli in guile, and to Richelieu in scorn for humanity. To tell the truth, the Chancellor does not know himself very well; he does not know today what he will do tomorrow, and, although director of world events for years, in reality he lets himself be led by the circumstances which accompany the events. The great secret of his power consists in the facility with which he changes his mind, abandons his friends, courts his enemies, and profits by the spite of one, the hatred of another, and the egotism of all. His completely elastic conscience knows no scruples, his soul has no other ambition than that of absolute power over men and things, kings and peoples. . . . He has seen so well that the destinies of sovereigns and empires have come to be concentrated in his person that he has come to the point of forgetting that this person does not represent the world. That's why he crushes all who are not his, all who serve him ill or do not obey him blindly, all who resist him or contradict him. Formerly—a long time ago—, Bismarck was ambitious for his country, desirous of seeing Prussia occupy the first rank among the European powers; today it can be affirmed boldly that this ambition has disappeared, making way for a violent desire to dominate by his own personality. As long as he worked for his King, just as long has he applied himself—at the present when the King has become Emperor—to preventing him from giving the slightest glance at affairs of state. The German Empire certainly owes its actual existence to the perseverance and audacity of the Prince, who founded it, reared it, and made it steadfast and strong, but now that this colossal work is finished he cannot decide to consolidate it, to let it develop by itself. He wishes to maintain unlimited authority in this empire and from that results the hesitations, the vacillations of his policy, which astonish us so often in this man of iron. . . . The Chancellor's energy has ended by becoming obstinance and spite. He is so used to succeeding in everything that he imagines that he has obtained the right to impose his caprices continually on all who surround him. In the main, his is a completely impulsive nature, which often acts by fits and starts, which, at present when his dearest projects have succeeded, no longer conceives plans, but acts only according to the impulse and exigency of the moment. He only dominates because he has know how to make himself feared. . . . Such as he is, the Chancellor does not exhibit the less a great historical image, especially when he is viewed from afar and when he is imagined on a pedestal in the same fashion as he will present himself to posterity one day. But when one examines him closely, one immediately discovers the meanness, the pettiness, the forgetfulness of great interests that are confided to him in favor of his sympathies or personal antipathies. Bismarck has always desired to see the entire world bow before him; in order to establish his authority he has made use of all the means within his reach. One of the most terrible traits of his character consists in his penetration into men, whose weak side he discerns at the first glance, whom he flatters, whom he blandly excites, and whom he knows how to profit from. . . .

There has been much talk of the Chancellor's plans; his recently published correspondence has even been cited as evidence that all that he has done was calculated in advance. For my part, I am firmly persuaded that, above all, he has known how to profit from circumstances and that taking power in hand he has had no other object than that of setting up his own self. Later his ambitions developed; then he recalled the dreams of his youth and, after the triumph of the man, wanted to ensure that of the country. Still later he wished to become greater by making the world believe that he owed his success not to good luck, but expressly to a preconceived determination and succeeded by the simple fact of a will as indomitable as it was resolute.

Few politicians have had so many enemies, and none has known how to get rid of them so adroitly. To tell the truth, it is not only his enemies he has cast aside; his friends suffer the same fate when they thwart or bore him. But it is certain that he is terrible in his rancors, implacable in his resentments, and without mercy in his vengeance. It is known what he was to Count Arnim and one need only recall Delbrück, Count Stolberg, and Count Eulenburg, all his former friends and colleagues who have displeased him and whom he knew how to dismiss, obliterate, annihilate, and, with marvelous skill—in a word—make disappear from the political and parliamentary arena. On good terms with all the parties in turn, he made use of each one, solely to discredit them in the eyes of the public by his alliance. A cunning tactician, he loves to appropriate the success of others and has the talent of succeeding in this difficult enterprise. One of his favorite tricks consists in mastering some ambitious intriguer and persuading him that he has the makings of a great man in him. The victim always falls into the trap, and it is thus that the Prince has collected a certain number of lost souls, who serve him with love and adoration, who naïvely imagine they are indispensable to him. . . .

. . . The motive which has impelled the Chancellor to surround himself with merely busy nobodies has its greatness, for it has permitted him to execute all projects without the slightest opposition. . . . But, on the other hand, Bismarck's tyranny has had the disadvantage for Germany of destroying all the men capable of replacing the colossus to which it is committed today. The Prince is the living incarnation of a system, of a policy, of all that constitutes a nation's life and organism. With the colossus gone, the German Empire will doubtless continue, but, of those who maintained it, there remain only feet of clay.

WILLIAM II: THE DISMISSAL[12]

The British ambassador to Berlin, Sir Edward Malet, records a conversation with William II. The emperor emphasizes the personal conflict of authority, especially over the calling of an international conference on the plight of the workingman, and Bismarck's desire to continue a policy of domestic repression. The state of his health is also brought in as a plausible pretext. Other conflicts are ignored as unsuitable for communication to a foreign ambassador.

The Emperor said to me: "I should like to explain to you the train of circumstances which has brought about the present state of affairs. The Chancellor has been staying at Friedrichsruh for eight months, and was ignorant of what was going on at the capital.

"It was not my intention to launch into a Socialistic policy, but things occurred which forced this course upon me. . . . The strikes which had recently ocurred in Germany had created a deep impression of anxiety, and there was a feeling in the air that, in order to prevent future disorder and even calamity arising from the state of things which had produced the strikes, something must be done. . . . Under the circumstances I had to choose between yielding hereafter, perhaps with the appearance of bad grace, to the popular movement or of taking the initiative myself. When Prince Bismarck came to Berlin on the last days of the debate on the Socialist Bill, it was evident that the Government was about to suffer the defeat which eventually came; but I learnt that the Conservatives would even at the last moment be willing to vote with the Government, if the Government would abandon the Expulsion Clause in the Bill, or if they would even only make an announcement that they would not press that clause during the present session, but would hold it over in order to take the opinion of the new Parliament. I implored Prince Bismarck to adopt this course, but he absolutely refused. The result was, as you know, that the Conservatives and the Socialists voted together.

"About this time I spoke frequently to the Chancellor about the

---

[12] Secret memorandum of Sir Edward Malet, 22 March 1890. In G. E. Buckle, ed., *The Letters of Queen Victoria: Third Series* 3 vols. (London: John Murray, 1930), 1: 584–87. Reprinted by permission of the publisher.

necessity of taking up the Socialist question, but he was dead against it. One night I sat up for two hours by myself and wrote down my own views as to what ought to be done on a paper which now forms the basis of the Bill, which will be laid before Parliament. I gave this to the chancellor, but he treated it lightly, and I could make no way with him. . . . In the meanwhile I had been endeavouring to gain over the Ministers separately to my views, but I found that they were one and all in complete subjection to Prince Bismarck, and dared not help me. Prince Bismarck did not differ with me in the view that the Socialist question must soon take an acute form, but his policy was to allow it to progress until it should be necessary to call out the troops to sweep the streets with grape-shot, and so to make short work of the whole affair. Such a policy as this might be possible, if my grandfather were still alive. The whole German people regarded him with such confidence, admiration, and respect that if he had thought it wise to allow things to come to such a pass, it would have been believed that he acted with a full sense of justice and responsibility, and he would not have alienated their affection. But for me, a young monarch, just come to the throne, to have allowed my people to be shot down in the streets, without making an effort first of all to examine their grievances, would have been disastrous to me and my whole House. It would have been said that my only idea of governing was by bayonets.

"I do not expect by the course I have taken to be able to remedy their grievances, but at least I have given a proof of my desire to do so, and my view is that although this Conference may not find a solution of the difficult questions before it, it may serve as a prelude to frequently recurring Conferences, in which foreign nations shall take part, doing perhaps little each time, but producing a conviction, in the minds of the classes whose affairs they examine, that their welfare is a constant object of solicitude, and that by this means we may have some hope that we may separate the large mass of honest Socialists from those who merely use the name as a cloak to their republican or anarchical designs.

"When Prince Bismarck finally accepted the idea of a conference, I hardly like to say it, but I can assure you that he used small and undignified means to prevent its ever coming to anything. For instance, without my sanction he put into the programme the question of limiting the hours of adult labor, no doubt thinking thereby to frighten your Government and the French Government into refusing to take part in it. In my discussions with him he treated me like a schoolboy. When I urged that I believed the Ministers were really in favor of my views, although they would not venture to say so because he was opposed to them, he told me that they were all blackguards and cowards. He became so violent on occasions that I did not know whether he would not throw the inkstand at my head. The moment came when I was obliged to think of my own dignity.

"On the other hand, I was assured by the doctors that his state of mental excitement was such that it might end in a crisis at any moment. He told me six weeks ago, when I urged that he should lighten his labors, that he intended to resign the Presidency of the Prussian Ministry and remain only as Chancellor. A short time after he told me he should resign the Chancellorship as well, and a short time after that he sent to me to say that he had changed his mind and that he should resign nothing, and he began to take upon himself increased work. I finally decided that, if I wished his life to be preserved, I must relieve him of his duties. He and all his family are at present incensed against me, but I hope that in a few months they will see that they have reason to thank me."

THEODOR BARTH: CREATOR AND DESTROYER [13]

Left Liberal member of the Prussian Chamber of Deputies and the German Reichstag and editor of the Nation, *Theodor Barth reveals the ambiguity with which liberal opinion regarded Bismarck. On the one hand, he was a national hero who had unified Germany. On the other, he aided in the destruction of liberalism.*

No one can escape the stirring impressions of this personality. A mixture of Junker daring and diplomatic cunning in a powerful figure with the bold head and glances darting forth under bushy eyebrows; caustic wit; flexible, elegant style; unerring aim in expression; humor of conversation; crafty frankness; animal vitality, which was even expressed in eating and drinking—all that worked together to make the great Chancellor a monumental figure in history. If one searches for the principal feature of his being, then one is tempted to find it in want of respect. . . . From this feeling of *nil admirari,* there developed in Bismarck that sovereign contempt for the existent, which gave the courage to cross over the boundaries of custom, to lay the old in ruins, and erect the new on these ruins. He was not blinded by the appearance of things, whether the appearance of the crown or the appearance of revolutionary torches. When he maintained that the majority of the Reichstag, that Europe, did not im-

[13] Theodor Barth, *Politische Porträts* (Berlin: Franz Schneider Verlag, 1923), pp. 12–21. Translated by the editor.

press him, that was in his mouth no empty boast, but the expression of a superior feeling of power.

Bismarck has often been praised for his vassal's loyalty and veracity. He liked to call himself the loyal servant of his master, but the vassal was very impatient when the master did not bow to the will of his loyal servant; the vassal delivered many temperamental oaths about his gracious master, when he followed his servant's counsels too hesitatingly. Once on his return from an audience with the King, he pitched his hat into a corner, exclaiming . . . : "I can never be a servant of princes." Bismarck interceded for his King's rights in foreign as well as domestic policy, because he saw the only firm support of his far-reaching plans in the Prussian monarchy. But his royalism bore so much the character of realpolitik, it was so specifically Prussian, that when Prussian interests collided with the principle of legitimacy, he at times tossed the reproach of "the swindling of sovereigns" at the heads of the oldest princely lines.

Bismarck's veracity also is only to be understood in that he scorned all illusions. But foreign diplomats who took his public assurances as gospel truth for all time would have been badly advised. . . . When it appeared necessary to him for the achievement of a great goal, Bismarck by no means shrank even from offering violence to truth. . . . He forced the world to regard matters in the light that appeared desirable to him; with that, understandably, objective truth did not always receive its due.

Bismarck was not the hero of a moral tale; such a person would have had difficulty in unifying Germany, and Bismarck is the unifier of Germany.

From the German peoples' strong impulse to political unity . . . one has, to be sure, often enough derived the assertion that even without Bismarck Germany would have succeeded in achieving political unity in another fashion. . . . There is no real meaning to this historical-philosophical speculation, which, on the other hand, leads to the certainty, circumscribed by historical proof, that, in that time, in the years of the sixties, unity would not have been completed without Bismarck. In the history of all times and all peoples there are few grand historical evolutions which can be traced back with such assurance to the activity of a single man as the political creation of existent Germany can be to Bismarck's statesmanlike performance.

Not only did Bismarck, with the greatest dexterity, use existing situations for his goals. He did more; he made situations entirely new in order to exploit them for himself and his political aims. Considering the well-established fact that the work of 1866 would never have taken place by far greater action of the powerful statesman, if the material means of strength concentrated in Prussia's monarchical

THE WORLD LOOKS AT BISMARCK / 119

power could not have been directed to an aggressive act, and considering the further unquestionable fact that King William not only had no intrinsic inclination for a basic conflict with Austria, but actually felt repugnance for that, it is to be ascribed exclusively to Bismarck's statesmanlike energy that the clash with Austria, which was the necessary pre-condition for German unity really came about. Around the King there was neither a statesman nor a general who was strong enough or who felt strong enough to take up Bismarck's great plans, if the minister of the conflict had broken down in their execution. There were enough reactionary Junkers who were ready to follow the King into the constitutional conflict and who would also have happily taken part in the most public breach of the constitution, but there was none among them who would have been willing and able to find the path out of the constitutional conflict into a new national creation. Even Roon, by far the most significant of Bismarck's helpers, was also to be had for any reactionary power policy; he was, however, in the first instance, the royalist swordsman, to whom it was incumbent above all to hew a way for his royal master from the midst of the democrats, who pressed him hard. For Bismarck, on the other hand, the conflict in which the Prussian King was entangled was a means to higher ends. He needed the conflict to bind the King to himself. The King trusted Bismarck's reactionary energy; his foreign policy was strange to him. But Bismarck appeared to the King as the only man who was able to fight through the military conflict victoriously. If this conflict had been concluded by a peace with the peoples' representatives, it would have been highly unlikely that Bismarck would have found the King's support for his far-reaching plans in foreign policy. Even among his most intimate friends he found hardly any understanding for this, his foreign policy. They were still up to their ears in all sorts of legitimist prejudices, while Bismarck had already freed himself to the point that he thought very seriously of a political connection with Napoleon III, a thought that covered even Leopold von Gerlach with gooseflesh. Nothing is more characteristic of Bismarck's way of looking at things than a remark in the correspondence with Leopold von Gerlach in the fifties, which refers to this Bismarckian heresy. As a paternal friend, Gerlach reproached Bismarck with his coquetting with the crowned Bonaparte, whereupon Bismarck excused himself with the remark that even medieval princes had at times not been ashamed to escape into the open through a sewer. That is the Machiavellian statesman Bismarck to the flesh. The constitutional conflict which he found in existence and whose continuation he used to win King William for himself and to bind him permanently to himself was to him a sewer through which he wished to escape into the open.

Without any doubt the sixties mark the high point of Bismarck's statesmanlike power. He impressed the stamp of his will on all events of the sixties. Despite the support which the Duke found in the entire royal family, including King William, it was Bismarck who snatched back the duchies of Schleswig and Holstein from the Augustenburg, who already supposed he had them secured. Contradicting all traditions of old Prussia, Bismarck alone was able to dare to throw the high card of a German national parliament based on *suffrage universel* upon the rickety table of the Confederation Diet in order to ruin the play for Austria. Only he could undertake to so muddy the diplomatic waters that King William could be brought to the conviction that the honor of the Prussian crown demanded a military decision with Austria.

Even the great success of the years 1870–71 recedes behind Bismarck's performance in the year 1866. One can imagine that if Bismarck had died at the end of the sixties the shaping of the North German Confederation into the German Empire and even the military decision with France would nevertheless have been completed in a fashion similar to what actually happened; but, if there had been no Bismarck, one surely would not have experienced an 1866 with the huge historical consequences it hid in its bosom. Bismarck's astonishing successes at the high point of his statecraft have misled undiscriminating admirers of the great man into praising all his later performances as statesmanlike masterpieces. Blind admiration never understands how very much it harms its hero when it never finds anything to censure in him. . . . Bismarck's historical physiognomy shows deep wrinkles, which intractable passions imprinted upon it. This North German Junker was made of the material from which, according to Machiavelli, the unifier of Italy would arise. In such figures the powers of hell likewise play as strong a part, and it appears unthinkable that they operate only beneficently and not destructively as well. This destructive influence of the Bismarckian spirit and Bismarckian statecraft take up a broad place in the entire picture of his historical activity. To a certain degree every great man corrupts his people; he is not only admired, he is imitated. But what in great matters is often termed virtue often is vice in the small. The ruthless realism, which constituted the statesman's greatness when crowns were at stake, is distorted into a comic or offensive caricature when it is adopted into the catechism of an immature youth or stimulates vulgarians to emulation. And such strong spirits who have perceived the great man's hawking and spittle and consider idealism an outmoded viewpoint unfortunately roam about German lands more than appears serviceable for the future. There is something senescent in this practical wisdom, which only reckons with real factors, with power, with interests, and with desires, considers an opinion dominated by opposite convictions an irresponsible luxury, and recognizes nothing outside its own and, at most, the national sphere of interests generally that one must take a lively interest in. Renan's epigram: *"Bismarck a agrandi l'allemagne et amoindri les allemands"* is not entirely without truth. If our entire political life at present turns on struggles of interests, then Bismarckian instruction has surely contributed not a little to this development. With the end of the sixties the great practitioner of realpolitik entered into the decadent period of his life; the unerring aim in judgment of the most important factors of public life which had characterized him to such an unusual degree in the golden age of his activity slackened off.

He did not understand clearly enough that under his hands the German Empire founded by him was advancing more and more irresistibly into the world economic system and could not let itself return to the narrow agrarian basis of the Prussia of his youth. Nor did he wish to see in the continual development of Social Democracy a powerful economic-political evolution of the wage earning class, but, on the contrary, he still hoped to be able to enchain this young giant with the cords of the police.

His statecraft, to be sure, produced one further success; he succeeded in splitting liberalism and deeply decreased its influence. It may be conceded that he acted with demonic skill in that, but it is impossible for unbiased historical writing to forgive a statesman when he swings the hammer of destruction against the firmest partisan support of the national state . . . without concerning himself that he thereby paved the way for the most dangerous adversaries of his work. The decline of liberalism to which Bismarck contributed so much stands in unmistakable relation to the strengthening of the Center and the development of Social Democracy. The speculation of the great practitioner of realpolitik that only as soon as he was free of the uncongenial friends who wished to eat with him out of one bowl —if also only quite modestly—would he be able also to defend himself with certainty against his real enemies showed itself to be false. . . .

But Bismarck misled himself not only in the effect of the whip, but also in the effect of the cake he dispensed—for, above all, the benefits of compulsory insurance legislation were thought of as such, especially in relation to Social Democracy. Even in his last Reichstag speech on 18 March [*i.e.,* May] 1889 on the occasion of the second reading of the old age and invalid insurance law, Bismarck made known what he was driving at with this legislation. To a sceptical remark I made he responded: "When one of the members of the Left Liberal party has said that we will not win Social Democracy over with this bill, then two things are mistaken for one another; there are Social Democratic leaders and Social Democratic masses." That the Social Democratic masses as well were not to be won in this fashion is quite clear today.

It is no injustice to Bismarck's historical greatness to recognize that the Chancellor's dismissal in March, 1890—however one thinks about the form in which it was accomplished—was a political necessity. . . . Bismarck's great time, however, was past. His authority, founded on immortal deeds, stood in the way of all decisive innovations. He could reconcile himself neither to the abrogation of the Socialist law nor to the introduction of the two-year term of military service and least of all to the free trade policy which had become an imperative necessity. For his fame, the Iron Chancellor was not called away any too soon from the helm of the imperial ship.

The sudden elimination of a man of such a past and such authority without the world getting out of joint, yes, without even the slightest political convulsion occurring at the time correctly produced astonishment and then serious reflection.

Abroad, particularly in France, one had often indulged in the opinion that the German Empire was so much the creation of Prince Bismarck that it could not be maintained in its previous fullness of power without his strong hand. And yet it was no voluntary resignation; it was a dismissal. How assured must the structure of the Empire appear and how strong the power of the imperial crown when, astonished, one experienced an alteration whose consequences justified no fears and no hopes.

It was not in Bismarck's character to accept such a fall with philosophic calm. The man who had once noted down the confession: "Again I hated the whole night through" was not to be consoled for loss of power through external testimonies of honor. Whether he uttered the words: *"Le roi me reverra"* is not established with certainty, but such an expression would not be foreign to his passionate mood. . . . When Count Keyserling once said to him that it was now his task, despite all the difficulties he had encountered, to display a harmonious personality, Prince Bismarck responded brusquely: "For what reason should I be harmonious?"

. . . Bismarck was a destroyer and a creator in grand style; certainly not a pure blessing for his people, but one of those powerful personalities, which fate is only accustomed to employ when it desires to achieve greatness.

PART THREE

BISMARCK IN HISTORY

Historians of Germany, whatever their nationality, have tended to see Germans either as a peculiar people or as a people with a peculiar history. The events following Bismarck's death, World War I, the collapse of the German Empire, the establishment of the Weimar Republic, and, above all, the domination of Hitler, have caused them to ask how Bismarck contributed to these events. The following selections, largely directed to particular aspects of the chancellor's career, reflect these general attitudes.

EUGENE N. ANDERSON: THE AMORALIST [1]

Writing after World War II, Eugene N. Anderson, now emeritus professor of history at the University of California, examines the long-range effects of the settlement of the constitutional conflict in 1866. He stresses the failure of Bismarck to create a viable constitutional state.

Although the struggle dragged for another two and a half years, a disinterested observer must have concluded at the beginning of 1864 that the liberals were defeated. They had no plan and no means of winning against the government. Bismarck continued in power; the administrative apparatus functioned as usual; the people paid their taxes; the government expended the public money; the soldiers remained loyal; and as a crowning act the hated ministry successfully participated in the war against Denmark. The denunciation of all these deeds by the liberals handicapped the hated government very little and failed utterly to block or even delay its actions. The march of industrialism continued vigorously, and the people were more prosperous than they had ever been. The liberals were so successful in their private economy that they eased the gov-

---

[1] Eugene N. Anderson, *The Social and Political Conflict in Prussia, 1858–1864* (Lincoln, Nebraska: University of Nebraska Press, 1954), pp. 441–43. Reprinted by permission of the publisher.

ernment's road to victory with mounting tax returns. Although Bismarck knew too little economics to be aware of the fact, he enjoyed the blessing of coming to power during an upswing of the business cycle. He was not merely powerful, he was fortunate.

The liberals did not surrender until Bismarck won the Austro-Prussian War and set about unifying Germany in the *klein-deutsch* sense. They had held out during two wars, in itself an almost unparalleled achievement; but when the second war gained one of their major objectives, German unity, they succumbed along with the Austrians. The liberals had opposed the King, the military reforms and Bismarck partly because they had feared a repetition of the defeat of 1806. They had not believed that an unreformed, increasingly militaristic Prussia could muster the resources and arouse the patriotic spirit necessary to protect itself. They saw their moral and political assumptions being wrecked, and they came to believe in the superior efficiency of *Realpolitik*.

The solution to the Prussian and German conflicts which Bismarck imposed had facets that affected the Hohenzollern King, the Conservatives, and the liberals, each in a different way. The ruler preserved as much absolutism as one could possibly command under a free constitution. The King remained in Prussia a sovereign by the grace of God, and in the German Reich his authority was scarcely less impressive. Bismarck retained the military reorganization, and by his use of the army in three wars of national unification he assured in the German Reich the popular as well as the legal continuation of Prussian militarism. For the King and the Conservatives he succeeded in keeping the social and political system of the Old Regime in local government and imparted to a declining agrarian nobility a new political vigor which kept that group in authority for two generations. With respect to the constitution he made the gap theory valid and kept it as an ultimate sanction for a government that remained to a large degree irresponsible. He transferred the legal position of the ministry in Prussia to the chancellorship in the Reich. In each case the government, declared nominally responsible in law, actually wielded authority out of harmony with the fact of constitutionality. To the liberals Bismarck gave national unity and a considerable amount of free economic legislation, although not all that they wished. The King on the whole was satisfied with the results. Many conservatives disliked intensely German unification and the liberal economic legislation. The liberals remained disgruntled with the vestiges of absolutism and caste. The remarkable fact was, however, that this political master, Bismarck, made it impossible for any one of these forces fundamentally to change the system which he proposed to introduce. Bismarck had won not merely over the liberals but in different respects over the Conservatives and the King as well.

The political and moral effects of the victory of *Realpolitik* were scarcely felt by the King and the Conservatives. The ruler and his Conservative supporters believed in power politics and practiced them in internal as well as international affairs. They continued as they always had to pursue *Interresenpolitik* under the guise of moral principles. Bismarck's victory meant the dominance of these methods in Germany in an age in which Western peoples were seeking to introduce universal principles of liberal conduct.

In the case of the liberals the success of *Realpolitik* destroyed the moral foundations of their beliefs. Wrong had proved to be effective; right had failed. Most of them swung to the side of Bismarck and joined the host of his adorers. The irreconcilable ones were doomed to continue a life of frustration. Until the end of the Second Reich in 1918 the pro-Bismarck liberals could not be depended upon to support a principle in a crisis; the anti-Bismarck ones could talk little but principles. Deprived of the opportunity to learn responsibility in government and faced with the reality of living in an anti-liberal society, the latter continued to defend generalities. Germany became a country largely of doctrinaires and believers in *Machtpolitik* à la Bismarck.

Did Bismarck settle the constitutional conflict in Prussia? The answer can only be that he did not, that he glossed it over by nationalism and by success in international relations. He solved none of the crucial internal social and political problems; he only postponed a settlement. The evidence for this conclusion is found in the fact that within less than three generations the Bismarckian Reich was destroyed, the Junker Conservatives were ruined, and the Hohenzollerns had lost their throne. The predictions of the liberals during the Constitutional conflict have proved to be basically accurate. In the case of Germany, history has substantiated the belief in the validity of moral principles in public life.

EGMONT ZECHLIN: PRIMACY OF STATE INTERESTS [2]

Egmont Zechlin in 1930 viewed Bismarck as the master of foreign policy whose aim was to act according to Prussia's interests. In this, according to Zechlin, he was successful.

[2] Egmont Zechlin, *Bismarck und die Grundlegung der deutschen Grossmacht* (Stuttgart and Berlin: J. G. Cotta'schen Buchhandlung Nachfolger, 1930), pp. 618–21. Reprinted, and translated by the editor, by permission of the publisher.

The diplomatic war of maneuver which permitted the loosening-up of the state system at mid-century and in which his statesman's superiority could come into account . . . permitted the foundation of the German Empire. Bismarck's foundation of the Empire grew from the basic conception of the years of Frankfort. The German governmental system had as its object the participation in organic cooperation with the life of the state of the historical powers whose contrariety had retarded national unity and could be played out in conjunction, in any case, according to the necessities of general policy, through the intervention of Prussia's power. And similarly his European alliance system also aimed at using the opposition of the great powers' interests and fusing them simultaneously to practical cooperation. In this system, each of the great powers had a place corresponding to its interests; each of them, however, was also hindered by a counterweight from pursuing a "power policy" exceeding the limits of their vital interests; and with each the German Empire could put its weight of power in the balance. Bismarck created a special function of the country of the center, which, while it served its own state egoism, also benefited the entire arrangement. Germany became the "center of gravity" of the balance of power system . . . but not, according to the proposals of Konstantin Frantz, the center of a Central European allied group to hold the powers on the flank in check. Bismarck understood how to evaluate the central position even more positively. He avoided challenging the other great powers to a counter-alliance by an eastern, western, or central European orientation and thereby risking a test of power by both groups, which could lead to a military collision. . . . He warded off the powers of coalition against Germany and this itself left "every chance open" as far as possible and increased his value as an ally still more in order to decide under the best conditions in case further developments or German military aims made an option necessary again. With this system Bismarck led Prussia . . . to the strength and position of a great power.

Of course, close consideration of his first years in office shows that the strength of circumstances and his opponent's policy forced him again and again into paths which he himself did not desire. It confirms his conviction and experience that events are stronger than human plans. Constitutional conflict, three-year term of service, and the gap theory were taken over by him, although he honestly wished to put demonstrations of "public opinion" as a "means of action" in the service of his foreign policy and therefore sought "good understanding between the government and country's representatives" and "free play for the Chamber and the press." The conflicts of Prussia with the coalition of Austria and the secondary states at the Federal

Diet and the danger of war which grew out of that were likewise found in existence by him. If he wished to use this situation to force Austria to recognize Prussian vital interests in North Germany, uncertainty about France forced him to moderation. Because he now renounced the fulfillment of Prussia's German mission, the opportunity at the time to put an end to domestic difficulties through external success also eluded him. The sending of General von Alvensleben to Petersburg already (in this negotiation with the Tsar) departed from the path Bismarck had in mind. Then Napoleon III wrested the initiative to himself, so that Bismarck fell into one of the most difficult embarrassments of his life. At the decisive moment England helped him out of danger. And yet Bismarck . . . brought his will into account and at the end of the year 1863 reached the central place of one sought after. If the picture which unfolds of his policy does not at this time reveal the bright colors in which one would like to see the heroic epoch of the years of the Empire's foundation, it is still not less admirable in the tough and likewise bold as well as cautious dialogue with the interests of the powers and practical-organic dovetailing into general development. Although his actions now also appear more constrained and dependent, they fulfill the quality that he himself postulated as the highest criterion of a statesman's achievement: that he achieve the freedom to utilize the conditions, which had developed without his assistance and perhaps against his wishes, according to the demands of the security and interests of his state.

GEORGE G. WINDELL: REVOLUTIONARY REALIST [3]

George G. Windell, professor of history at Louisiana State University, New Orleans, depicts Bismarck as a realist whose policy was in many ways revolutionary. The particularist nature of the Center party and its call for international intervention in the Pope's favor sparked the Kulturkampf, according to Windell's analysis.

The Reichstag convened on March 21 [1871], and on the same day the *Zentrums-partei Deutschlands* was formally organized. A few days later it published its first official program. The document was headed by a quotation from Mallinckrodt's famous Reichstag speech

---

[3] George G. Windell, *The Catholics and German Unity, 1866–71* (Minneapolis: University of Minnesota Press, 1954), pp. 289–94.

of 1867, *"Justitia fundamenta regnorum,"* and listed three objectives of the party. . . . The Center, it stated, would strive to preserve the federal character of the Empire; it would seek "civil and religious freedom for all citizens of the Reich"; and it would not attempt to compel its members to vote in accordance with any official party viewpoint, which viewpoint, however, would always be arrived at through free discussion.

Although the program made no mention of the Roman Question, it was upon this that the imperial *Zentrum* chose to make its first parliamentary fight. On February 18 the Prussian Center had moved in the *Landtag* an address to the throne protesting Italy's appropriation of Rome. The motion was, of course, voted down. During the first days of the Reichstag, the National Liberals, under Bennigsen's leadership, in order to forestall a similar move there, moved an address to the Kaiser declaring the willingness of the Reichstag to see Germany intervene in the internal affairs of any country, *i.e.,* in this case, Italy. Immediately, August Reichensperger introduced an amendment which would have substituted a request that the government take action to secure the Pontiff's traditional rights. The lines were clearly drawn, and practically the entire membership, other than that of the *Zentrum,* combined to defeat the Reichensperger amendment. The house then proceeded to adopt the original draft by the overwhelming majority of 243 to 63. Thus the *Zentrum* began its parliamentary career with a crushing defeat. This was followed only a few days later by an equally impressive rejection of Peter Reichensperger's motion to include the Prussian guarantees of religious freedom in the *Reich* constitution. These two debates form the prelude to the *Kulturkampf.* The *Kölnische Volkszeitung,* which had called Peter Reichensperger's motion "an excellent test for judging the prevailing spirit within the other parties," had its answer. Windthorst predicted darkly that "in the new Germany the legal rights of Catholic citizens will be crushed." The National Liberal, Miquel, expressed the view of a large part of the Reichstag: "Germany has come into existence against the will of these gentlemen; they are now the defeated party." Bismarck regarded the Center's proposals as a declaration of war against himself.

To him they appeared an attempt to secure by parliamentary maneuver what Ketteler's letter of October 1, 1870, and Ledochowski's November mission to Versailles had failed to achieve by negotiation. Moreover, Ketteler had repeated his demands when he called on Bismarck in Berlin on March 9, shortly after the latter's return from Versailles. This time Bismarck had courteously refused. Both projects of the *Zentrum* impinged upon areas in which Bismarck was inordinately sensitive to interference. His general dislike of parliamentary intervention in foreign policy has been remarked upon before. In this case, having just completed a great war which seriously upset the European balance of power, he had no wish to involve Germany in avoidable difficulties with any country, particularly over an issue so complex as the Roman Question.

Furthermore, Bismarck was understandably annoyed that north German Catholics, who in the past had fought savagely any effort to widen the competence of the federal authority, and their southern friends, who had in some cases been willing to defend state sovereignty literally to the death, were now demanding exactly what they had always opposed; a significant extension of the area of federal jurisdiction. Beyond that, the *Zentrum's* proposals for altering the constitution could hardly have been accepted without opening up again the whole question of the Reichstag's functions in all its aspects. It is not impossible that he suspected this to be the real purpose behind the moves.

In addition to these specific grounds, Bismarck had many other reasons to hate and fear the *Zentrum*. Its membership was a patchwork of discordant elements. It included *hochkonservative* aristocrats from Prussia and Bavaria, moderately liberal bourgeois from the Rhineland, and radical democrats like Krebs of Cologne, who, had he not been a Roman Catholic, would doubtless have joined Bebel and Liebknecht. Among its leaders were intimates of the old deposed dynasties, such as the Hanoverian, Windthorst. The Polish faction, although it retained its own individuality, likewise supported the party on many occasions. Finally, on the national level the *Zentrum* absorbed the Bavarian Patriot party, though the Patriots for a long time remained a powerful force in state politics, where they persisted in their extreme particularism. These widely divergent elements were held together by a single principle. As defined by the *Zentrum* itself, this principle was merely the desire to prevent individual states and the Catholic Church from being crushed by an omnipotent central government. As defined by Bismarck and his National Liberal allies, it was *Reichsfeindlichkeit*, not significantly different in the Chancellor's eyes from hostility to him personally.

These two viewpoints, one merely the converse of the other, posed a dilemma which was incapable of peaceful resolution in the political and intellectual frame of reference which dominated Germany in 1871. Thus the *Kulturkampf*, covertly under way since 1866, broke into the open. It was apparent in the increasingly fanatical tone of the press on both sides during the spring of 1871, and it acquired official status when, on July 8, 1871, Bismarck, in his capacity as Prussian minister-president, abolished the Catholic section of the Prussian *Kultusministerium*, after his renewed efforts to secure papal intervention, in the hope of forcing moderation upon the Center, had failed. A new era in his relations with German Catholics opened.

This new era, which was to be dominated by the *Kulturkampf*, grew directly out of the old. . . .

. . . Much of the hostility of Catholics toward Bismarck is attributable to their attachment to intellectual, political, and ecclesiastical traditions which were alien to the mainstreams of middle and late nineteenth-century culture. They distrusted secular education, liberty of conscience, separation of Church and state, and all these they saw advocated, if not by Bismarck himself, at least by his allies, the National Liberals. In south Germany Catholics were, in many cases, also convinced that a Germany united under Prussia would mean ultimate strangulation of the Church itself. These fears appeared all the more justified when so many northern, and especially Prussian, liberals persisted in identifying Protestantism as the true German religion and Catholicism as the symbol of reaction and foreign domination.

The tendency of political opinion to polarize around confessional viewpoints had unfortunate, even disastrous, results. Persons who should have been natural allies found themselves in opposite camps. In retrospect, at least, the basic cleavage of the age appears to have been between a traditional, morally and religiously oriented *Weltanschauung*, shared historically by both confessions, and the secularistic, realistic, amoral outlook typified in Germany most spectacularly by Bismarck. The gulf between the confessions, which had narrowed considerably during the first half of the century, was now artificially widened by political maneuvers on both sides. This helped to push the majority of people south of the Main into a sterile particularism, and thereby indirectly forced nationalists of all varieties, in both North and South, willy-nilly into the arms of Bismarck.

To Catholic writers, of whom the Bavarian, Jörg, is the outstanding example, Bismarck after 1866 stood as the embodiment of the revolution in Germany. In this judgment they were not far from the mark. Where they erred disastrously was in their constant efforts to identify him with liberalism. Whatever else the great Prussian may have been, he was not a liberal, and Catholics, in so trying to label him, betrayed a striking lack of understanding of either the man or the movement. Rarely did they show any appreciation of his honest sympathy for federalism, in which they, too, generally professed a belief. Their federalism, of course, was quite incompatible with their constantly reiterated demands that the central government undertake to guarantee the freedom of the Catholic Church from interference by state governments. Such inconsistencies were products of the political immaturity of most German Catholics. Had their leaders possessed a better understanding of Bismarck's true purposes, much of the bitterness of the last sixties, as well as the *Kulturkampf* of the seventies, might have been avoided. Moreover, it is not beyond the realm of possibility that, under such circumstances, a working alliance between the Chancellor and Catholic political leaders might have developed before 1870, instead of a decade later.

That Bismarck would have welcomed such an alliance in 1868 and after is clear from his correspondence. The unexpected victory of the hostile clerical-particularists in the *Zollparlament* elections in Bavaria and Württemberg, and their near victory in Baden, both angered and frightened him, for it brought to a sudden halt the slow but consistent progress toward a *kleindeutsch* union which had begun with the War of 1866. The south German faction was able, for the most part, to prevent any action on the problem of national unity at the *Zollparlament* sessions of 1868 through 1870. In the two latter sessions the question was scarcely mentioned. Between the middle of 1868 and early 1870 control over the political situation in Germany gradually slipped out of Bismarck's hands. That period of a year and a half was marked by the rise of the Patriot party in Bavaria, its victory at the polls, and the ensuing overthrow of Hohenlohe; by the founding of the *Volkspartei* in Baden; by the beginnings of a revolt against Bismarck's military policy in these states and in Württemberg; and by an open revolt of the National Liberals in the North German Reichstag. Together, these ominous developments, all of which culminated in February, 1870, spelled potential catastrophe for Bismarck, for they destroyed his long-cherished belief that time was on his side. The necessity of counteracting these multiplying disasters is primarily what induced him to press the Hohenzollern candidacy when it was taken up by the Spaniards for the second time in February, 1870. That he was able to use the candidacy to bring about a solution for his many problems satisfactory to himself is a measure of his political genius. It is, moreover, in no way uncomplimentary to that genius to underline the fact that he was in a sense grasping for a straw, and that it was the inexcusable French blunders of July, 1870 which insured the success of his almost desperate stratagem.

C. GRANT ROBERTSON: VICTIM OF IDEAS [4]

Writing during World War I, the liberal English historian C. Grant Robertson portrays Bismarck as the foe, and the victim, of ideas. In the Kulturkampf, for which he was responsible de-

[4] C. Grant Robertson, *Bismarck* (London: Constable and Co., Ltd., 1918), pp. 316–19, 321, 326–27. Reprinted by permission of the publisher.

*spite later disclaimers, he ignored the spiritual basis of belief
and consequently suffered defeat, Robertson maintains.*

Bismarck's decision to crush the Clerical Centre was momentous.
After 1878 he argued that he was not responsible for the policy of
the *Kulturkampf*, nor for the May Laws and their execution. The
argument will not stand the test of facts nor of probability. In 1872,
1873, and 1875 he spoke repeatedly both in the Reichstag and the
Prussian Landtag in defence of the coercive legislation and of the
general policy of Prussia and the Empire in the controversy. He
complained bitterly in private letters to Roon of the desertion of the
Conservative party in the "Catholic controversy"; he was responsible
for the appointment of Falk, and supported him until 1878 against
the attacks in Court circles. It is, in the absence of all corroborative
evidence to the contrary, impossible to believe that Bismarck as Chancellor and Minister-President would have allowed a subordinate colleague to embark Prussia and the Empire by legislation and administrative action in a life-and-death struggle, which involved the most
delicate and fundamental issues of high policy at home and abroad,
without his complete concurrence. It is demonstrable that the correspondence between the Emperor and the Pope, which stated very
tersely the Prussian attitude, was on the Emperor's side drafted by
Bismarck; the withdrawal of the German mission from the Curia—
the rupture, in fact, of diplomatic relations—was Bismarck's act, and
in the negotiations after 1878 Bismarck assumed that the May Laws
would not be withdrawn unless the Vatican made substantial concessions. The later assertion (in 1878 and repeated in his Memoirs)
that he regarded the struggle as mainly a recrudescence of the chronic
problem of Poland was an afterthought, and the blame subsequently
laid on Falk, as the author of the mischief and the failure, was a
characteristic trait of ingratitude. A scapegoat had to be found, and
Falk, the hero of the National Liberals and Radicals, served the convenient purpose of exculpating the Chancellor and affronting the
parties with which Bismarck broke between 1878 and 1879.

In 1874 Bismarck told the Reichstag that since 1862 his previsions
and forecasts in all the great issues had been wonderfully accurate.
The remark had a side reference to the *Kulturkampf*. But in 1871
Bismarck plainly miscalculated. The diplomacy with which he had
hitherto crossed swords successfully had not had the traditions, skill,
fertility in resource, and pertinacity of the Vatican. The Roman
Curia could and did pull many wires throughout Europe, and it
could afford to wait. It had no capital that could be stormed, leaving
the defence impotent. Its capital was everywhere, planted in the

consciences of millions of its communion. Heads can be cut off, but the obedience of heart and will cannot be enforced by prison or the guillotine. Bullets or wristcuffs cannot kill ideas. The extermination of the faithful is not the same thing as the extirpation of a faith. Indeed, the seven years from 1871 to 1878 were an instructive object-lesson in the limits of power even when exercised by a State with the executive strength of Prussia. In the constitutional conflict in 1862 Bismarck had rightly assumed the Liberals would not raise barricades, defy the laws, or refuse to pay taxes, and that, if they did, the whiff of grapeshot would settle the first outbreak. In 1872 he apparently calculated that the Catholics would either not resist, or, if they did, would soon surrender to a rigorous coercion. He was completely mistaken. When Cardinal Archbishops, with the applause of their congregations, defied the law and went to prison, the State as Power could only, as Windthorst remarked, bring in the guillotine—if it dared. For when a state by its own action converts law-breakers into martyrs for conscience it loses the sympathy of the law-abiding. . . . Universal suffrage proved a terrible weapon in the hands of the Centre party. At the general election of 1874 the National Liberals increased their numbers to over one hundred and fifty, but the Clericals polled a million and a half votes and returned not sixty but ninety-one members. Bismarck therefore had to face a National Liberal party stronger than ever and more indispensable to the government, and a Centre opposition enormously encouraged by its success. . . .

The ministerial conduct of the fight was vitiated also by serious blunders. The punitive measures against the inferior clergy—the hardworking priest of the village and small town—threw hundreds of parishes, ignorant of the deeper issues of Vaticanism, into opposition. The government made no effort to enlist the sympathy of educated Catholicism with the cause of freedom of opinion. Instead of concentrating on the narrower issue of Vaticanism and assisting the German hierarchy, placed in a grave perplexity between two allegiances and influenced by a genuine antipathy to the more profound consequences in the Decrees and by a patriotic reluctance to defy the law binding on German citizens; instead of trying to find a compromise for the bishops coerced by Rome and menaced by the State; instead of rallying the Catholic laity to the support of its episcopate in the struggle with the Curia, the government struck right and left at high and low with the indiscrimination of brute strength. Falk fought with the ability of a trained lawyer who assumes that a juristic answer, expressed in well-drafted legislation, and backed by executive action, can settle every problem of life and conduct. Bismarck left the law to Falk, the administration to the Home Office, and thought of the higher politics alone. The limitations in his statecraft were at once exposed. . . . The subtle yet deep intellectual and moral implications in the controversy did not interest him, nor had he the time, the inclination, or the accumulated knowledge to master them. And . . . the ingrained contempt for ideas as ideas, for "ideologues," and for men to whom ideas have a more inspiring import than material force warped his judgment and blinded his intuition. To Bismarck, as to Napoleon, the Church was a necessity of an ordered life, but its action and position must be strictly correlated to the ends prescribed by reasons of State. In the *Kulturkampf* Bismarck found himself in deeper water than his strength and skill could manage. He was to repeat the experience in the struggle with Social Democracy.

ERICH MARCKS: ARCHITECT OF DIVISION [5]

Erich Marcks, in this account written during the first World War, saw Bismarck as a national hero but was not blind to his faults. The Kulturkampf was a defeat for the national idea, he argues, because it led to increased division.

But this is certain. Bismarck did not correctly evaluate the imponderable powers which lay in the vitals of his opponents; he was astonished at the power of the church and of the priesthood. And he had overestimated the energy of national sentiment. His parties did not remain behind him. The radicals deserted because basically they desired different things than he did and also because his repressive measures certainly did not please them. The Conservatives left his ranks easily because a battle with the church was inherently hazardous to them. Moreover, new state tasks arose for which he needed the Center. He was likewise responsible for this retreat and the loss is indisputable. Bismarck participated as the strongest in both the greatness and the blame. He had desired to complete his work, but, instead of unity, division had increased.

From 1878 Bismarck strove to alter his course. In 1879 he sacrificed his colleague Falk unwillingly, but yet from the inherent compulsion of this reversal. From that time on, he negotiated with the Center and the Curia and, nevertheless, sought to execute decisive state decisions independently. He dismantled the combative legislation that he considered unnecessary, always with the desire of gaining counter-concessions by that and yet never by the surrender of his own independ-

[5] Erich Marcks, *Otto von Bismarck: Ein Lebensbild* (Stuttgart and Berlin: J. G. Cotta'schen Buchhandlung Nachfolger, 1915), pp. 149–51. Reprinted, and translated by the editor, by permission of the publisher.

ence. Step by step until 1886 he made peace with the papacy. Of course, the principles of state self-assertion since 1872 were sacrificed and the domestic loss was painful—though not, in spite of everything, as much for Bismarck as for his allies. The struggle only rooted the Catholic party more widely and more deeply. He had to accept the fact and reckon with it. He had to press onward and recognize and form the living. He had really wanted to dissolve the Center; he had not achieved that. He was unable to eliminate it by a direct understanding with Rome. He had to negotiate in friendship or enmity and from case to case with his shrewd opponent Windthorst and to struggle for power with him. Two things are also not to be forgotten in that connection: as uncomfortable as the strength of the party, which was founded in opposition to him, remained to him, he, without too great concessions, without dependence, won its cooperation for the same empire whose founding in 1870 had brought it into the arena as an adversary or at least as a counterweight. That was an advantage for the empire and nation, in accustoming the Catholic part of the population to the new house. The moral loss was truly undeniable; this political advantage over him may not simply be overlooked.

The breaking-off of the struggle with the church shows that limits were set to the victorious course of the power of the nation-state in Germany and that many internal counter-effects were not outdistanced. Also Bismarck had seized, and overstrained, his means thereby. He corrected his error, and, if, in his way, he had herewith taken hold of spiritual matters in an all-too opportunistic and statesman-like manner, he had in any case strengthened his empire with new supports. At the same time, the breaking-off of 1878 shows that his alliance with liberalism was infirm on intrinsic grounds. As we have seen, Bismarck was never a liberal. That alliance had brought to maturity irreparable results and successes, but yet it had never basically satisfied the great statesman of power. Until it ended, his liberal decade retained for Bismarck the same traits: painful friction with the party itself, besides with the Conservatives and the court, and, moreover, a ferment of domestic unpleasantness.

W. H. DAWSON: COMBATTER OF SOCIALISM [6]

In 1919, the English publicist W. H. Dawson published his history of the recently defunct German Empire. It was the fruit

[6] W. H. Dawson, *The German Empire, 1867–1914, and the Unity Movement* (London: George Allen and Unwin, 1919), 1: 462–66. Reprinted by permission of the publisher and Archon Books.

*of years of thought and writing on German affairs. He was espe-
cially interested in social questions and here presents the factors
that he believed influenced Bismarck to fight the socialists.*

In 1876 Bismarck decided that the time had come to oppose
the further advance of movement which had become dangerous to
the State. He had watched its growth for a long time, marking with
alarm its decline from the innocent Socialism on a monarchical basis
which Lassalle had preached and in which he himself had for a
moment taken a more than platonic interest. His contemporary say-
ings, when in France the Empire gave place to the Republic in September, 1870, would appear to indicate his apprehension even then
as to the effect of the new political order upon the larger Continental
monarchies. At a later date he said that he became for the first time
conscious of the danger which threatened Germany when in the first
session of the Diet in 1871 the Socialist deputies had lauded the Paris
Commune. "That appeal to the Commune was a ray of light upon
the matter, and from that moment I regarded the Social Democratic
elements as an enemy against which the State and society must arm
themselves." Already in that year he had endeavoured to induce the
Governments of Europe to combine in resistance to the common
enemy of their peace, and in the following year he had supported
Spain in a proposal that the Powers should suppress the International
Association, as the root of the evil.

Both of these attempts had failed in the absence of agreement; England in particular refused to depart from her traditional standpoint,
which was that so long as the strangers within her gates obeyed the
laws of hospitality there was no good justification for ejecting them.
Busch, the revealer of so much of the secret political history of the
period, says that Bismarck's motive in proposing international action
on the Socialist question was not fear of Socialism at all, though that
was the standpoint which Busch was bidden to emphasize in his
Press articles on the subject, but rather a wish to keep Russia still
isolated from France, by prejudicing the latter as the land of the Commune, and also to win Austria more firmly to Germany's side. As ever,
Bismarck's motives were probably complex, yet it need not be doubted
that a genuine apprehension as to where the International and its
propagandism might lead influenced him greatly.

Failing thus to bring about international action, Bismarck turned
his attention to possibilities of action at home. In 1874 he proposed
an amendment of the Press Law which would have made the encouragement of illegal acts or of disrespect for the law an offence punish-
able by long imprisonment. The Diet resented that attempt to revive

the evil memories of Carlsbad and to manacle again an institution whose freedom had been so lately won, and the matter rested for a time. Two years later he proposed to amend section 160 of the Penal Code so as to make it an offence to incite, either by word or writing, to acts of violence or to attack the institutions of marriage, the family, and property. But the Diet as then constituted was still unfavorable to attacks upon liberty, even in the name of *raison d'état*, and this proposal was likewise rejected as inconsistent with the imperial constitution, which guaranteed to all German citizens the right of free thought and free speech. Windthorst, the spokesman of the Ultramontanes, declared: "If the Minister of the Interior and his colleagues have no better means of dealing with the Social Democrats, and these people are really as dangerous as they are represented, then may God help us!" A sense of partnership in suffering made the Clerical leader tender to the grievances of the Socialists. To him it was far more important to know in what respects the Socialists were right than to ferret out their heresies. Let error, he said, be combated with truth, and above all let the Government remove the consciousness of injustice and so dry up the springs of discontent.

Two more years passed before Bismarck again attempted coercive measures. In the meantime the German Social Democrats had at the Ghent International Congress (September, 1877) subscribed to a manifesto in which the working classes of all lands again, as in 1848, proclaimed blood brotherhood, and vowed to use "every political measure which can lead to the emancipation of the proletariat." In the following year an event occurred which seemed to justify drastic action. On May 11, 1878, a halfwitted tinker of Leipzig, named Hödel, a convicted thief of low character, fired a pistol shot at the Emperor in the Berlin Park. He missed his aim, but the attempt sent a wave of horror and indignation through Germany. The first thought of the reactionaries was to exploit the crime as the foul fruit of Socialist agitation. Hödel professed to be a Social Democrat, and from this fact they drew the conclusion that regicide was a recognized part of his party's programme. It was in vain that the Socialists disclaimed responsibility for the crime, and pointed to Hödel's earlier connection with the Christian-Social party, then in high favor.

Bismarck had long been waiting for the opportunity of applying to the new political movement his specific of physical force, and now the justification seemed to have come. It is said that on hearing of Hödel's crime his first exclamation was, "Now we have them!" At once he sent word from his retreat in Varzin that a law against Social Democracy should be immediately prepared. It was ready in two days, and after endorsement by the Federal Council was laid before the Diet by the 20th.

Conceived in such haste, the bill proved to be badly drafted, and in Bismarck's absence it was just as badly defended in the Diet by advocates who were only half-hearted in their work. The first provision set forth that "publications and associations following the aims of Social Democracy may be prohibited by the Federal Council," subject to subsequent approval or disagreement by the Diet. It was pointed out, however, that so wholesale an embargo upon the aims of Social Democracy was absurd, inasmuch as many of them were found on the programmes of the loyal and patriotic parties. To the Conservatives this objection was pure pedantry, and they were for passing the bill without discussion in any form the Government wished. The thoughtful section of the House, however, declined to allow itself to be stampeded in a moment of panic, and the bill was rejected by 281 votes against 57, without reaching the committee stage. The majority consisted for the most part of National Liberals, Progressists, and Clericals. The Socialists had not taken part in the debates. Observing how the wind was blowing, and assured that the Government would be more easily beaten without their help than with it, they declared it to be inconsistent with their dignity to take part in the discussion of a "law which constituted an unexampled attempt upon popular liberty," and discreetly remained silent. The Government prorogued the Diet in pique, yet admitted its decision to be prudent and just by promptly announcing that the defeated proposals would not be proceeded with.

Once again, however, events played into Bismarck's hands, though with a cruel irony. No sooner had the Diet refused to entrust to him the weapon against violence which he demanded than a further crime was perpetrated which both confirmed his attitude and confounded his opponents. On June 2nd a second attempt was made on the life of the aged Emperor, again in his capital and within sight of his palace. This time the would-be assassin was not a crazy youth, but a man of thirty years, a doctor of philosophy and a farmer. This man, by name Nobiling, awaiting his victim at the top window of a house in the Linden Avenue, fired two shots at him as he drove past, wounding him in the arm and neck, though not dangerously. Followed into the room by an infuriated crowd, which had rushed indoors from the street, Nobiling turned his still smoking weapon against himself with better effect, for the shot inflicted injuries to the brain, which brought on unconsciousness, and in this condition he lingered for several months, until death cheated the gallows of its due. The Emperor bore the blow bravely, suffering more in spirit than body. Recalling on the last day of the year the fate which had befallen him, he wrote in his Diary: "The physical sufferings were not to be compared with the pain that sons of Prussia should have perpetrated a deed which at the close of my life was doubly hard to overcome, and had darkened my heart and mind for the rest of my days."

Bismarck was now in no mood for temporizing with a reluctant Diet. Apprehensive that it could not be trusted to endorse the drastic measures which the occasion called for, he persuaded the Federal Council to dissolve it, and new elections took place on July 30th. In the meantime, the Crown Prince had been charged with the representation of his father in affairs of State. The result of the elections was the return of a Diet entirely pliable to the Chancellor's wishes. In the previous year the Conservatives of North Germany, comprising the feudalists, had joined with those of the South and formed the German Conservative Party. The blend was not a good one, but it secured greater unity of action, and as a result the confederates gained thirty-eight seats, while the National Liberals lost twenty-nine, the Radicals eleven, and the Socialists three.

A revised bill for the repression of Socialist excesses was introduced on September 9th, and its success was assured from the outset. Bismarck took charge of it, and the speeches which he made in the course of the debates on its several readings deservedly rank among his most remarkable political utterances. They were important as foreshadowing the era of social legislation which began several years later. Throughout the discussions the Chancellor carried with him the overwhelming sentiment of the Diet, and public opinion in the country was equally on his side. It was in vain that the Socialists protested; the bill was passed on October 19th by 222 votes against 149, the majority including all the Conservatives and National Liberals, with several Progressists; while the entire Clerical party, still in antagonism against the Government on the Church question, and most of the Progressists voted in the minority. With a true insight the Radical leader Richter, declared, as a parting shot at the bill: "I fear Social Democracy more under this law than without it." The Socialists received the result with defiance, warning the Government that repression would rather benefit than injure their cause. The law was to come into force at once.

ERICH EYCK: DESTROYER OF THE NATIONAL LIBERALS [7]

Erich Eyck, a German lawyer and journalist closely associated with the Left Liberals and later a British citizen, sat down during World War II to write a critical biography of the chancellor. He pictures him as a ruthless demagogue who used the attack on the Social Democrats to destroy the National Liberals.

[7] Erich Eyck, *Bismarck and the German Empire* (London: George Allen and Unwin, 1950), pp. 236–43. Reprinted by permission of the publisher.

On 11th May 1878 a plumber named Hödel fired at William I and missed. The Emperor was unhurt. Hödel was an utterly worthless scroundrel and a political weather cock. For some time he was a member of the Social-Democratic Party; later he joined Stoecker's Christian Socialist Party; Stoecker was court chaplain and an anti-Semitic demagogue. It is quite certain that there was no conspiracy and that Hödel had no accomplices. At the time of the attempt, Bismarck was at Friedrichsruh. As soon as he learned of it, he telegraphed to Bülow, his deputy at the Foreign Office, that the incident should be seized on as pretext for introducing a law against the Socialists and their press.

In earlier years Bismarck had entered upon confidential talks and negotiations with Lassalle, the founder of the German Socialist movement. At the time of the Prussian constitutional conflict he hoped to use him as a tool against the Progressive party. . . . Later he changed his attitude completely. . . . Bismarck grew steadily more determined to achieve repressive legislation in Germany. He opened his heart to Bamberger, the Liberal parliamentarian, who had written on the subject of Socialism: "If I don't want any chickens, then I must smash the eggs."

Bismarck's first step in this direction was a bill to amend the penal law, but this was thrown out by the Reichstag, led by Lasker, in the spring of 1876. . . . Now, after Hödel's attempt on the Emperor a second effort at oppressive legislation was made—a government bill openly directed against the Socialists, their agitation, and their press. This bill was a very careless and clumsy piece of work. It was plain that the Ministers who sponsored it had negligently strung together a few odd paragraphs, merely in order to meet their master's wishes. They probably felt it could not pass the Reichstag, provided that the National Liberals refused to betray their principles. For the bill was clearly discriminatory, that is to say, a measure which was not meant to be applied to every citizen alike, but only to persons of certain political convictions. Thus it grossly offended against the principle of equality before the law and against the freedom of the press and liberty of association. Indeed, the basic principle of the *Rechtsstaat* was at stake.

Some of the National Liberal deputies were nonetheless sufficiently scared of Socialism to support the bill. These were not the industrialists or big capitalists, but university professors such as Treitschke and Gneist. Treitschke, the prophet of power politics, was a Liberal only in name. But Gneist, the great constitutional lawyer and admirer of the English constitution, had been one of the Opposition leaders during the constitutional conflict. It was calamitous for the development of the national mentality that the German universities gradually ceased to be the strongholds of liberty which they had been in the middle of the century. But these professors had not yet gained the ascendancy in the National Liberal Party, which once more followed Lasker's lead by urging the rejection of the bill. The party voted against it almost to a man, after Bennigsen, its leader, had spoken in the name of all of them.

In this speech Bennigsen asked the government whether it was true that they had brought in the bill even though they knew full well that the Reichstag would reject it. He was all the more justified in putting this question as Bismarck had not even taken the trouble to come to Berlin to give support to his own measure. This was, of course, quite in keeping with his tactics. He wanted to sow discord between the National Liberals and those who had returned them, for these latter, he was sure, were much more scared by the Socialist bogy.

Then came a second attempt on William's life. On Sunday, 2nd June 1878, a Dr. Karl Nobiling fired at him from the window of a house in the Unter den Linden as he drove past in an open carriage. William was seriously wounded; bleeding profusely, the old man of eighty-one had to be taken back to his palace.

Nobiling's attempt was the act of a lunatic. He came from a well-to-do middle-class family, had studied economics and taken his degree at Leipzig. He certainly had no political connections. Nobody in the Social-Democratic Party even knew his name. Whether his motive was a political one will never be known, for at the moment of his arrest he wounded himself mortally and died before a proper interrogation was possible. . . .

Bismarck was in Friedrichsruh when the attempt was made. The telegram with the news was handed to Tiedemann, his confidential assistant and secretary. Tiedemann went to meet the Chancellor, who was out walking in the woods surrounding Friedrichsruh. Here is Tiedemann's own account: "As I stepped out of the park, I saw the Chancellor walking slowly across the field in the bright sunshine, with his dogs at his heels. I went to meet him and joined him. He was in the best of tempers. After a little while I said: 'Some important telegrams have arrived.' He answered jokingly: 'Are they so urgent that we have to deal with them out here in the open country?' I replied: 'Unfortunately, they are. The Emperor has again been fired at and this time he has been hit. His Majesty is seriously wounded.' With a violent start the Prince stopped dead. Deeply agitated, he thrust his oaken stick into the ground in front of him and said, breathing heavily, as if a lightning flash of revelation had struck him: 'Now we will dissolve the Reichstag!' Only then did he inquire sympathetically after the Emperor's condition and asked for details of the attempt."

. . . When he made this decision, what did Bismarck know about the origin of the attack, about the assailant, or his political connexions? Nothing! But despite this he had already resolved to exploit the incident in order to suppress the Social-Democratic Party, of which, for all he knew at that moment, Nobiling might have been a strong opponent. Is it not the moral and political duty of a statesman to examine the facts before taking such a far-reaching decision? Bismarck felt under no such obligation, for he was totally uninterested in the real facts of the case. All he cared about was how much political capital he could make of it in whipping up the feelings of the masses. Like all demagogues in all ages, he wanted to appeal to instinct and not to reason. He did not wish to reveal his true aim to the electorate. For the object of his manoeuvre was really to break the power not so much of the Social Democrats, as of the National Liberals. This does not mean that he did not also desire the suppression of the Social Democrats, for he did. But—unlike the National Liberals—they were not a political millstone around his neck. These National Liberals, on the other hand, had voted against his bill to suppress the Socialists. Hence in the coming electoral struggle, which bade fair to be a heated contest, they could be held up as the men who had refused protection to the life and health of the dear old Kaiser. "Now I've got those fellows where I want them," said Bismarck to his intimates. "Your Highness means the Social Democrats?" somebody asked. "No, the National Liberals," was the Chancellor's reply. A popular rumor attributed to Bismarck the saying: "I shall squeeze the National Liberals against the wall until they squeal." In his *Reminiscences,* Bismarck denies using "a phrase so vulgar and in such bad taste." But, be that as it may, it sums up his feelings and intentions quite correctly. . . .

Thus the Reichstag was dissolved and Germany found herself amid the sound and fury of a general election. The government press did everything in its power to rouse the masses to anger against the National Liberals, who were accused of having denied protection to the Emperor's life by voting against the first anti-Socialist bill. Nobody could say, of course, how this bill, if it had been passed, could possibly have protected him against the shots fired by Dr. Nobiling. But that did not matter. Popular passion never likes cold logic. . . .

It is a symptom of the strength which the Liberal idea still possessed in Germany that the National Liberals lost only about 100,000 and the Progressives about 40,000 votes. But the loss of constituencies was larger: 30 National Liberals and 10 Progressives were deprived of their seats. The two parties could only muster about 140 deputies together, while the two Conservative Parties increased their number from 78 to 115 deputies; they had won almost 600,000 votes. The Social Democrats who, in the previous election, had polled half a million votes, lost no more than 60,000. The National Liberal Party still held a considerable number of seats, but most of the deputies had been returned only by promising the voters that this time they would support measures against the Socialists.

The government at once brought a fresh bill before the new Reichstag. . . . This time Bismarck himself was a frequent and very energetic speaker in the debate. His speeches are to some extent of special interest to the biographer, because the attacks of the Social Democrat Bebel and the Progressive Richter compelled him to justify his earlier attitude towards the Socialists and especially his confidential interchanges with the late Lassalle. Bismarck spoke of Lassalle with the greatest respect and appreciation and paid a tribute to his conversation. "It was," he said, "so interesting that he had always felt sorry when it stopped. . . ."

In the Reichstag the bill was opposed by the Social Democrats, the Centre Party, and the Progressives. The Conservative Parties backed it whole-heartedly. The National Liberal Party once more had the casting vote. The majority of its members were in favor of the bill. This time Lasker did not venture to oppose it. The current of feeling among the electorate was too strong. In any case, resistance would have been fruitless, for even without him there was an assured majority in favor of the bill. And so the best he could do was to try to tone down some of the clauses. In one important point he succeeded: he reduced the period for which the law was valid to two and a half years. The government wanted the law to be permanent, but had to give way on this point.

The consequence of this amendment by Lasker was that Bismarck had to apply to the Reichstag every second or third year for a renewal of the statute. On four occasions he got his way, but the opposition, particularly among the Liberals, was growing stronger. At last, in 1889, Bismarck tried to get a permanent law passed, but he failed. . . . In 1890 the *Sozialistengesetz* at last died, never to be resurrected.

The *Sozialistengesetz* had destroyed the whole Social-Democratic press and the whole Social-Democratic organization. No meetings could be held at which a Socialist wanted to speak. All the safeguards provided by the law (not that they amounted to much) were ruthlessly trampled on by the police. Socialist politicians and agitators were expelled from any cities in the most brutal way. And this inhuman persecution achieved precisely nothing. The law was quite unable to prevent an increase in the votes cast for the Social Democrats. In spite of the suppression of agitation by the spoken or written word, the votes given to Social Democrat candidates rose to 550,000 in 1884, to 763,000 in 1887, and to 1,427,000 in 1890. If we compare the aims of the law with what it did in fact achieve, it was a complete failure.

Bismarck's policy of naked force miscarried as badly against the
Socialists as against the Catholic clergy. The National Liberals, who
supported him in this campaign, were the real losers in the end, for
they had abandoned their principles, and for a political party that is
the crowning sin. And in any case their sacrifice proved in vain. Only
a year later they had ceased to be Bismarck's party and were to see the
Chancellor turning to their bitterest rivals in order to hound them out
of the position they occupied in parliament and on the political scene
in general.

VERNON L. LIDTKE: CHALLENGER OF THE SOCIALISTS [8]

*Associate professor of history at Johns Hopkins University,
Vernon L. Lidtke examines the political threat of Bismarck's
state socialism to the German Social Democratic party. He finds
that it was a severe, if temporary, challenge.*

Despite the difficulties in arriving at a clear definition of State
Socialism, some broad characteristics can be identified as they applied
at the time. First, State Socialism recognized an obligation of the existing state to undertake measures for the improvement of the working
classes. The specific measures set forth varied with the various pro-
moters of State Socialism. Second, it advocated some level of nationalization or monopolization, also varying in degree with different writers.
Usually the German State Socialists looked to the Reich and not to
the individual states (*Bundesstaaten*) or the municipalities for the
implementation of their program. Third, State Socialism was loyal to
the monarchical state and the values of the established churches and
generally aimed to attract the working classes to the existing system.
With some State Socialists, such at Todt and the Court Chaplain,
Adolf Stoecker, the chief motivation was to restore working-class
loyalty to Protestant Christianity. Political reform was not an aim
of the State Socialists, for most of them were deeply conservative.

The difficulties of the Social Democrats in confronting State Socialism on a theoretical level stemmed from the fact that they themselves
had absorbed so much of its thought in the late seventies. . . .

Bismarck's program of monopolization and social welfare confronted the Social Democrats with the practical challenge of State
Socialism. Although Bismarck made no pretense of being a theoretical

[8] Vernon L. Lidtke, *The Outlawed Party: Social Democracy in Germany, 1878–
1890* (Princeton: Princeton University Press, 1966), pp. 156–69. Reprinted by permission of the publisher.

spokesman for State Socialism, his program corresponded with its general tenets. Observers of the German scene commonly referred to his measures as examples of State Socialism, and the Social Democrats approached his projects with the same assumption. Thus, as the Social Democratic Reichstag deputies fashioned their response to Bismarck's program, they were also presenting the outlines of their own answer to the larger challenge of State Socialism as a theory.

The initial uncertainty of the Social Democrats about how to respond to the Bismarck program of monopolization and social welfare is apparent from many sources. The conflicting positions presented in the *Zukunft* discussions . . . on nationalization foreshadowed the ambiguity that characterized the Social Democratic response when confronted with a fuller version of Bismarck's State Socialism after 1880. Numerous party leaders expressed agreement with much of Bismarck's program, arising no doubt from their belief that nationalization necessarily meant a step toward socialism. Thus, in April, 1878, Wilhelm Bracke told Engels that he approved of the Imperial nationalization of the railroads; he even thought that the projected tobacco monopoly was "not unacceptable." He added hastily that he would nevertheless oppose any public Social Democratic support for Bismarck's economic program.

Other sources indicate that some Social Democrats thought of the monopolization program as a genuinely socialist measure. In the summer of 1880, two lead articles in the *Sozialdemokrat* unconditionally endorsed the tobacco monopoly. . . .

The confrontation with Bismarck's State Socialism posed a fundamental challenge to the party's democratic principles. If Bismarck's program of monopolization and social welfare had to be recognized as genuine socialist measures, then the Social Democrats had no grounds on which to oppose a socialism instituted by the authoritarian Reich. This posed a question of priorities for the Social Democrats. Could nationalization by Bismarck bring about socialism without a democratization of the German government? For those who viewed the democratic political principles of Social Democracy as its chief goals, the answer was "no." For others, democratization could wait. Thus a fundamental tension emerged between the traditional democratic-political principles of the party and what they took to be their socialist-economic ideas. This was the underlying problem posed by Bismarck's State Socialism. . . .

The full impact of the challenge of Bismarck's State Socialism did not hit the Social Democrats until 1881. On November 17, 1881, the well-known social message of the Kaiser was presented to the Reichstag, outlining the over-all scheme for Accident, Sickness, and Invalid Insurance. Deliberations on these measures occupied much of the

Reichstag's time through 1884. Combined with the tobacco monopoly, which came before the Reichstag in 1882, these measures forced themselves into the center of Social Democratic discussions. It is no exaggeration to say that Bismarck's State Socialism created a serious crisis in the Social Democratic party—a crisis which was largely hidden from public view.

The Imperial social welfare program posed a painful dilemma for the Social Democrats. In economics they had been tutored to think along the lines of State Socialism, and a number of leaders were sufficiently impressed by the insurance scheme to be tempted to approve it openly. This included many of the moderates. . . . It was impossible, however, for Social Democrats simply to accept the Imperial insurance program without undermining their political opposition to the Iron Chancellor. However, it was equally impossible for the Social Democrats, who actively demanded improvements for the working class, simply to reject a program of social welfare because of their political opposition to Bismarck. The radicals were especially determined to avoid the danger of undermining their political opposition by a too sympathetic response to the social welfare program.

Social Democrats—especially the radicals—had to find a course by which they could both accept and reject the insurance program. The course was found. In the spring of 1881, when a draft for the Accident Insurance was first debated in the Reichstag, the Social Democrats introduced a series of amendments to the bill. In essence the Social Democratic changes fully agreed with the principles of Bismarck's bill, but in detail they greatly extended the benefits for workingmen. Simply put, the Social Democrats affirmed that the Chancellor was moving in the right direction, but they complained that he was not prepared to move far enough. . . .

The Social Democrats had found the ideal tactic for responding to the welfare aspects of Bismarck's State Socialism. Thereafter, they followed the same practice of introducing amendments or parallel bills, giving themselves the opportunity to accept the principle of Bismarck's legislation and also specific reasons for voting against it. Since their amendments were never incorporated into the final bills, they could always vote against the welfare legislation on the ground that it was wholly inadequate and therefore fraudulent.

The public rejection of the Accident and Sickness Insurance Bills, beginning in the spring of 1881, merely camouflaged the fact that, within the party, Bismarck's State Socialism continued to exert a seductive appeal. . . .

The debate on State Socialism was stimulated by the events around the election of October, 1881, for the campaign focused on the issues raised by Bismarck's program for monopolization and social welfare.

Bismarck hoped to reduce the strength of all parties which objected to this economic program and to gain a Reichstag built on the conservative parties with assistance from the National Liberals and the Centrists. He likewise expected that the promise of social welfare would undermine the strength of the Social Democrats with the working classes. State Socialism thus became a direct challenge to the Social Democrats in the election. . . .

In addition to the difficulties created by the constant police harassment and the underlying appeal of Bismarck's unfolding welfare program, the Social Democrats had to contend with a political challenge from the camp of Adolf Stoecker and the Christian Social party. Although Stoecker's initial plan of January, 1878 to found a working-class party that would be loyal to Protestant Christianity and the Hohenzollern monarchy had already disintegrated, his movement still posed a threat to the Social Democrats. He attracted a small following, including some workingmen, by exploiting anti-Semitic sentiments and endorsing the State Socialist plans of Bismarck. In matters of social reform, Stoecker was far more radical than the Chancellor. Insofar as State Socialism had a spokesman who could speak to the masses, the Court Chaplain filled the bill. The fact that Stoecker had concentrated his efforts in Berlin also made his movement a significant threat to Social Democracy. . . .

The total Social Democratic vote in the election of 1881 dropped from what it had been in July of 1878, but it is difficult to determine whether this resulted from the challenge of State Socialism or simply from the restraints imposed by the severe policy repression. While it appears that the repression was most responsible, the evidence also shows that in those few districts where representatives of the State Socialists campaigned energetically the Social Democratic vote dropped markedly. . . .

It appears from this that State Socialism posed something of a popular threat to the Social Democrats. It proved, however, to be a transitory threat. The reasons for this may not be too difficult to fathom. For one thing, few State Socialists were also interested in becoming the popular leaders of working-class masses. Stoecker was unique in that respect, and so was Adolf Wagner, who, however, never ventured to harangue the masses as Stoecker did. For another thing, once the Accident and Sickness Insurance programs were passed by 1884, the Social Democrats could argue convincingly that these measures had not solved the problems of the workingmen.

J. C. G. RÖHL: THE AUTOCRAT [9]

In examining the cumbersome constitutional and administrative system of the German Empire, J. C. G. Röhl considers Bismarck an autocrat who provided the cement for it. He points out the built-in threat to the chancellor's position in the power given to the monarch.

The confusion in the country as a whole was necessarily reflected in the unfinished structure of its Government. That there could be no Cabinet with parliamentary responsibility is obvious. . . . That there could be no Reich Cabinet of any sort is equally clear. There were twenty-five Governments in Germany, most of them with their own monarchs and parliaments, their own loyalties and traditions. In 1866 and 1870–71 they had been forced, tricked and even bribed into joining the Reich. They looked to Berlin with utmost suspicion, watching for signs of further encroachments. A Reich Cabinet with real powers could only have ruled over them, and this was totally unacceptable. . . . The Constitution of 1871 gave the German Kaiser only the rights of a *primus inter pares* and declared sovereignty to reside in the Bundesrat or Federal Council, to which each State sent its representative. This was quite plainly a fiction, for the delegates to the Bundesrat could only act on instruction from their home Governments. These in turn were more or less dependent on the support of their monarchs and parliaments. In this way, the Reichstag faced not a responsible Government but a nebulous, anonymous and faceless body which simply faded away under attack.

A Reich Cabinet was impossible for another reason. Prussia was not just a member State but covered three-fifths of the area of the Reich. Her King was always the Kaiser, and eighteen of Germany's twenty-one Army Corps were Prussian. Berlin was the capital both of Prussia and the Reich. . . . Prussia was where real power lay in Germany. A Reich Government beside or above the Prussian Government was unthinkable. The King of Prussia and the Prussian Ministry of State were bound to play a leading role in determining the policies of Germany as a whole.

There was, however, a strong case for a *single* Reich statesman, responsible for mediating between the Prussian Government and the non-Prussian Governments and for ensuring that things operated

[9] J. C. G. Röhl, *Germany Without Bismarck: The Crisis of Government in the Second Reich, 1890–1900* (London: B. T. Batsford, Ltd., 1967), pp. 20–26. Reprinted by permission of the author, the publisher, and the University of California Press.

smoothly in the Bundesrat and Reichstag. . . . In 1867, Bismarck—who already held the posts of Prussian Minister-President (Prime Minister) and Foreign Minister—had himself appointed Reich Chancellor. As such, he became President of the Bundesrat and the only man responsible for those questions (foreign policy, the Navy, customs, trade and postal services) which the Constitution had declared to be "Reich matters." In the course of the next decade, the Chancellor became the focal point for the development of seven Reich offices under a Secretary of State. . . . In 1878, Bismarck formed a small Reich chancellery to enable him to control the increasingly complex business of the Reich. The Secretaries of State did much of the routine work in the Bundesrat and Reichstag, but they remained Bismarck's subordinates in a very real sense. Before 1878, he insisted on signing every Reich document in person. After that date, he forbade two Secretaries to sign the same document, since this obscured the fact that they were only deputising for the Chancellor. He abhorred the idea of collective government and only twice convened a meeting of the Secretaries to discuss policy. He even stopped them from corresponding with each other without his express permission. . . . All contact with the Kaiser was strictly prohibited "without my express consent, unless that consent is self-evident." By 1890, the Foreign Office alone possessed thirty-two volumes of his instructions on such matters as the size of blotting paper, the pagination of heavy documents, abbreviations, and the use of red covers that would not stain. . . . It was little wonder that most of the Secretaries sighed with relief when, in 1890, the Chancellor's grip was relaxed.

If Bismarck could keep a strict eye on his subordinates in the Reich, his position in the Prussian Ministry of State was—in theory at least —quite different. The principle was upheld that "the real, *de facto* Minister-President in Prussia is and remains His Majesty the King." Consequently the powers of the nominal Minister-President were virtually non-existent. As defined by a Cabinet Order of 1852, he had the right to be informed of important decisions, to add his own comments to the reports of Ministers before passing them up to the King, and—except in the War Minister's case—to attend any audience between a Minister and the King. Because the King had the right to decide all matters, majority decisions were not binding in the Ministry of State. Any Minister overruled by his colleagues had the right to appeal to the King. . . . Bismarck often complained of having "to ask eight donkeys for permission whenever he wished to eat a spoonful of soup. . . ." After 1879, however, such complaints ceased altogether. By dismissing recalcitrant Ministers and replacing them with his own nominees, and by exercising an overwhelming influence over the aging King Wilhelm I, Bismarck achieved an unprecedented position of authority in Prussia. . . . The danger was, of course, that under a different monarch and a different Chancellor the old disunity would reassert itself.

One method used by Bismarck to strengthen his position in the Ministry of State was to appoint some of the State Secretaries, who were his subordinates, as Prussian Ministers without Portfolio. . . . In the years 1878–81 he tried another experiment. Count Stolberg was appointed Vice-Chancellor in the Reich and Vice-President of the Prussian Ministry of State. . . . In 1888, Boetticher, head of the Reich Office of Interior and thus in practice Bismarck's foremost deputy in the Reich, was made Vice-President of the Ministry. . . . On the other hand, Bismarck's constant experimentation in this field shows that even he regarded his control over the Prussian Ministers as less than complete.

Another way of exercising control was to insist that *all* correspondence between the Prussian departments and the Reich Offices passed through Bismarck's hands. In the Reich he could insist on this right as Chancellor. In Prussia he argued that the Prussian Government must deal with the Reich Offices through its Foreign Minister, as all the other German Governments did, otherwise the latter would suspect "that the Reich institutions stand within the Prussian Ministry." As time went on, it became increasingly difficult for Bismarck to uphold this privilege. . . . Indeed, toward the end of his rule he wrote a letter of complaint, as Prussian Foreign Minister, to himself as Reich Chancellor and President of the Bundesrat!

The post of Prussian Foreign Minister was an integral part of Bismarck's authority as Chancellor, for the Chancellor alone had no vote in the Bundesrat and could not, strictly speaking, appear before the Reichstag. It was as Prussian Foreign Minister that he cast Prussia's seventeen votes in the Bundesrat, and as one of Prussia's delegates that he spoke in the Reichstag. Because he dominated the Prussian Ministry of State so completely, Bismarck had little trouble on this score. But officially he could cast the Prussian vote only "in accordance with the decision reached in the Ministry of State" by the usual processes. Any weakening of his authority in the Ministry therefore threatened his authority in the Reich.

As Bismarck grew older, the Government's dilemma presented itself with increasing clarity. Bismarck's autocracy was intolerable and his pedantic insistence on formal distinctions seriously hindered efficient government. There was a widespread feeling that the Government must accustom itself to take decisions collectively, as other Governments did. And yet Bismarck's autocracy was necessary to hold the conglomerate of departments together. Without his authority, the Prussian Ministers would fall into disunity and be tempted to appeal to the King for support against their colleagues. They would tend to treat the Minister-President and Chancellor as an equal and dictate how the Prussian vote in the Bundesrat should be cast. This would raise the insoluble issue of Reich-Prussian relations. The South German Governments, who regarded a strong Chancellor as a guarantee that their wishes would be respected in Berlin, would feel that the Reich institutions were simply a front for Prussian domination. As the authority of the Government as a whole declined, the influence of the parliaments, the press and public opinion would grow. But these pressures would operate in different directions. In Prussia the influence of the Conservatives on Government policy would increase, whereas in the Reich the need to win the approval of the Centre party in the Reichstag would lead the Chancellor and the Secretaries to pursue a more moderate course. The attempt to normalise the system of government would thus lead, in a short space of time, to confusion. Consequently, when the crucial test came, the Government would prove incapable of effectively countering the Kaiser's bid to pick up the reins which Bismarck had dropped.

It was the crowning irony of Bismarck's achievement that, by rescuing the authority of the Prussian monarchy from certain destruction, he unwittingly prepared the ground for his own downfall. Both in fact and in theory, the Prussian King and German Kaiser had tremendous powers. He was in personal command of the Army and Navy, and neither the Chancellor nor even the War Minister and Navy Secretary had any say in "command" matters. In direct consultation with his Military Cabinet and (after 1889) his Navy Cabinet, he made all appointments and promotions in the armed forces. The men in attendance on him were almost all of them Army Generals who owed no allegiance to—and very often despised—the civilian politicians. In Prussia he still had all those prerogatives of an absolute monarch which had not been curtailed by the promulgated Constitution of 1851 [sic]. In particular he had the right to appoint and dismiss Ministers at will and to determine policy. . . . In the Reich, the Kaiser had no ancient prerogatives, but only those rights explicitly granted him by the Constitution. But even these included the right to appoint and dismiss the Reich Chancellor and all the Reich officials at will. And in practice, the personal union between the Prussian King and Kaiser on the one hand and the Prussian Minister-President and Chancellor on the other meant that Prussian principles were extended to the Reich. . . . Under . . . Wilhelm I (1858–88), Bismarck soon established for himself such a dominant position that the monarch did not intervene. Yet Bismarck . . . was acutely aware of the danger that the Kaiserin or some other person at Court might try to use the Kaiser against him. Wilhelm's son Friedrich . . . ruled for only ninety-nine days. Yet there is little doubt that he would have dismissed Bismarck and decided many political questions in person if he had survived. His son, Kaiser Wilhelm II, was certainly determined to rule. In 1887, when both his grandfather and his father were still alive, he exclaimed to one of Bismarck's most loyal Ministers that "one would need Prince Bismarck very urgently for some years to come, but then his functions would be divided up and the monarch himself would have to take over more of them."

E. MALCOLM CARROLL: ALIENATOR OF PUBLIC OPINION [10]

E. Malcolm Carroll, writing before World War II, concentrated on the interpenetration of Bismarck's foreign and domestic policy through study of diplomatic documents and newspapers. Here he probes the chancellor's strengths and weaknesses, devoting particular attention to the unfavorable public response he evoked at home and abroad.

In contrast to the praise usually lavished upon Bismarck, the conclusions presented in this study have been critical. There is, of course, another side to the picture. His extraordinary command of diplomatic technique cannot be denied. No statesman of his generation, and none of his successors in Germany equaled his skill in using the interests of other countries to advance those of his own. Since the maintenance of the status quo would assure Germany's preeminent position in Europe, there is no reason to doubt his desire for peace. Few of his achievements were lasting (even the national unity which he hastened was more superficial than real), but their immediate value was inestimable. He assured Germany's security and predominance in Europe for twenty years. If, for ulterior purposes, he often represented latent as immediate dangers, if he sometimes purposefully increased existing tension, he always succeeded in keeping the decision for peace or war in his own hands. He was partly responsible for Germany's reputation abroad for brutality and unscrupulousness, but his system of alliances insured her against the hardening of this unfavorable opinion into a hostile coalition. If his greatest successes were palliatives rather than permanent solutions, statesmanship perhaps may not fairly be judged by a more exacting standard. His foreign policy, nevertheless, is open to criticism from the point of its

[10] E. Malcolm Carroll, *Germany and the Great Powers, 1886–1914: A Study in Public Opinion and Foreign Policy* (Englewood Cliffs, N.J.: Prentice-Hall, Inc., 1938), pp. 337–41. Reprinted by permission of the publisher.

methods, its relation to the dominant economic and social trends in Germany, and especially its use of public opinion. He would have been remiss in his duty had he not taken advantage of international tensions, but Germany's permanent interests were not served by purposefully increasing them. He may not have been directly responsible for the Franco-Italian friction in Tunis, but Italy's membership in the Triple Alliance, which that antagonism made possible, was never more than of limited value, because the approach to England which it opened was not effectively exploited. His encouragement of the friction between England and France in Egypt was extremely skillful; but, because their statesman saw through his game, it tended to defeat its own purposes. It added to the already abundant suspicion and dislike of Germany on the part of the Western powers. Much has been made of Germany's fear of being used as England's lightning rod or sword upon the continent; but England also suspected that Germany valued her friendship chiefly as a tool against France, and suspicion of Bismarck's intentions was likewise an important cause of the failure of Franco-German cooperation under Ferry. His manipulation of the Austro-Russian rivalry in the Balkans is often regarded as his greatest diplomatic achievement. His encouragement of Russia to attack Turkey in 1877 doubtless served Germany's immediate interests by diverting Russia's attention from Central Europe, but the powerful Pan-Slavs, and even the Russian government, never forgave Germany for Bismarck's failure to support her interests during and after the Congress of Berlin. By maneuvering Russia back into his system of alliances in 1881 and 1887, he erected a temporary defense against these dangers; but the belief that Russia's friendship was essential to Germany's security, for which he was largely responsible and which revived in many quarters after his fall, was not an unmixed blessing. It tended eventually to deprive German foreign policy of the adaptability to circumstances which her situation required.

That Germany was and should remain primarily a continental power was one of Bismarck's basic assumptions. He believed that colonial expansion should be left to the initiative of individuals rather than that of the state, although he was responsible for the acquisition of almost all of the colonies which Germany possessed before 1914. There was much to be said for this point of view. An imperialist policy was certain to increase the friction with the established world empires—England, France, and Russia—but it was toward this result that the most significant economic and social movements in Germany were working. The rapid industrialization of Germany, accelerated by Bismarck's adoption of the protective tariff system of 1878, with the attendant rapid increase of population, created a powerful demand for markets, sources of raw materials, and suitable areas for colonization. Some of this dissatisfaction might have been averted by the negotiation of commercial treaties opening new and widening old markets or by legislative support for the settlement of the surplus population upon Germany's own soil. But Bismarck showed no interest in using his incomparable diplomatic ability for the benefit of German industry, nor did he even consider the possibility of extending the social security laws to an attack upon the great landed estates. His entire career shows that, in his opinion, diplomacy, commerce, and industry were entirely different branches of statecraft. He had no adequate solution for the problems that were pointing Germany toward imperialism.

Although public opinion was certainly not among the more obvious of the determining factors of Bismarck's foreign policy after the establishment of the Empire, his attitude toward it had momentous consequences both to himself and to Germany after his fall. Not until the problem of Germany's relations with Russia and Austria became acute, when popular sentiment threatened the nice balance which he wished to maintain between these powers, did he show much appreciation of its importance. Through the press bureau of the foreign office and in his speeches to the Reichstag he gave a good deal of attention to the education of opinion in regard to the proper solution of this fundamental problem. The results, though difficult to estimate, were doubtless considerable, but even more important was his success. The nationalist sections of the middle classes united with the Conservatives in an unquestioning support of his foreign policy, but it was nevertheless under Bismarck that a cleft developed between the official conduct of German policy and a section of public opinion that neither he nor his successors ever bridged. For the most part, neither the Progressives nor the Social Democrats—who were making good their claim of speaking in the name of the working classes—accepted his aims and methods as those which were required by the country's true interests. While the former applauded his strong speech against Russia, February 6, 1888, their reaction would have been different if they had been aware of the Reinsurance Treaty. Neither of these opposition parties had any sympathy for the principles of *Machtpolitik,* and both saw Germany's salvation in a diplomatic association with the Western powers. They also agreed in condemning Bismarck's use of the press. The existence of official and semi-official newspapers was a standing grievance; but even more offensive was the publication of alarmist communications—the famous *Kaltwasserstrahlen*—during periods of international tension. Innumerable protests were directed against the practice of exaggerating foreign dangers to drum up sentiment for increases in the army and to secure pliant majorities in the Reichstag. By his abandonment of the *Kulturkampf*, Bismarck neutralized the Centrist's criticism to a considerable extent, but his domestic policy, especially in its refusal of any concession to the principle of ministerial responsibility and in its reliance upon indirect taxes, which bore most heavily upon the working classes, continued to alienate liberal opinion. Taxation and military service bore most heavily upon the masses, but their spokesmen were refused any real voice in German policy at home or abroad. Instead, Bismarck dismissed them cavalierly as *Reichsfeinde* or as sentimentalists who were incapable of understanding the realities of international politics. No wonder that his dismissal was accepted not only with indifference but even with the hope that it would mean a change for the better. If he was largely responsible for the divorce between German policy and the masses, his influence upon nationalist opinion had serious consequences. He knew that every country must pay for the windows broken by its press; Germany eventually paid the bill for Bismarck's use of the press for alarmist purposes in the form of a public opinion that was increasingly susceptible to panic and hysteria. He was responsible to no small degree for the conviction that the chauvinists would always dictate France's action in a crisis—an assumption which inevitably militated against a cool steadiness in relations with her—and for the ingrained suspicion that England would never be a reliable friend.

It is customary to trace the first weakening of Germany's diplomatic position to Bismarck's fall and the subsequent failure to renew the Reinsurance Treaty. While his advanced age made impossible a much longer period of power, even a few more years of contact with him might have steadied the Emperor. The circumstances of his dismissal undoubtedly weakened Germany's prestige abroad and, eventually, that of the Empire at home as an act of ingratitude. Despite the increasing alienation between German and Russian public opinion, it was of value to Germany that a diplomatic relationship should be retained as a barrier to the dangerous pressure of popular passions for as long a period as possible, especially in the absence of a clearly thought-out substitute. The failure to act on Russia's desire for the renewal of the treaty was, as events proved, an irreparable blunder never to be corrected by later efforts to repair the broken line to St. Petersburg. It did more to win Russia for an alliance with France than the latter's ardent courtship.

GORDON A. CRAIG: RECOGNITION OF LIMITATIONS [11]

Gordon A. Craig, professor of history at Stanford University, has established himself as an authority on Bismarck's foreign policy as well as on the role of the army in German history. He believes the chancellor's greatness lay in realizing the limits of statecraft and in acting accordingly.

There is no doubt that Bismarck would have accepted the proportion [sic] that the first law of politics—and especially of foreign politics—is that one can rarely do exactly what one would like to do. The course that theory would define as the best in a given contingency, circumstances usually render impracticable; and the statesman finds himself compelled to settle for the least harmful of a number of unpleasant alternatives. Bismarck never forgot this, and, from hard experience, he came to know the factors that, in given cases, could, and generally did, limit his freedom of choice and action.

Prussian, and later German, foreign policy was, for one thing, limited in its freedom by the nation's geographical position. This made a vigilant and active foreign policy essential, for, as Bismarck wrote in 1857: "a passive lack of planning, which is content to be left alone, is not for us, situated as we are in the middle of Europe." On the other hand, it forbade adventures in exotic and exciting areas remote from the nation's main sphere of interest, activity, and danger. Thus, Bismarck could say to a colonial enthusiast in the 1880's, "Your map of Africa is very beautiful, but my map of Africa is in Europe. Here is Russia and here is France, and here we are in the middle. That is my map of Africa."

Germany's policy was limited also by her power at any given moment, and Bismarck's appreciation of this—so dramatically illustrated during the years of the constitutional conflict—need not be elaborated, except to note that—unlike some later statesmen in his own and other countries—he never took too restricted a view of power and always recognized that it included both a nation's actual and potential military and economic strength, and its reputation as well. He knew . . . how much a nation's diplomacy depends upon its reliability in the matter of promises and threats; and he guarded Germany's reputation as jealously as he did her military resources.

And there were other limitations that had to be observed. The

---

[11] Gordon A. Craig, *From Bismarck to Adenauer,* rev. ed., (New York: Harper and Row, 1965), pp. 16–19. Reprinted by permission of the Johns Hopkins University Press.

freedom of Prusso-German diplomacy was always limited by the nature of its international setting. Opportunities like those that were offered to it when the European Concert was riven by dissension, as in the years from 1856 to 1870, were not likely to recur in times when there was a consensus among the powers, and a wise statesman had to adjust his policy accordingly. At any given moment, moreover, Germany's freedom to act was limited by the groupings of the powers, the strength and reliability of allies, and other facts of international life. It was equally affected by the nature of its domestic constitutional arrangements; and, while Bismarck did not have to reckon with anything like democratic control of foreign policy, he could never completely ignore public opinion; and even his relative freedom in this respect was balanced by the way he was limited, and his policy disrupted, by the prerogatives and prejudices of his sovereign, to say nothing of those forays into politics by military and other irresponsible agencies that were so much a part of the Prusso-German system. Finally, German diplomacy was limited by the effectiveness of its representatives, who, despite their schooling at Bismarck's hands, remained subject to human frailties, and by the nature of the problems with which they, and he, had to deal—some of which (the problem of Austro-Russian rivalry in the Balkans, for example) were not susceptible of easy solution, if, indeed, they were soluble at all.

If Bismarck had refused to recognize any of these limitations—and he did not—he would still have been held back from *hubris* by one more that he never forgot. Diplomatic plans, like all human designs, are always subject to the intervention of chance or providence. . . .

His reflections on this ultimate limitation of diplomacy were influenced, like so much of his political thought, by his religious beliefs, and specifically by his view of God's providence. To Bismarck as to Luther, God was a *Deus absconditus* whose will determined the fate of nations but whose purpose could never be perfectly apprehended by man. The statesman is like a child in a dark room; he can only hope that God will allow him an occasional glimpse of light so he can hobble after it. He dare not anticipate the ways of providence (it was for this reason that Bismarck, in 1867 and in 1875, steadfastly repudiated the doctrine of preventive war) and must have the humility to recognize that "by himself he can create nothing; he can only wait until he hears the step of God sounding through events and then spring forward and seize the hem of his garment—that is all." And aside from this—and here was the hardest thing of all to contemplate—the statesman must admit that God may have willed the utter defeat of all his plans and even the destruction of his country. . . .

Bismarck is generally described in the textbooks as the first *Real-*

politiker; but unfortunately so much has been written about *Real-politik* that its meaning has become obscure and mixed up with blood and iron and incitement to war by the malicious revision of royal telegrams. This is neither the place nor the time to correct what has become a traditional view. Even so, it may be permissible to suggest that the essence of Bismarck's realism was his recognition of the limitations of his craft, and that it was this, coupled with the passion and the responsibility that he brought to his vocation, that made him a great statesman.

ADALBERT WAHL: THE GERMAN HERO [12]

Writing at the time of the Weimar Republic, Adalbert Wahl looked with nostalgia at the days before the first World War. He presents the chancellor as an unique hero, but also as an essentially German one.

. . . In his nature and in his actions Otto v. Bismarck was completely divorced from the usual standards. The restoration of German unity, which at least in the beginning was in opposition to the passionately aroused Prussian and German people, to a great number of separate German states, and to foreign countries which were partially envious, partially openly hostile, borders throughout on the miraculous, and really has no parallels in the history of all epochs and peoples. But the man was even more miraculous than the achievement. Anyone who would maintain that he understands him completely, in whose soul—according to his own magnificent words—there were whole provinces into which he granted no one a look, only bears witness to his superficiality. It is quite clear that there stands before us a being of a different kind than we are ourselves, formed from different material, produced by a different age—we would say that if we could name the age to which he belonged. His powers of body and spirit appear not only to soar into the gigantic, into the demoniac nature of his passions, but also to be differently blended and combined than with others. When the report was brought to him of the serious wounding of the old King by Nobiling, his first words were: "Now we'll dissolve the Reichstag"—then only did he inquire about the condition of the wounded man. Is that not a man of calculating intelligence alone, hard, unfeeling, in whom the human

[12] Adalbert Wahl, *Deutsche Geschichte* 4 vols. (Stuttgart: W. Kohlhammer Verlag, 1926), 1: 10–12. Reprinted, and translated by the editor, by permission of the publisher.

recedes far behind the political? Nothing would be falser than this conclusion. Bismarck was capable of the most tender feeling: at his departure from office he shed tears easily even before people who were not close to him; he wept at the report of the hopeless illness of the Crown Prince, to whom nevertheless he had never been close; deeply moved he could throw himself on the floor and take into his lap the head of a dying old dog, with frightful self-reproaches because he believed he had caused the dog's death by an otherwise merited punishment. He had times when he, as a landed proprietor on his estates, often lived for weeks simply as a human being in the midst of his sincerely loved family, seriously giving himself trouble to remain aloof from politics which then at times completely engulfed his entire will. It was also incalculable in what form his personal and practical reaction would be manifested in every single event, in every single situation. Nothing would be falser than to see in Bismarck only the cold, practical calculator and also to wish to *eliminate* the greatest and weightiest personal passion and impulse for retaliation. But even far more biased would be an interpretation (which perhaps may be presented more frequently in the near future) by which he acted even in many of his great undertakings *preponderantly* from personal motives of the designated kind. No one will understand him who does not recognize his sublime practicality, in virtue of which, even in moments of greatest passion, he elevated himself above things, countless times wrote state documents which are of a magnificent calm and objectivity as if the author were not a politician subject to the pressure of business, but a cool retrospective historian. But there are still numerous unsolved puzzles. The man who could be the most friendly host in the middle of princely hospitality, spread on other occasions, even in his own house, an atmosphere about him which made a strange, disturbing, even sinister, impression on the visitor.

If in many things he thus remains to the observer strange and foreign, he is still also close to us again. We understand the Prussian in him, the loyalty of a vassal to his own king. We also have a presentiment of the German in his innermost core, though, to be sure, in countless things he raised himself above the all-too German. We find him German in the search for God, in the absolutely sincere struggle over belief, in submission to God after he found Him, in the frequent struggle with God, in the modest silence in public concerning his belief. He is German in his family, in his attitude to his wife, and above all in the superabundant love for his eldest son, Herbert. He is German in the thoroughness of his work and knowledge. His is German in the way he loved the woods and animals and in the way he brooded over the phenomenon of nature.

If, besides the genius which is not to be comprehended nor to be described, and besides the incomparable astuteness—never reached before or since—which characterized this diplomatic technician, one falteringly seeks to describe what made him so great and at the same time so formidable, then we would put in the first place the passion, which gave to his undertakings monstrous force; then his unbounded courage, which not only attempted the great, but even resisted and defied the opinion of his people; the bellicose drive, which made him accept any challenge offered; and the apparently innate "thought of the results," which permitted him with unbelievable speed to foresee the possible consequences of any event. From the time he became a minister he was free of any trace of party spirit or doctrinairism and yet rich in belief and strong in belief in God and in Prussia. That remained the cornerstone of his being.

HAJO HOLBORN: PRACTITIONER OF REALPOLITIK [13]

The late Hajo Holborn, Sterling Professor of History at Yale University, here distills his years of historical investigation and writing to examine the underlying basis of Bismarck's thought. He devotes particular attention to the chancellor's views of the influence of ideology and religion in politics.

What made Bismarck a fiery enemy of Gladstone was both the liberalism and insistence of Gladstone on a Christian program in politics. Bismarck soon parted company with his early conservative associates, the members of the so-called Christian-Germanic circle, with regard to the application of Christian principles to practical politics. In Bismarck's view, the world and its orders were created by God and the course of history directed by him. The existing political institutions, consequently, were not made by men nor could they be altered by ideal constructions of human reason, as the liberals proposed. But the concrete plan of God was unknown to man, except that it was clear that in all history the decisions had been reached by power used for selfish interests, and that this *raison d'état* could be studied and acted upon. This nature of the political life of the world was to him divinely instituted and, therefore, essentially immutable, although life was a continuous conflict and struggle. To hope that men could change the nature of politics would be sinfully arrogant

[13] Hajo Holborn, "Bismarck's Realpolitik," *Journal of the History of Ideas* 21 (1960): 88–91. Reprinted by permission of the *Journal of the History of Ideas* and Mrs. Holborn.

and would meant to meddle in divine government. The statesman might gain, however, at rare moments a fleeting adumbration of divine action on a higher plane.

These ideas excluded the possibility of Christianizing the state and international life. There was no ideal state, let alone an ideal international order, but only the concrete order of history which demanded from everybody obedience to the positive law. This Bismarckian attitude has been called Lutheran by historical students of Bismarck, and it is quite true that his political conceptions showed the earmarks of the political thinking that had developed in German Lutheranism. But it would be erroneous to assume that Bismarck's and Luther's opinions were identical. The world of states was for Luther not the arena for the realization of the kingdom of God. Luther admitted that statecraft required special political knowledge though to him this was not identical with the *raison d'état*. And while Luther did not believe that the state as such was a Christian institution, he considered it the duty of every individual Christian to assert within the public life a special moral attitude derived from his Christian faith. In this respect Bismarck's early conservative companions, particularly Friedrich Julius Stahl, were closer to Luther than Bismarck.

But Bismarck did not deny that at least the statesman himself, if he was a Christian, was bound by certain specific principles. The exercise of power was not to aim at personal ends but was a calling to preserve the natural order of things and to serve the state. No doubt, these were important moral restraints which reflected genuine ideas of Luther, though in somewhat weaker fashion. Luther justified war only in self-defense and recommended that Christian princes should rather suffer some occasional injustice and forget about their own "reputation" than go to a war that would bring calamitous suffering to their people. Bismarck repeatedly condemned preventive wars and never accepted war lightheartedly, but he did accept it as a means for accomplishing his political aims. Also, he ruled out wars for prestige, but not for the honor of the state.

The outlook on life and history with which Bismarck entered politics endowed the prevailing political conditions of Prussia with an aura of sanctity. Not only the monarchy but also the traditional class society of Prussia, with the junker estate as the dominant social group, was in his eyes the God-willed order of things, and its maintenance by all means of political cunning the unquestionable duty of the statesman. Liberalism, which for him comprised every movement derived from the ideas of the American and French Revolutions, was the sworn enemy of a healthy political life, since it attempted to replace historically developed forms of life by an arbitrary system of man-made institutions. In Bismarck's thought any kind of liberalism was bound to lead to government by parties, and this weakening of the authority of the state would bring forth the chaos of a social republic, from which a people could be freed only by a regime of fire and sword. On the other hand, a regime of naked force was disliked by Bismarck, although many governmental measures which he recommended or adopted were of highly doubtful legality. He was not even a champion of an unrestricted absolute monarchy. He objected to the suppression of the independent rights of the nobility by rulers. Moreover, absolutism fed that "boa constrictor," bureaucracy, which was tyrannical but at the same time a breeding ground of liberal notions.

These Bismarckian conceptions might have made this junker a radical reactionary after the breakdown of the German revolution, radical to the extent of demanding the suppression of those moderate German-national and liberal trends that had existed in Prussia before 1848, and even more of the concessions made during the revolution of which the Prussian constitution was the most important grant. But in spite of his brazenly contemptuous attitude toward democracy and liberalism during the revolution, Bismarck was not found among the extreme die-hards in the 1850's. A parliament, in particular, seemed to offer many potential advantages. Through it the conservatives could assert their views—if need be even against crown and bureaucracy—and Bismarck never forgot that the king had faltered in the early months of the revolution. But the chief value of a parliament was the chance it provided for entering on a contest with the liberal forces. Bismarck realized that these forces could not be conquered by mere repression and that the ideological errors and the political futility of modern democracy would have to be shown up by word and deed.

While Bismarck, therefore, accepted a parliament, he remained a deadly foe of parliamentary government. The monarchical government was always to retain a basis of power of its own and for this reason never surrender its exclusive control of the army and foreign affairs. During the revolution of 1848–49 Bismarck had seen that the Austrian and Prussian monarchies recovered their strength because their armies remained loyal to the dynastic cause. He had also observed the weaknesses in German liberalism, how the fear of social revolution had impaired its aggressive spirit, how the political moderates and radicals had divided, and how the ideas about the forms of the desired national union, *gross-deutsch* vs. *klein-deutsch,* had produced further splits in German liberalism. He had also noticed that the social and economic program of the liberals failed to keep its early large following united, and that individual groups could be bought rather cheaply by the old governments. It had not escaped his attention that the majority of the German people, especially the peasant and working classes, were still politically quiescent and that it might be feasible to mobilize them for the support of monarchical government, as Louis Bonaparte had done.

These were Bismarck's formative experiences as he rose to become the leading statesman of the Prussian state. His supreme goal was and remained the preservation and the elevation of the Prussian military monarchy. He was convinced that the power of Prussia in Germany and Europe could be enhanced once her policies were freed from the shackles which the Christian principles of the old conservatism imposed. This applied not only to foreign affairs but also to domestic politics. As long as the sanction of force remained firmly in the hands of a sovereign king, he saw no danger in adopting some of the aims of what he called "the revolution."

OTTO PFLANZE: THIEF OF NATIONALISM [14]

> *Otto Pflanze, professor of history at the University of Minnesota, has embarked upon a monumental biography of Bismarck. In this selection, he reflects upon Bismarck's actions and their general consequences, stressing the "theft" of nationalism from the liberals.*

With but few exceptions, therefore, Germany's leading scholars have rejected the view that there was any direct relationship between the Bismarckian and Hitlerian Reichs. Later Meinecke himself appeared to retreat from his position of 1945 (that the "seeds" of the "German catastrophe" were sown in the Bismarckian Reich). The Bismarckian *Machtstaat*, he concluded, was a geopolitical necessity for Germany. Ritter has detected an upsurge of "Bismarck veneration"; Bernhard Knauss writes of a "certain tendency to repopularize Bismarck" by picturing him as the George Washington of German history; and Wilhelm Mommsen rejoices that a "much more positive judgment" of Bismarck has developed in recent years, while cautioning against "too much of a good thing." Comfort is found in the fact that the first German chancellor was not highly regarded by Nazi ideologists. Conservative historians have been inclined to trace the origins of the Nazi revolution to the breakdown of the old aristo-

[14] Otto Pflanze, *Bismarck and the Development of Germany: The Period of Unification, 1815–1871* (Princeton: Princeton University Press, 1963), pp. 7–14. Reprinted by permission of the publisher.

cratic society and bureaucratic state under the impact of liberal and democratic ideas and the emergence of the masses as a factor in politics. There is also a tendency to see these ideas and movements as importations from abroad, foreign influences which had a cancerous effect upon the sound organism of German society. It is assumed that the German Reich created by Bismarck and overturned in the revolution of 1918 was essentially a healthy institution whose destruction eliminated the most effective obstacle to the rise of totalitarianism.

One of the purposes of this book is to question this assumption on grounds more valid than those previously advanced by critics of Bismarck. The history of Scandinavia, western Europe and the Anglo-Saxon world shows that there is no necessary causal relationship between popular sovereignty and the rise of totalitarianism. It cannot be denied that Germany has been influenced for the worse by some unfortunate trends common to the whole of European civilization. But it is also true that during the last two centuries a cultural cleavage opened along the Rhine. In the development of her political attitudes and institutions Germany followed a course largely independent of the west.

The unique development of Germany began, of course, long before Bismarck. Its origin lay in the character of the Prussian political and military system, the late appearance of the German middle class, the subjection of church to state in the Lutheran faith, the link between authority and freedom in German political thought, the victory of historical over natural law, the idealization of the state and its power, and the German view of nationality as a matter of common culture rather than common citizenship.

Because of Bismarck the gap widened still more. He compounded a new synthesis in German political attitudes between German nationalism, Prussian militarism, and Hohenzollern authoritarianism. Through the moral power of the German national idea he constructed a new and firmer basis for traditional autocratic and militaristic institutions in the emergent age of mass democracy. He legitimized and preserved for Germany the political system of "mixed powers" (that is, an authoritarian executive combined with a popular legislature) which elsewhere in western Europe was but a transitional stage in the growth of a liberal-democratic order. His career heightened the already dangerous adulation of power in Germany and accentuated the popular belief that what matters in the employment of power is success. He perpetuated in a far different age the Frederician tradition of the genius-statesman, unlimited in the last analysis by any constitutional restrictions and responsible alone to his own inner conscience for his conduct of public affairs.

Undoubtedly there was much in Bismarck's statesmanship reminiscent of the political style of the eighteenth century. The diplomatists of the age of reason did not seek to remake the world in the image of their own religious or political faiths, but to strengthen the power and security of their states within the framework of the European equilibrium. The latter was regarded as the pre-condition of political stability and the protective mechanism which preserved the independence of the powers. Bismarck's motives were those of *raison d'état* and *arrondissement* typical of eighteenth-century statecraft. His aim was not to unify the German cultural nation, but to expand the Prussian state within the limits of the European balance of power. Like Frederick the Great, he insisted upon the supremacy of political over military strategy. With Clausewitz he believed that war is properly but a continuation of diplomacy "by other means."

The "cabinet diplomacy" of the eighteenth century was possible, however, only because of the relative homogeneity of social and political conditions in that age. Europe possessed a common political structure, a common political outlook, and a common ruling class. Monarchical government, the concept of divine right, and aristocratic rule were universal. While the status of the nobility depended upon the survival of the monarchical order, no international crusade was necessary to rescue that vested interest. England was the only exception to the general consensus, but the English revolution was not accompanied by a violent social upheaval, and furthermore it was not deliberately exported.

The French revolution and Napoleonic conquests disrupted this harmony and introduced a new era of crusading idealism in European politics. But the old order, while severely damaged, was by no means destroyed, and its restoration in the settlement of 1815 created the possibility of a return to classical diplomacy. For a time conservative doctrine and the fear of revolution delayed its reappearance. During the fifties, however, the drift toward realism in the European psyche brought about a revival of the eighteenth-century diplomatic style. In many respects Bismarck, Buol, and Gorchakov were closer to Kaunitz, Choiseul, and Frederick the Great than to Metternich, Alexander I, and Frederick William IV.

Nevertheless, it is utterly incorrect to depict Bismarck as a man out of his age, belonging more to the past than the future. The practice of cabinet diplomacy in the nineteenth century became increasingly difficult because of the erosion of its social and political foundation. Bismarck was one of the first to grasp that the emerging age of popular movements required a new kind of politics. No longer could the masses be ignored in the conduct of either domestic or foreign affairs. Whatever the ends of the statesman, war and foreign conquest required the moral approbation of a righteous cause. At home the doctrines of legitimacy and divine right no longer sufficed to justify authoritarian rule. If monarchical institutions were to endure in an age of dynamic economic and social change, they had to be rooted in the more fertile soil of national sentiment.

Bismarck was the political surgeon who amputated nationalism from liberalism and conservatism from legitimism. Following Louis Napoleon, he comprehended that nationalism and liberalism were not necessarily compatible and that the former might actually be converted into anti-liberal force. "It was only through Bismarck," Bertrand Russell shrewdly observed, "that German patriotism became respectable and conservative, with the result that many men who had been liberal because they were patriots became conservative for the same reason." In the process German nationalism lost what remained of that humanitarian and cosmopolitan outlook which was its endowment from Herder and the ages of reason and romanticism. His exploitation of nationalism for imperialistic and authoritarian purposes is what makes Bismarck, like Napoleon III, a transitional figure between the politics of the eighteenth and twentieth centuries, between the age of aristocratic absolutism and that of authoritarian nationalism.

Moral forces provided Bismarck with means rather than ends, with objects to be manipulated rather than with guides for political action. What moved him was not the ideal of German national unity, but the quest for greater internal stability for the Hohenzollern monarchy and greater external power for Prussia in Europe. Had Austria been willing to continue the dual domination of Germany on a basis more favorable to Prussia, or had the constellation of European politics been less favorable for Prussian expansion, he would have followed a conservative course in foreign policy, co-operating with Austria and Russia against popular forces in Germany and Europe. Within Prussia he would have endeavored to outflank the liberal opposition by appealing to the artisan and proletarian classes through a policy of state socialism.

Nevertheless, it is doubtful that Bismarck would have been permanently satisfied to follow the conservative course. The radical, even revolutionary, one of alliance with German nationalism was more in keeping with his volcanic temperament and, furthermore, it promised the greater gains. At one stroke it provided a common solution to the double crisis he faced at home and abroad. It gave him the moral means with which to justify simultaneously the expansion of Prussia and the retention of Hohenzollern authority. Finally it enabled him to travel with the "stream of time" by steering into a current of great potential strength.

In stealing the national plank from the liberal platform Bismarck had a number of precedents to follow. Since 1806 the Prussian government had either preempted or appropriated much of the liberal program. The Stein-Hardenberg reforms, the Zollverein, the Prussian constitution of 1848–1850, and the free-trade treaty of 1862 pointed the way for his action. But the theft of the cause of national unity was the most persuasive act of all in reconciling the German liberals to authoritarian rule. It demonstrated with finality the truth of Bismarck's statement to Napoleon that "only the kings make revolution in Prussia."

He owed his success in raiding the liberal program in large part to the absence of any genuine popular movement in Germany. Despite the remarkable changes in the economic and social structure of Germany during the late fifties, there was as little mass support for the liberal cause in the constitutional conflict of 1862–1866 as there had been during the later stages of the revolution in 1848. This weakness arose from the inadequate penetration of liberal ideals into the lower strata of German society, but also from the deliberate unwillingness of the liberals to look after the material needs of the working class. The alliance of the aristocratic and middle classes consummated by Bismarck in 1866 left the working class no other recourse than to find in proletarian socialism its spiritual home.

As an autonomous movement German nationalism was also patently lacking in vitality before 1870. For six decades German nationalists had been confronted with the challenging task of uniting a badly divided people, but only once, in 1848, did the ideal of national unity generate sufficient popular support for the attempt. Within weeks, however, the patriotic fervor evaporated. By May 1849 only a few were still willing to sacrifice for the cause. At other times only the external stimulus of a crisis with France (1813–1815, 1840, 1859, 1867, and 1870–1871) succeeded in bringing any life to the national movement. Only on two of these occasions (1813–1815 and 1870–1871) was anything accomplished, and this was due entirely to the leadership provided by the Prussian state, whose ministers exploited German nationalism for their own political ends. The achievements of 1864 and 1866 were attained by the Prussian state over the bitter opposition of the national movement. In 1864 the efforts of the Nationalverein through popular agitation to push through the claims of the Prince of Augustenburg to Schleswig-Holstein ended in complete failure, and in 1866 the nationalists could not prevent civil war over issues believed in the beginning to be alien to the national cause.

The common view of German nationalism as an irresistible current sweeping down the decades to fulfillment in 1870 is a fiction of nationalistic historians, derived from the hopes and aspirations of those *kleindeutsch* leaders, like Sybel and Treitschke, who were their intellectual forebears. Only under the stimulation provided by Bismarck for his own political ends did German nationalism begin to move the masses. It is a fact of fateful significance that German national sentiment could gain sufficient momentum to overcome the particularistic loyalties of the German people only in combination with Prussian militarism and Hohenzollern authoritarianism.

The lethargy of German nationalism before 1870 does indeed leave open to doubt the assumption that the Bismarckian Reich was the only possible solution to the German question. At Königgrätz, however, the concept of a unified national state, represented by Prussia, was completely victorious over the older concept of universal empire, represented by the Hapsburg monarchy. Under the Holy Roman Empire and the German Confederation the German people possessed no precise frontier delimiting the area of their political and cultural influence. For centuries their fate had been joined with that of the peoples of central Europe. By restricting their horizon, the decision of 1866 greatly accelerated the growth of that inverted national sentiment which was to devastate Europe in the twentieth century. The achievement of national self-determination by Italy and Germany accentuated the ambitions of the subject peoples of the Hapsburg monarchy to divest themselves of German leadership and assert their cultural and political autonomy. The ultimate consequence was the disintegration of central Europe into its many national components.

Throughout Europe the constitutional system of "mixed powers" underwent changes in the nineteenth century which call into question its inherent stability as a governmental form. Either the power of the legislature penetrated the executive creating parliamentary government, or the reverse occurred with a consequent devitalization of parliamentary life. England, France, Italy, the Netherlands, and the Scandinavian countries experienced the former process. In Prussia the possibility of such a development arose during the constitutional conflict of the sixties. Owing to Bismarck's genius the chance was lost and the contrary current set in. Through the victories of 1866 and 1870 the essential features of the Prussian system, with some diminution of parliamentary authority, were extended over the rest of Germany. Another important consequence was the disorganization of the major political parties. Bismarck's manipulations fragmentized the party structure and reduced the possibility of stable majorities. His stark realism weakened the attraction of political ideals and exalted in German political attitudes the prestige of power at the cost of principle.

His undeniable sense of ethical responsibility is inadequate as a justification for Bismarck's arbitrary actions. The possession of an active conscience, grounded in religious faith, is never a sufficient substitute for legal and institutional checks on the use of power. Although he deplored absolutism, Germany's first chancellor demonstrated by his willingness to break the constitution that he recognized in the final analysis no higher authority than the expediency of power. The priority he gave to might over right in both domestic and foreign affairs established an unfortunate precedent in German history upon which men of other aims and other conscience were eventually to capitalize. It was the precedent of the man of titanic will, to whom success is the major criterion, who appears in a time of chaos and weakness to lead his people over seemingly insuperable obstacles to the promised land of internal stability and external power.

Bismarck himself was deeply skeptical of the capacity of individuals to shape history. But his own career shows that his pessimism was unjustified. To be sure, he did not create the forces with which he dealt. By manipulating, however, he altered them. The combinations he achieved became a historical influence of the first magnitude. Bismarck belongs to that category of men whom Hegel called "world-historical individuals" because through them the world is changed.

Afterword

Most historical attention has rightly been devoted to Otto von Bismarck's years in office, but the eight years of his retirement are also instructive. If the dismissal, portrayed in Tenniel's classic cartoon, "Dropping the Pilot," seemed the end of an epoch to many, the former chancellor vehemently disagreed. His life had been devoted to the pursuit of power, and he waited noisily in the wings for a call to return to office which never came. The stormy circumstances of his departure increased his isolation; few officials found the choice between the rising and the setting sun difficult. They chose William II. This isolation was reinforced by a tacit boycott of the old man.

Still conscious of an unimpaired intellect and the wisdom of his policies, Bismarck reacted in a characteristic fashion. His rage at the dismissal and his vindictiveness toward his successors lessened only, if at all, when despair at his futile existence and desire for death increased.

Yet his supplanters quaked in almost comic fashion at the very notion of his return to power. And they had reason. Stripped of official position, he appealed to public opinion. Though refusing to take his seat in the German Reichstag to which he was elected in 1891, he found a spokesman in the *Hamburger Nachrichten.* Through this newspaper, interviews, and speeches to the hordes of admirers who flocked to Friedrichsruh, he initiated a torrent of propaganda directed against the policy of his successors. The bitterness engendered during his quarter-century in power was not lessened by his disclosure—his critics said "betrayal"—of state secrets, notably the Russian Reinsurance Treaty. Bismarck even incongruously proposed greater parliamentary criticism of the government. Generally, however, he held consistently to his earlier principles: the importance of preserving the German Empire and national feeling, the necessity of avoiding wars for aggrandizement or prestige, and the primacy of continental interests over colonialism.

Official counter-moves could only too embarrassingly be made to appear as part of an unrelenting vendetta against a defenseless old man, to whom only gratitude was owed for unifying Germany and guiding the destinies of the new nation. Clumsy in the extreme, these measures reached their height in 1892, when Bismarck traveled to Vienna for his son's wedding. Under strong German pressure, the

Austrian official world reluctantly ignored him, but he was greeted everywhere by rapturous popular acclamation. Nor did the Reichstag majority forgive its old antagonist; it refused to send its congratulations on his eightieth birthday in 1895.

The years of Bismarck's retirement, unlike Napoleon's at St. Helena, engendered no new legend, although his utterances strengthened the old. To defend his policies and savage his opponents he dictated his memoirs, to be published after his death. Incomplete, disorganized, and unilluminated by self-criticism, they are an imperfect monument to his anger and genius. Yet they will continue to be read as long as nation states exist, defying premature announcements of their imminent demise, and as long as men value individual achievement. Bismarck will remain a focus of interest—and controversy.

Bibliographical Note

The literature on Bismarck and his times is vast, comparable to that on Lincoln in the United States. A convenient listing is K. E. Born, *Bismarck-Bibliographie* (Cologne and Berlin, 1966). The following references are limited to some of the more useful works in English.

Among the sounder general histories of modern Germany are W. H. Dawson, *The German Empire, 1867–1914,* 2 vols. (London, 1919); H. Holborn, *A History of Modern Germany,* 3 vols. (New York, 1959–69); E. J. Passant and W. O. Henderson, *A Short History of Germany* (Cambridge, 1959); K. S. Pinson and K. Epstein, *Modern Germany* (New York, 1966); W. M. Simon, *Germany: A Brief History* (New York, 1966); V. Valentin, *The German People* (New York, 1946); and A. W. Ward and S. Wilkinson, *Germany, 1815–1890,* 3 vols. (Cambridge, 1916–18).

Bibliography and interpretation of Bismarck may be found in A. Dorpalen, "The German Historians and Bismarck," *Review of Politics* 15 (1953): 53–67; G. P. Gooch, *Studies in German History* (London, 1948); H. Kohn, ed., *German History: Some New German Views* (London, 1954); and L. Steefel, "Bismarck," *Journal of Modern History* 2 (1930): 74–95.

Bismarck's writings have generally been indifferently or inexactly translated. Some of his correspondence may be found in *Love Letters* (New York and London, 1901); *The Correspondence of William I and Bismarck,* 2 vols. (New York, 1903); and H. Schoenfeld, ed., *Bismarck's Speeches and Letters* (New York, 1905). His memoirs from an imperfect German edition appear as *Bismarck: The Man and the Statesman,* 2 vols. (New York, 1899); and *New Chapters of Bismarck's Autobiography* (New York, 1960); both works are abridged in one volume, with an introduction by T. S. Hamerow (New York and Evanston, 1968). Some Bismarck selections, together with contemporary reactions, appear in W. M. Simon, ed., *Germany in the Age of Bismarck* (New York, 1968). Of the great body of interviews, some appear in C. Lowe, ed., *Bismarck's Table Talk* (London, 1895); H. Ritter von Poschinger, *Conversations with Bismarck* (New York and London, 1900); and S. Whitman, *Personal Reminiscences of Prince Bismarck* (London, 1902). A prime, though not always completely reliable, source is M. Busch, *Bismarck: Some Secret Pages of His History,* 2 vols. (New York, 1898).

General studies of Bismarck are many. A convenient compilation of varying opinions is T. S. Hamerow, ed., *Otto von Bismarck: A Historical Assessment* (Boston, 1962). J. G. L. Heskiel, *The Life of Bismarck* (New York, 1870) is an early view with much on Bismarck's youth. C. Lowe, *Prince Bismarck: A Historical Biography,* 2 vols. (London, 1896) is adulatory, but valuable for its contemporary appraisal. C. G. Robertson, *Bismarck* (London, 1918) gives the liberal viewpoint, while the psychological approach is attempted in E. Ludwig, *Bismarck: The Story of a Fighter* (Boston, 1927). Presenting some novel interpretations are W. N. Medlicott,

Bismarck and Modern Germany (Mystic, Conn., 1965); and A. J. P. Taylor, *Bismarck: The Man and the Statesman* (London, 1955). A critical view from the Left Liberal standpoint, stressing the domestic scene is E. Eyck, *Bismarck and the German Empire* (London, 1950). It lacks the colloquial style and rich documentation of the three-volume German original, which is critically examined by H. Rothfels, "Problems of a Bismarck Biography," *Review of Politics* 9 (1947): 363–80. The view of Bismarck after World War II is presented in F. Meinecke, *The German Catastrophe* (Boston, 1950). Dramatic presentations of Bismarck's character and career are W. Richter, *Bismarck* (New York, 1965); and, including selections from primary sources, L. L. Snyder, *The Blood and Iron Chancellor* (Princeton, 1967). Bismarck's political philosophy is examined in H. Holborn, "Bismarck's Realpolitik," *Journal of the History of Ideas*, vol. 21 (1960). O. Pflanze, *Bismarck and the Development of Germany: The Period of Unification, 1815–1871* (Princeton, 1963) is a solidly based and perceptive study of Bismarck's public career.

A useful guide to major interpretations of unification is O. Pflanze, ed., *The Unification of Germany* (New York, 1968). Primary sources include K. Ringhoffer, ed., *The Bernstorff Papers* (London, 1908); Count F. F. v. Beust, *Memoirs*, 2 vols. (London, 1887); Ernest II of Coburg, *Memoirs*, 4 vols. (London, 1890); and J. L. Motley, G. W. Curtis, ed., *Correspondence*, 2 vols. (New York, 1889). R. Weymess, *Memoirs and Letters of the Right Hon. Sir Robert Morier*, 2 vols. (London, 1911), is particularly perceptive. Morier's feud with Bismarck is described in F. B. M. Hollyday, " 'Love Your Enemies! Otherwise Bite Them!' Bismarck, Herbert and the Morier Affair, 1888–1889," *Central European History* 1 (1968): 56–79. General accounts include F. Darmstaedter, *Bismarck and the Creation of the Second Reich* (London, 1948); W. E. Mosse, *The European Powers and the German Question, 1848–71* (Cambridge, 1958); and H. v. Sybel, *Founding of the German Empire by William I*, 7 vols. (New York, 1890–98). On liberal, nationalistic opinion, there is E. N. Anderson, *The Social and Political Conflict in Prussia, 1858–1864* (Lincoln, Neb., 1954); and A. Dorpalen, *Heinrich von Treitschke* (New Haven, Conn., 1957). The struggle with Austria is the subject of C. W. Clark, *Franz Joseph and Bismarck* (Cambridge, Mass., 1934); H. Friedjung, *The Struggle for Supremacy in Germany, 1859–1866* (London and New York, 1935); and L. D. Steefel, *The Schleswig-Holstein Question* (Cambridge, Mass., 1932). Indispensible for the study of the conflict with the military is G. A. Craig, *Politics of the Prussian Army* (New York, 1964). See also Craig's "Military Diplomats in the Prussian and German Service: The Attaches, 1816–1914," *Political Science Quarterly* 64 (1949): 65–94; "Portrait of a Political General: Edwin von Manteuffel and the Constitutional Conflict in Prussia," *Political Science Quarterly* 66 (1959): 1–36; and *The Battle of Königgrätz* (Philadelphia and New York, 1964). Military and constitutional questions in Prussia and the empire are considered in F. B. M. Hollyday, *Bismarck's Rival* (Durham, N.C., 1960). A theoretical discussion of constitutional aspects is B. E. Howard, *The German Empire* (New York, 1906). On the crisis of 1870, the documents contained in G. Bonnin, ed., *Bismarck and the Hohenzollern Candidature for the Spanish Throne* (London, 1957) are essential. Studies on the crisis are E. M. Carroll, "French Public Opinion on War with Prussia," *American Historical Review* 31 (1926–27): 679–700; R. H. Lord, *The Origins of the War of 1870* (Cambridge, Mass., 1924); H. Oncken, *Napoleon III and the Rhine* (New York, 1928); and L. D. Steefel, *Bismarck, the Hohenzollern Candidature, and the Origins of the Franco-German War of 1870* (Cambridge, Mass., 1962). On the annexions of 1871, see C. D. Hazen, *Alsace-Lorraine under German Rule* (New York, 1917).

The chief sources, primary and secondary, of Bismarck's diplomacy may be found in the bibliography of the stimulating A. J. P. Taylor, *The Struggle for Mastery in Europe, 1848–1918* (Oxford, 1954). Anglo-German relations are stressed in Volume I of E. T. S. Dugdale, ed., *German Diplomatic Documents, 1871–1914* (New York and London, 1969); and P. Knaplund, ed., "Letters from the Berlin Embassy, 1871–1874, 1880–1885," Vol. II, *Annual Report of the American Historical Association for the Year 1942* (Washington, D.C., 1944). J. Y. Simpson, ed., *The Saburov Memoirs* (Cambridge, Mass., 1929) is illuminating on relations with Russia. For the United States, there is A. D. White, *Autobiography*, 2 vols. (New York, 1905). The memoirs of German diplomats reflect the same social milieu and political assumptions and should be used with especial caution in regard to references to domestic affairs. Of particular value are Prince C. zu Hohenlohe-Schillingsfürst, *Memoirs*, 2 vols. (New York, 1906); Prince B. v. Bülow, F. A. Voigt, trans., *Memoirs*, 4 vols. (Boston, 1931–32); and F. v. Holstein, N. Rich and M. H. Fisher, eds., *The Holstein Papers*, 4 vols. (Cambridge, 1957–63). Holstein is the subject of an admirable biography, N. R. Rich, *Frederick von Holstein*, 2 vols. (Cambridge, 1965). The classic account of Bismarck's diplomacy is W. L. Langer, *European Alliances and Alignments, 1871–1890*, 2nd ed. (New York, 1950). A greater connection between foreign and domestic affairs is argued by E. M. Carroll, *Germany and the Great Powers, 1866–1914* (New York, 1938). Still useful is J. V. Fuller, *Bismarck's Diplomacy at Its Zenith* (Cambridge, Mass., 1922). Sharply critical of Bismarck is W. N. Medlicott, *The Congress of Berlin and After*, 2nd ed. (London, 1963), and *Bismarck, Gladstone and the Concert of Europe* (London, 1956).

German imperialism is discussed in the outdated M. E. Townsend, *The Origins of Modern German Colonialism, 1871–1885* (New York, 1921), and *The Rise and Fall of Germany's Colonial Empire* (New York, 1930). P. Gifford and W. R. Louis, eds., *Britain and Germany in Africa* (New Haven and London, 1967) contains much of interest, especially H. A. Turner, Jr., "Bismarck's Imperialist Venture: Anti-British in Origin?" pp. 47–82. Also useful are W. O. Aydellotte, *Bismarck and British Colonial Policy: The Problem of Southwest Africa* (Philadelphia, 1937); W. O. Henderson, *Studies in German Colonial History* (London, 1962); H. R. Rudin, *Germans in the Cameroons, 1884–1914* (New Haven, Conn., 1938); and A. J. P. Taylor, *Germany's First Bid for Colonies, 1884–1885* (London, 1938).

The Kulturkampf is examined in its many aspects in the excellent L. P. Wallace, *The Papacy and European Diplomacy, 1869–1879* (Chapel Hill, N.C., 1948). The background is examined in the essential G. Windell, *The Catholics and German Unity, 1866–1871* (Minneapolis, 1954). A contemporary critique is R. Morier, "Prussia and the Vatican," *Macmillan's Magazine* 31 (1875–76): 1261–80. Also valuable is S. W. Halperin, *Italy and the Vatican at War* (Chicago, 1939). The religious aspect is stressed in K. S. Latourette, *The Nineteenth Century in Europe: The Protestant and Eastern Churches* (New York, 1959); and J. N. Moody, ed., *Church and Society: Catholic Social and Political Thought and Movements, 1789–1950* (New York, 1953). Volume I, "The Conservative Phase, 1815–1871," of W. O. Shanahan, *German Protestants Face the Social Question* (Notre Dame, 1954), gives perspective to Bismarck's religious views, the Kulturkampf, and anti-Semitism. The specific nineteenth-century context of anti-Semitism is examined in P. W. Massing, *Rehearsal for Destruction* (New York, 1949), and P. G. J. Pulzer, *The Rise of Political Anti-Semitism in Germany and Austria* (New York, 1964).

Evocative of the atmosphere of the empire in its first decade is H. Vizetelly, *Berlin under the New Empire*, 2 vols. (London, 1879). One aspect of the abandonment of cooperation with the liberals is treated in F. B. M. Hollyday, "Bismarck and the Legend of the 'Gladstone Ministry,'" in L. P. Wallace and W. C. Askew, eds., *Power, Public Opinion, and Diplomacy* (Durham, N.C., 1959), pp. 92–109. Though dealing primarily with a later period, L. Cecil, *Albert Ballin* (Princeton, N.J., 1964) sheds light on the new protectionist age. Economic developments are treated in J. H. Clapham, *The Economic Development of France and Germany, 1815–1914* (Cambridge, 1923); W. H. Dawson, *Industrial Germany* (London, n.d.); G. Stolper, K. Haüser, and K. Borchardt, *The German Economy, 1870 to the Present* (New York, 1967); and T. Veblen, *Imperial Germany and the Industrial Revolution* (New York, 1915). Earlier developments are considered in W. O. Henderson, *The Zollverein* (London, 1959).

Bismarck's social policy is discussed in W. H. Dawson, *German Socialism and Ferdinand Lassalle* (London, 1899), and especially in *Bismarck and State Socialism* (London, 1891). Of particular excellence are V. Lidtke, *The Outlawed Party: Social Democracy in Germany, 1878–1890* (Princeton, 1966); and H. Rothfels, "Bismarck's Social Policy and the Problems of State Socialism in Germany," *Sociological Review* 30 (1938): 81–94, 288–302. Also penetrating is L. P. Wallace, *Leo XIII and the Rise of Socialism* (Durham, N.C., 1966). Other useful works are R. T. Ely, *French and German Socialism in Modern Times* (New York and London, 1900); F. C. Howe, *Socialized Germany* (New York, 1915); C. Landauer, *European Socialism*, 2 vols. (Berkeley and Los Angeles, 1959); G. Landauer, *Social Democracy in Germany* (London, n.d.); and G. Roth, *The Social Democrats in Imperial Germany* (Totowa, N.J., 1963). Two primary sources are A. Bebel, *My Life* (London, 1912) and E. Bernstein, *My Years in Exile* (London, 1921).

The chancellor's later years are touched upon in J. A. Nichols, *Germany after Bismarck* (Cambridge, Mass., 1958); K. F. Nowak, *Germany's Road to Ruin* (London, 1932); and J. C. G. Röhl, *Germany without Bismarck* (London, 1967). M. Harden, *Monarchs and Men* (London, 1912) is the reaction of a contemporary.

Index

GREAT LIVES OBSERVED

Gerald Emanuel Stearn, *General Editor*

Other volumes in the series: